Tennessee Rivers

# Tennessee Rivers
# A Paddler's Guidebook

## Bob Lantz

**Outdoor Tennessee Series**

Jim Casada, *Series Editor*

**THE UNIVERSITY OF TENNESSEE PRESS**

Knoxville

The Outdoor Tennessee Series covers a wide range of topics of interest to the general reader, including titles on the flora and fauna, the varied recreational activities, and the rich history of outdoor Tennessee. With a keen appreciation of the importance of protecting our state's natural resources and beauty, the University of Tennessee Press intends the series to emphasize environmental awareness and conservation.

Library of Congress Cataloging-in-Publication Data

Lantz, Bob, 1938–
Tennessee rivers: a paddler's guidebook/Bob Lantz.
    p. cm.—(Outdoor Tennessee series)
ISBN 1-57233-232-8 (pbk.: alk. paper)
 1. Canoes and canoeing—Tennessee—Guidebooks.
 2. Rivers—Tennessee—Guidebooks.
 3. Tennessee—Guidebooks.
 I. Title.
 II. Series.

GV776.T2 L36 2003
797.1'22'09768—dc21          2003006427

*To the members,*

*past and future,*

*of the Tennessee*

*Scenic Rivers*

*Association.*

# Contents

# Editor's Foreword

**W**aterways are the earth's life blood. From tiny rivulets to mighty rivers, they provide sustenance as surely as they capture our imaginations. Tennessee is particularly blessed in this regard, for from the high country of the Great Smokies and Unakas to the fertile bottomlands of the Mississippi, waterways wend their way across the state's landscape like so many wrinkle lines on the face of Mother Earth. The paths traversed by these streams are as varied and unpredictable as the prospects they provide, but all waterways that are of appreciable size share certain things in common.

For as long as human beings have lived in this fair land, the rivers have been highways for them, winding and sometimes torturous, to be sure, but nonetheless watery pathways leading to new horizons. Generally, though not always, those new horizons, like the manifest destiny of the United States of which Tennessee would become a part two centuries ago, lay westward. This was thanks to the fact that all of the Volunteer State lies west of the eastern continental divide, with her drainages moving in unison toward union with the Mississippi.

Long before the coming of the first Europeans, Native Americans used these waterways not only as travel routes but also as a fruitful source of food, for wildlife was found in greatest abundance along creeks and rivers. In their skillfully crafted and highly utilitarian canoes, Indians could navigate all but the smallest and swiftest of streams, moving as they did in suitably unobtrusive fashion through the natural world with which they lived in close harmony. Much the same was true of the first white people, because the hardiest and most successful of these interlopers learned their skills in woodsmanship from the indigenous peoples they encountered.

In time, though, these newcomers brought changes to the landscape. Most of those changes were in the form of one type of worship or another at the altar of that sometimes false god they called progress.

Clumsy barges and rafts replaced the canoe, only to be succeeded in turn by ever faster (and noisier) craft, such as steamboats, flotillas of huge, diesel-driven transport, or bass boats sporting 150 horsepower engines. Hardwood bottoms gave way to cotton fields. Mushrooming populations sent coliform counts soaring as water clarity and cleanliness declined dramatically. With these changes came others that were, to the conservationist's eye, equally unwelcome. Dams sprang up across much of the state and inundated untold acres. Government agencies, such as the U.S. Army Corps of Engineers, worked endlessly to undo nature's artistry. Despite human ravages, thousands of miles of Tennessee streams clung tenaciously to the characteristics that so entranced pioneers of the ilk of David Crockett and Daniel Boone.

They retained their tree-lined shores, if for no other reason than that periodic flooding mitigated against agricultural fields reaching to the water's edge, and timber cutting was difficult in such places.

In the fullness of time, there came a growing awareness of the importance of clean water, control of agricultural runoff, and streamside management zones. As a result, while the state's waterways will never return to the pristine days and unsullied ways that were their hallmarks before feeling the effects of human carelessness, they are today a source of hope. Better sewer management, a growing awareness of the far-reaching importance of rivers in recreational and related senses, and expanded public intolerance for the travesties of pollution are all having a positive impact.

An earlier book in this series looked at a worst-case scenario, the sad saga of the Pigeon River, and how madness for Mammon could destroy a waterway for decades. That is why it is somehow heartening to have a work which is, in many ways, a celebration of rivers. That is, I believe, the perspective most anyone who takes paddle in hand and sets out on a Tennessee stream with a canoe as a companion will have.

That celebrant will be caught up in the ceaseless rhythms of moving water, listening to its songs and sensing its pulsating power. While doing so he will be enchanted by the flavor of the natural world he is privileged to savor. It is a time that gladdens the heart and uplifts the mind, and those with a historic bent can look back in fond longing to what it must have been like when massive stands of the American chestnut lined the streams of the Cumberland Plateau or when virgin forests cast verdant shadows on streams teeming with bass, trout, and bream. It is, of course, impossible to call back yesteryear fully, but the effort is nonetheless one which is well worth making, for such recollections reward and renew. Taking to the water in a simple, sleek, silent craft is the ideal way to create them.

In a canoe, whether paddling madly through Class IV or V rapids or drifting sedately along a sleepy, slow-moving stream in the Mississippi Plain, one develops a serenity of spirit and enjoys the solace of solitude. Both are qualities that are at a premium in today's world, and that is why this work is so welcome and timely. We need the closeness to the natural world that waterways bring, and as ever more Americans are discovering, movement back to the water is as intriguing and invigorating as that back to the land. Canoeing skills, at least at their most elementary level, are easily mastered, and they can open up a veritable host of new recreational horizons. The sportsman will find hunting territory where whitetails and wild turkey abound suddenly within his reach, or perhaps he will rediscover the nearly lost art of paddling up ducks. For the angler, fishing holes that are beyond the pale of weekend warriors with their shiny, decibel-dealing devils we call powerboats, beckon invitingly. Camping enthusiasts will realize that the canoe is a fine friend for those with a desire to venture, as the Dean of American Campers, Horace Kephart, once put it, "back of beyond." Or perhaps the appeal of nothing more than a day's float, with a hearty lunch on some sandbar and the welcome wonder of bone-weariness at trip's end, will be enough.

Whatever one's passion or pleasure, *Tennessee Rivers* is sure to meet it in full measure. On one level, the book is of the straightforward "how to, where to" genre; its two primary sections, "Prepare to Paddle" and "River Descriptions," deal with such subjects in some detail. By the same token, and this is particularly true of the portion of the work related to individual streams, Bob Lantz manages to infuse his personality into the book in a fashion that enables it to transcend the pedestrian pace so common to volumes of this nature. The reader is carried, albeit vicariously, to streams of dreams, knowing as he is so transported that his companion is a stellar guide and "hale fellow well met."

In other words, this book has charm and character. Chatty in nature but with a common-sense outlook, it takes the reader by the hand and says "let's go canoeing." Indeed, the overriding message Lantz conveys is one of "do it." He rightly realizes that an advanced level of expertise is not and should not be a prerequisite for taking to many Tennessee streams. Instead, all that is required is a love of the natural world and a desire to see it from the perspective provided by rivers—though certainly paddling skills come in handy.

Arguably there is no finer way to see and know the real Tennessee. Only after one has traveled mile after enriching mile on the state's rivers, rejoicing in the experience all the while, does realization dawn regarding just how much beauty, little touched by human hands, the Volunteer State has to offer. These waterways beckon with a siren's call, and be fore-warned—they can also bewitch. Once you take to Tennessee streams, it will be to return again and again, like a moth drawn to the flickering and elusive beauty of a candle's flame. Each time one does so the experience is uplifting and renewing, and when paddles are stored away and the everyday world reasserts its mastery, gladness reigns in your innermost being. You know that the water is always there, predictable and permanent, a bastion of certainty sustaining life. It blesses those who choose to travel along its myriad courses by kayak or canoe with an additional bounty, for they come to know rare contentment, true peace in the heart.

For me at least, the only activity that can produce comparable sensations is fly fishing, and that pursuit also involves the mesmerism of moving water. These pages direct us to Tennessee's ever-soothing streams, and as they do so it is well to remember the wealth that is water that nature gives us. We tend to take its presence, in abundance, for granted. Yet our streams are to be cared for and cherished, kept clean and clear. So treated, they, like the good earth of which they are an integral part, will never, ever let us down. Thoughts of that nature should fill your mind as you travel Tennessee's waterways, and one could scarcely ask for a better companion to that travel than this book. Certainly it is a welcome and well-chosen addition to the series of which it now becomes a part.

Jim Casada
Series Editor
Rock Hill, South Carolina

# Acknowledgments

**O**ver twenty years ago Bob Sehlinger wrote a river guide for the neighboring state of Kentucky. He then began promoting and inspiring river guides for the rest of the southeastern paddle-active, river-rich region. His energy, enthusiasm, foresight, and exploratory river-running skills (when needed) were (and are) greatly appreciated. A different type of river appreciation was provided in that same time frame by Jim Robertson, a nature photographer by both trade and avocation. He inspired the understanding of our rivers in many diverse ways. He showed how paddling was a superb tool for more intimately experiencing the truly natural world of free-flowing waters. He not only personally experienced this rich riverine environment but he also captured exceptional visual representations of it to pass along to others, wherever they might be. I am especially pleased to have some of his classic Obed River interpretations in this book.

In no particular order, I also thank the following river runners who provided measureless amounts of river inspiration throughout the years:

Murray Johnson, Don Bodley, Don Hixson, Bill Griswold, Bill Mitchum, Dick Wooten, Mac McLean, Henry Wallace, Ann Tidwell, Clark Tidwell, Ebeth McMullen, Chester Butler, Carl Storey, Dick Creswell, Roz Goudeau, Doug Cameron, David Brown, Don Dial, Roy Guinn, Alice Middleton, Bob (K) Lantz, Bill Lantz, Bertha Chrietzberg, Frank Fly, Ed Young, Victor Ashe, Bob Todd, Don Todd, Ray Norris, Sam Venable, Carl Leathers, Susan Neff, Ohio Knox, Buddy Caldwell, Bob Hemminger, Barbara Stagg, John Gilliatt, Lester Levi, Mike Long, Walt Mayer, David Mason, Marge Davis, Bob Miller, Ruth Neff, Libby Napier, Jack Grosko, Pat Shaw, Barnett Williams, Bill Kelsey, Bob Pyle, and Dottie Adams (who taught me to canoe!). I was continually inspired by my late mother, Maxine Lantz, who paddled into her late eighties (and would have paddled longer had she lived longer) and handily demonstrated that river canoeing is indeed a life skill and life love.

I would also like to thank Jennifer Siler and the staff at the University of Tennessee Press for having the vision and keeping faith for too many years (I'm embarrassed to admit how many) while the river maps were researched and produced.

And especial thanks and gratitude goes to my wife, Joyce, who married into an ongoing river-book revision and then lived with it for over a decade . . . which included too many discussions of needed computer upgrades and too much time spent on river map production. She gained little in the way of river running except for quick runs over to the Hiwassee (we'd run the river for upper-body exercise, then hike back to the automobile on the John Muir Trail to complete the activity) just to get away from the computer maps and to remember what canoeing was all about.

This book is dedicated to the members, past and future, of the Tennessee Scenic Rivers Association. For over thirty years, TSRA has been an effective statewide source for two important river outreach activities.

Most importantly, they zealously (and economically) provide safe paddling instruction. They aggressively push even the mildly interested through their open door to river enjoyment. For anyone who will invest a weekend, they pass on lore and enthusiasm needed for safe river running. Years ago the pioneers of TSRA taught me that safe river paddling skills were not necessarily intuitive, and my capacity to enjoy those flowing waters made an immediate quantum jump.

At the time I was surprised to discover that TSRA's canoe school track actually prepared the student as a new paddling instructor. And that has worked for decades! Safe paddling techniques have evolved and been passed on, year after year. Thousands of people have enjoyed our rivers due to this learn-and-teach system.

And it is a small step from enjoying our resources toward concern and then active protection of those same resources. This is the second major river outreach activity of TSRA. Many outstanding river conservationists have stepped forward from the paddling ranks of TSRA and led significant local (and even national) river protection and enhancement efforts. All those concerned river activists knew that TSRA, as a committed and viable organization, would back their river-protection efforts, time and again.

TSRA (P.O. Box 159041, Nashville, TN 37215-9041) has taught us to appreciate our river resources in many ways. And they continue to be effective to this date. Thank you TSRA!

*Part 1*

# The State, Its Rivers, and the Elements of Paddling

# Tennessee's Geologic Diversity

Tennessee is a strung-out and oddly shaped state. Eight states border Tennessee, and the long northeast-to-southwest diagonal distance is greater in length than straight-line distances in most of the larger western states. Bristol, in northeastern Tennessee, is closer to the Canadian border than it is to Memphis in southwestern Tennessee; Memphis, in turn, is closer to the Gulf of Mexico than it is to Bristol. Tennessee's predominant east–west axis cuts directly across the grain of the region's geology; hence, Tennessee offers a varied array of landforms and waterways. From the small watershed, cascading mountain whitewater in the east, to the Yazoo meanderings of bottomland swamp water in the west, Tennessee offers a wide variety of experiences to canoeists, all a direct result of its cross-the-grain geology.

Scientists break Tennessee into nine distinct geologic regions, each with different topography, underlying and outcropping rocks, soils, minerals, and, of course, streamways.

In this book, the stream descriptions cross geologic boundaries somewhat to combine float streams into similar watershed groupings, but since geology and topography are strongly related and the characteristics of the various float streams are similarly dependent on the landforms through which they flow, there is a strong relationship between the divisions described here and those of the geologists. The second map shows the five divisional boundaries found in this book as they relate to the nine geologic ones in the first map. By knowing some of the geologic details of each major canoeing division the paddler can get a better feel for the type of streams and river runs to be expected there. The description of these areas will follow an east to west trajectory.

## Mountains, Ridges, and Valleys

This area actually contains two geological regions: the mountainous, hard rock Unaka Range Province, containing the well-known Great Smoky Mountains National Park, and the Valley and Ridge Province, containing the Tennessee River's Great Valley of East Tennessee. Both of these regions contain highly faulted, distorted subterranean rock layers, and both are geologically complex. Generally, these two provinces are a part of the overall Appalachian mountains, with the Unaka Range in Tennessee being parallel to the lower but better-known Blue Ridge range in North Carolina. The centrally positioned Great Smokies are a part of the Unakas and contain the highest and broadest parts of the range. All the Unakas are characterized by a hard rock, thin-soil structure. Heavy-metal mineral deposits are near the surface and often exposed. (These deposits provide an opportunity to stop and pan for

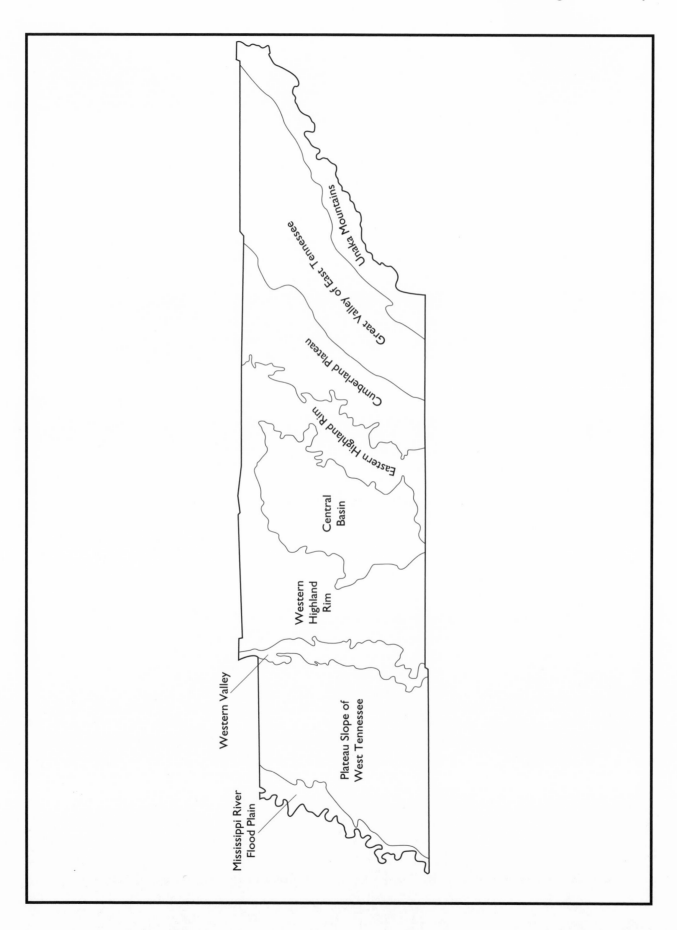

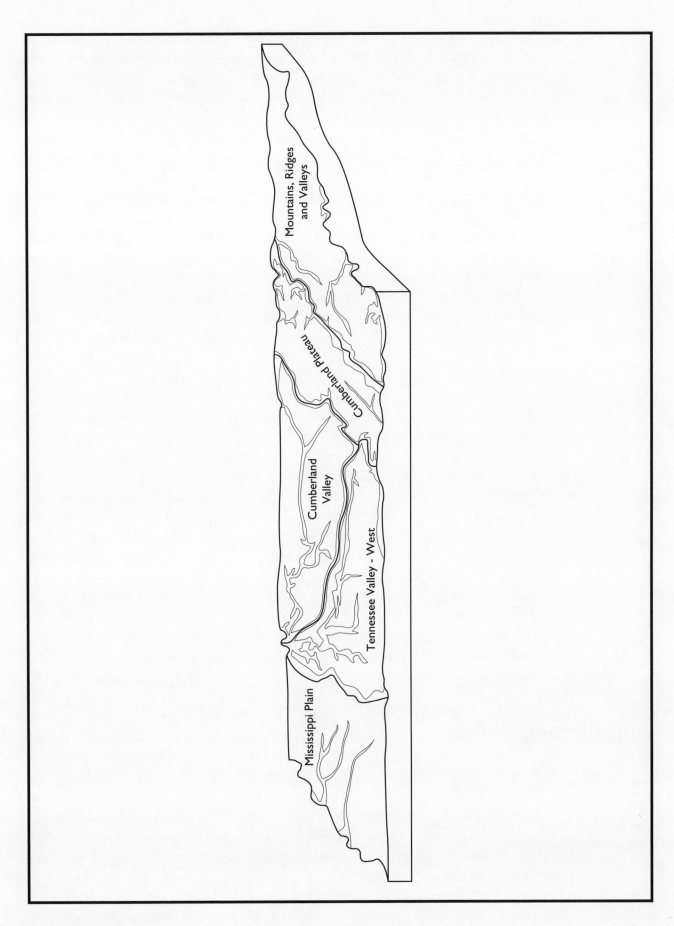

Mountains, Ridges and Valleys

Cumberland Plateau

Cumberland Valley

Tennessee Valley - West

Mississippi Plain

gold on the way down the mountainside. The Coker Creek gold run in 1831 trained many of the later Forty-Niners, and several productive Unaka fields, including the underlying copper resources in the southeast corner of the state, are continually being re-examined as worldwide precious-metal values change.) Jade, rubies, and other minerals are exposed as the thin cover over the fire-and-brimstone rockbase erodes. Expect to see rockwall or forest in the Unakas. There is little soil depth to support any agricultural use; similarly, there is little water-retention capacity in these thin-soil deposits. When it rains, the streams flow; when it doesn't, they don't. Fast runoff, steep slopes, rocky terrain—by definition, these are ideal conditions for the seasonal, highly technical whitewater streams that predominate in the Unakas.

All those crashing mountainside cascades (and a few larger, intermountain drainways) coming from the Unakas work their way westward toward that major southbound interceptor, the Tennessee River. This major regional waterway drains down the middle of a large hill-and-dale valley that is actually as geologically complex as the structure of the eastern mountains. Long ago, the valley was a fjordlike arm to a southeastern sea that received the erosion sediment from the then-new Rocky Mountain–like Unakas. Over time the submerged valley bottom continued to sink, fold, and buckle. Its hard rock base eventually turned on edge, here and there causing the lines of linear north–south low ridges now found in this valley. The foundations of many of the ridges were pinched off, and some of the hills simply drifted away. (For instance, a hill on the University of Tennessee campus in Knoxville derives from its foundation near Dolly Parton's homestead outside Sevierville. But that was a long time ago.) Basically these lines of ridges do not abruptly alter the stream flows of the nearby rivers. Rather, they simply redirect these streamways to funnel the masses of water to the south. Drainages coming from many miles away are all brought together in this complex Great Valley of East Tennessee. The Clinch, Powell, Holston, Nolichucky, French Broad, Little Tennessee, and Hiwassee are all major rivers brought together in a relatively limited area to feed the Tennessee River. Expect slackwater impoundments downstream on these major riverways; however, often long-season, free-flowing, easy-water overnight trips are possible upstream. Few technical whitewater challenges will be found in the valley, but, because of the extensive watershed, exploring upstream tributaries (like those just mentioned) is worthwhile. A word of caution, however: going too far up a tributary will lead to a different geological province (probably back in the mountains) and to those crashing cascades again.

# Cumberland Plateau

After leaving the Great Tennessee River Valley and continuing west, the paddler again encounters mountains. This next geologic province is the Cumberland Plateau (called the Cumberland Mountains in the northern part of the area). This highland range is a continuation of the more northern Alleghenies and remains a part of the eastern Appalachians. In fact, the Cumberlands are home to more mountain settlers than the better-known Unaka Range to the east.

The Cumberland Plateau is geologically less complex than the Unaka Range. Eons of seabed layers have left a wear-resistant, deep sandstone caprock over the softer underlying limestone and shale. Beds of coal intermingle with the sandstone deposits, and oil and natural gas are common in subterranean pockets. The area has had its share of uplift, faults, and overthrust, but the topography did not succumb to all these mountain-forming influences because (even during the long span of geologic time) little of the hardcap sandstone eroded away. So far, all this may not sound too interesting to a canoeist, but these geologic details have a significant impact on the exhilarating Cumberland Plateau streamways.

Probably some of the best wildwater canoeing in Tennessee can be found in the Cumberlands. Because of the hard caprock, drainage waters have managed to cut only narrow passageways, which slice deeper into the sandstone caprock the farther downstream the canoeist ventures. Unlike the normal mountain streams that start steep, fast, and difficult and then flatten out as they reach the rolling foothills and valleys, the "backward" plateau streams start small, slow, and flat, then pitch over to a steeper gradient, receive more feeder waters, and penetrate deeper into the gorge cuts where big (house-sized) gorge-wall rock falls litter the passageway. These falls create exciting, technical canoeing—high class white-water! When there is enough water, upper watershed creeks are Class I's and II's; midway tributary floats are II's and III's; downstream runs are steep, technical III's and IV's (the same runs are Class IV's and V's and up when there is too much water in these narrow confines of the rock bluffs).

The nature of the geology leaves little soil buildup atop the plateau, hence rain retention is minimal and a fast runoff from any rainfall should be expected. Additionally, the close-walled gorges along the waterways have little floodplain capacity, and this same fast runoff will cause a stream to rise higher and faster than normally expected. The progression from whitewater to wildwater to flushwater can and does occur on a rainy day's run.

The river gorges of the plateau are visually striking. The canoeist will develop an intimacy with rockways. Sheer rockwall bluffs guard the stream. House-sized boulders litter the streambed. Canoeists dart blindly to the side of, through, and occasionally under these eons-old undercut obstructions. Strange river currents, surprising rock falls, and overestimated canoeing skills all wring out a memorable trip in these remote, one-way gorges. Tangles of rhododendron and laurel line the banks. Road crossings are rare and wildlife is plentiful. The rivers rise and spend 95 percent of their run in this rural highland plateau. Many streamways have clear, refreshing waters, but feeders coming from active (or even abandoned) coal-mining sites are usually loaded with silt and fish-killing mine acid. Upstream, water quality is either great or terrible—the canoeist either floating on clear, see-through streams or on opaque, dead mine drainage. Downstream, the feeders mix and all the water gets somewhat murky. No matter; canoeing in the Cumberlands is an unforgettable experience.

# Cumberland Valley

Continuing westward, the landscape drops off the backside escarpment of the remnant Pennsylvanian sandstone plateau and onto some chert-infested Mississippian limestone known as the Highland Rim. This is the Cumberland Valley canoeing region, which contains parts of three geologic provinces: the Eastern Highland Rim, Central Basin, and Western Highland Rim. The two Highland Rims are lower than that eastern Cumberland Plateau but compared with the Central Basin, they are high, and they do indeed form an enclosing rim.

The rims together form an elevated base that completely surrounds the Central Basin, a 60-mile-wide (east to west) by 120-mile-long (north to south) depression in the center of the state, which contains Tennessee's bluegrass, walking horses, and, of course, Nashville's country music scene. Eons before the long-hunters of early history arrived, the ground Nashville sits on used to be at the level of the Cumberland Plateau. The present site of Music City rode atop a large, uplifted dome anchored by the "lower" Highland Rims. But the uplift cracked the surface of this limestone dome and erosion ate it all into the basin of today. And the remnant limestone rim still surrounds the basin below the level of the sandstone Cumberland Plateau to its east and above the depths of the bluegrass basin at its core. Erosive forces do not rest, so the basin imperceptively enlarges daily. Someday, the Highland Rim will completely yield and the western Cumberland Plateau escarpment drainageways will become something else again as they plunge all the way into a newly formed "Highland Basin." Presently, they just plunge halfway, onto the existing, soluble Eastern Highland Rim. The Eastern and Western Highland Rims are actually connected, with the main difference between them being that the western rim once was under a sea immersion that did not reach the eastern rim. Hence the eastern rim displays more general geological erosion (while the western side rested under water), and the western rim contains a deposited iron-ore concentrate (from that short immersion) not found on the eastern rim. (In fact, the western rim's low-grade ore once supported a rudimentary iron industry that provided Confederates with cannonballs, among other useful products.)

Basically, both rims are composed of limestone. And limestone has a peculiarity: it dissolves over the years. The rivers draining the limestone rims are peculiar, too. They flow along for a while, then just sink out of sight among the riverbottom gravels. Because of the large amount of water in the springtime "tides," the river channels are usually well-defined rock-ways. But often several miles of babbling brook will be followed by several miles of pure rockbed, and this may be followed by several miles of babbling brook again. One dramatic example of this in-again, out-again river flow came to light a few decades ago when aerial photographs indicated a falls no one even knew existed. Now called Virgin Falls, this full-size stream was found to spring from a cave-like opening on the mountainside, travel about 50 feet along the ground, tumble over a dramatic 110-foot fall, and then promptly re-enter the underground drainage in a "sink" cave among the boulders at the foot of the falls.

Riverways are well developed on these limestone slopes of the Highland Rims, yet there are probably bigger drainages underground. (A particularly famous one emerges in the state's smallest county, Moore County, right behind the Jack Daniel's Distillery in Lynch-burg.) Canoeing in limestone country is a scenic adventure. Greener grasses cannot be found. All the ground cover wildflowers are hardy and plentiful; their hues are brilliant. The flora thrives to rich, deep foliages. The topography is interesting: elevation differentials are not great, but slopes are steep. The valleys were formed through chemical dissolution as well as through long-term weathering erosion, so it contains hummocks and knobs, rock outcrops, springs, sinks, and caves. The Highland Rim is truly one of nature's grand and secret places. But beware. Because of these atypical stream-formation mechanisms, probably some of the most treacherous and downright dangerous canoe runs are found here. The smaller, extremely seasonal Cumberland Plateau/Eastern Highland rim escarpment streams are the most dangerous. Once a canoeist is far enough downstream so that water erosion becomes the predominant form of stream formation, the hazard lessens, but the stupendous scenery continues—all the way into the Central Basin.

Within the Central Basin, the canoeing experience will change. Bigger watersheds mean more year-round floating; deeper soil means more stabilized flows. The terms "water table" and "ground charge" begin to mean something. Typical mud riverbanks with towering streamside trees create blowdowns and strainers to avoid around the next bend in the river. Yet the agrarian nature of this bluegrass basin also means that floats with a definite rural flavor are available just outside the city limits. Pastoral canoeing abounds in the basin. And all the major drainageways are steeped in remnants of the area's early history (with an abundant share of prehistoric puzzles, too). Within the Cumberland Valley the canoeist is in the heart of mainstream Tennessee.

## Tennessee Valley—West

This section contains four of Tennessee's nine major geological provinces. The Tennessee Valley—West section cuts across the southern parts of the Eastern Highland Rim, Central Basin, and Western Highland Rim. The geology and the resulting canoeing in these three provinces are the same as described for these areas in the Cumberland Valley section. This Tennessee Valley—West section, however, also completely encompasses a fourth geologic province, the Western Valley of the Tennessee River. Unfortunately, almost all of this province lies under the immense slackwaters of Kentucky and Pickwick Lakes. These backwater reservoirs inundate almost the entire northbound crossing of the Tennessee River on this side of the state. And with the valley submerged, there remains little of geologic interest to the fast-water canoeists in this western valley province. But bass anglers, tugboat captains, duck hunters and waterfowl watchers, however, find a lot to be interested in, because Kentucky Lake produces many forms of water-dependent wildlife. It is interesting to note that in all past times of recorded history, this northward drainage of the great Tennessee River has always been a flatwater float, even back in the flatboat days of the early Nashboro settlers. This section of the Tennessee offered a float similar to what can presently be found on Kentucky Lake (but without the barge wakes). The underlying alluvial deposits and the repeated sea submergence had pretty well flattened the valley. In fact, the Tennessee River only turned north at all because the Ice Age trapped so much of the world's free water and fouled up flow patterns of so many major drainages. Before that, the Tennessee–Tombigbee Waterway probably already existed, and the Tennessee did not make its northbound crossing to the Ohio River. And yet another Tennessee–Tombigbee Waterway could reasonably be expected to exist again in a brief eon or two as the geologic processes grind out more changes.

## Mississippi Plain

At first glance, these last two geologic provinces (Plateau Slope and Mississippi River Valley) may seem flat and singularly uninteresting. But since the major formations of all our geologic provinces are continually undergoing slow (on our time scale) changes, the flat provinces in Tennessee's Mississippi Plain are probably the most dynamic, geologically speaking, of them all. The top eighty feet of soil were air-deposited (in the world's worst dust bowl) after the last Ice Age. The Mississippi River carved a several hundred-foot-deep gorge during that Ice Age and has now completely filled it with bits and pieces of the Rocky Mountains from the west and the Blue Ridge Mountains from the east—all since the Ice Age. Thousands of feet of sand (which will someday make an uplifted sandstone plateau) have been overlaid on a now-cracked limestone and dolomite dome (like the old Nashville dome). As recently as 1812—which is very recent in geologic time—as the steamboat *New Orleans* worked its way on its maiden voyage from Pittsburgh to New Orleans, that overlaid rock dome shrugged and the water-soaked countryside erupted in an awesome earthquake, causing unbelievable surface disturbance. The Reelfoot Lake basin was formed, and the Mississippi River drained backwards to fill it. The same river formed gigantic "sinks" to fill ruptures in the soft-bottomed bed. Eruptions of steam and sulphurous gases leveled whole stands of native forests. The naturally water-soaked ground heaved up in waves like the gelatinous mass that it was. Bottomless quicksand developed. Riverbanks collapsed. Dry land became lakes, and lakes became dry land. (Although running late and presumed lost in this wilderness cataclysm, the *New Orleans* dodged the shifting riverbed and hazardous currents and flotsam and completed an unforgettable maiden voyage.) This was very dramatic demonstration that the geologic process continues. To this day, earthquake-prone Los Angeles and western Tennessee share common earthquake code restrictions because of their respective hazards.

But a canoeist does not operate on a geologic scale of time, and, in fact, rarely operates on any common time frame at all. The canoeist likes to sense the natural flow of the river, the weather, and the seasons. And canoeing in the Mississippi Plain offers a relaxed time frame as nowhere else can. The thick deposit of loess (air-laid soil) atop the sand and silt deposit of the long-duration sea embayments on the Plateau Slope and Mississippi Valley guarantee a meandering flatwater drainage system. Giant hardwoods broken by clustered cypress bogs can be found thriving along these deep-soil, swamp rivers. Wood and gumbo mud are the paddler's constant companions, and if you want a rock to set a camp stove on, you'll have to bring your own.

Note: Much of the information in this section was derived from the excellent book *Our Restless Earth: The Geologic Regions of Tennessee*, by Edward T. Luther (Knoxville: University of Tennessee Press, 1977). For further study into Tennessee's unique and multifaceted geology, this eloquent, readable, and inexpensive book is highly recommended.

# Prepare to Paddle

## The Paddler

**W**e're in a river canyon and twilight is upon us. The day's light fades. A dull rosy color tones the features of the river. But it's getting harder to discern any telltale details within the water's flow. We've completed our river paddling for the day. We're tired. We cannot even see very well. But we can still hear the river, every bit as loud as before. We're moving slower. The river isn't. The schedule of the river knows no twilight. The river runs on through the night, and through the next day, and the day after that. The river even runs on through the following work-a-day week while we're all elsewhere plying our respective trades.

And I have often marveled at that idea. As best I can figure, water continues to flow over that midriver ledge, even in the dark of night when no one is there to thrill to its presence or fear its pounding power. We sometimes get a little crazy when we spend too much time mulling the obvious. Is there any lessening to the magic of that drop when the flow pounds on in its own world of riverine isolation? Surely not. I suspect the magic is continuously there, always available to those who might pass within its radius of influence. For how would the river know when it is 2 P.M. on a Saturday and paddlers will shortly float on by? So I decided to test this definition of river wildness. I paddled the Obed on a Tuesday morning and found that same weekend afternoon boat-swamping wave at Widow Maker rapid. At another time I introduced my Yankee bride to the Hiwassee as we floated it by full moon at midnight. We found those same midrapid thrills in the middle of the night (and more fear than I thought would be there).

The good news is that the river keeps on moving on. It seems that only the paddler is needed to make the river scene a complete experience.

So let's get you out there . . . and safely back! What will you need to experience the river?

> Personal flotation devices (PFDs).
> A Canoe.
> Canoe outfitting.
> Two (or more) paddles.
> Suitable wearing apparel.
> Training in the use of a canoe.
> Information on the stream section.
> Provisions for an automobile shuttle.
> Most importantly, other canoes in the party!

Winter paddling in the city. Even the metro streams increase their flow in wintertime. Paddle Mill Creek through Nashville and stop at Murfreesboro Road for a hot cup of coffee or a pizza. (Be careful at the breeched dams, old bridge piers, and pipe crossings.) Photo shows an organized TSRA club trip. Photograph by Ann Spencer.

Chapters and even books have been written about each of the above topics. And, indeed, it is worthwhile to study, learn, and obtain the necessary information. You will enjoy your outdoors ventures much more when you do them right. And your chances of comfortable survival increase dramatically with each increment of knowledge added to your general canoeing expertise.

This chapter will not make you a seasoned river rat. For that, you need to paddle, talk with others, help others, ask others for help, paddle, join canoe clubs, lobby for free-flowing rivers, paddle, read newsletters, read magazines, read maps, read water, paddle, make mistakes, take advanced training, provide training for others, paddle, install canoeing hardware, make roof racks, sight down the keel line of your canoe, buy a different canoe, paddle, buy synthetic underwear, buy wool, buy fleece, paddle, teach, preach, beseech, paddle, paddle, paddle. Paddle carefully during the short, cold days of winter; paddle in control during the cold-water flush of springtime; paddle and endure during the tepid droughts of fall. You learn by doing. That's a major lesson from life. And it's not unique to canoeing. So get out and paddle. And wear your PFD.

# Personal Life Jackets

Your body is more important than any canoe. So the very first consideration for a paddler is to choose a proper PFD (Personal flotation device) and to wear it. Find a comfortable, well-fitting one. Make sure it is big enough for you when fully fastened. Then fasten it up!

We already know that you are a great swimmer. So are the rest of us. But when you are concerned about your floating camping gear, the status of the other swimming paddlers, and a canoe full of water moving down on you in the current (while the rocks from downstream move up at you from the other direction), the last thing you need to do is to practice your breathing rhythm with that winning crawl stroke. You want positive flotation and protection for your body. You want the ability to twist around in the water, keep your head up, kick your feet to the surface, use your arms to grab things, use your PFD cushioned upper body to bounce off things. Your prefastened PFD allows all this. An unfastened PFD floats well, too, but usually without your body anywhere nearby.

Look for the vest style of PFD. A horse-collar type will be uncomfortable after a few hours. Do not even consider using a floating cushion as a substitute. You want to wear your PFD all day, fully fastened. This means that as you zip up your PFD, you also reach around and fasten the straps usually found around the chest and waist. Wear such a PFD in a size that fits you. If the PFD is too big you will find it riding up in your face while in the river. If too small, the PFD will not keep you sufficiently afloat in the river. You want room in the arm holes for comfort while paddling. You want room at the neck to keep it from abrading your chin during the movements of paddling.

Along with your canoe and paddle, your PFD will become one of the three most cherished items of paddling gear. You will develop a personal bond with each item. The PFD will keep you warm during a chill wind on the river. You will sit on it at lunch time to smooth the bankside stones. You will roll it up and use it for a pillow. And, of course, you will swim in it. You will even begin to think that you look better when wearing it. Don't miss out on all this pleasure. Get a good PFD and wear it!

# Hardware—The Canoe

You need a canoe. The shape of your chosen craft will be dependent on the type of water on which you plan to paddle. A canoe for sheltered, small lakes will be different from one for open, wind-exposed inland seas, which again will be different for moving flatwater rivers, and different again for wild rivers with turbulent rapids, or again for small cascading whitewater streams. All these different canoe designs have varying heights of the ends, midsection depths, amounts of fore-to-aft keel-line curvature (called "rocker"), degrees of side-to-side roundness (or flatness) of the bottom, ends parting the water as blunt or sharp or combinations, and much more.

At first a canoe simply looks like a long, narrow open shell with two pointed ends. But a closer look at different models will show the many variations of the basic design elements that are possible. All these changes in shape go to make this manually propelled craft as efficient and seaworthy as possible. No one design can satisfy all such conflicting conditions. Canoes for high winds are low cut in the ends and midsection. Canoes for high waves are higher cut and generally fuller in the ends. Canoes for flat water are straight keeled and rounded across the bottom. (These are efficient designs that provide less energy-absorbing wakes behind them.) Canoes that must be quickly maneuvered in whitewater have rockered keel lines and are usually blunt in the ends.

This book generally addresses river canoeing. A canoe used for such moving waters will have a greater depth to the ends and midsection than the more wind-resistant, fast flat-water craft. The keel line may be slightly curved or even straight along most of the length with a rise or lift at the ends. The ends of the canoe will be somewhat full (to gain buoyancy fast in foamy whitewater), but will provide a narrow waterline entry to be efficient in the pools. The canoe might not be symmetrical front-to-back, but it loses certain versatilities of use if it isn't. The canoe will not be extremely narrow, nor will it have a rounded transverse profile across the bottom.

You have your choice of paddling tandem or going solo, and, generally, the length of the craft will be dependent upon that choice. Keep in mind the boundary length of 16 feet. A solo canoeist can handle a 16-foot canoe, yet that canoe also has the inherent load carrying capacity for the weight of a tandem team. Popular solo canoes are usually 13 to 15 feet, but they can be as short as 12 feet or as long as 17 feet. In the past, standard tandem canoes were 17 feet. But today good tandem canoes are produced in a range from 14 to 19 feet. Please realize that there are specialty exceptions to any of the values listed here.

You are about to choose your canoe. You have measured the length, width, and depth. Now, when sighting down the keel line, do you see an external keel? Do you want such a keel? No. A protruding external keel is neither desired nor needed (except, maybe structurally). A keel is *not* an effective mechanism to keep the canoe tracking in a straight direction. The paddlers, working together, make the desired track. The entire underwater wetted shape of the canoe hull, itself, is designed to either aid in straight tracking or to allow easy maneuverability. A protruding external keel does not provide enough square inches of wetted material to counteract that underwater surface. The keel will only hang up and catch in the shallows. It also scrapes when beaching the boat and can get in the way when pulling a loaded canoe over barely submerged logs. Although this comment is somewhat simplified, a keel basically appears only when needed to hold the two halves of a canoe shell structure together. It used to be the base upon which a wood-based shell was constructed. Later it became a convenience for metallic construction and then a nuisance for various plastic constructions. A keel is not a performance enhancer.

What material should the hull be made from? Don't worry about that now. You'll find out soon enough that whatever material you choose will have its advantages and too many disadvantages. You will be choosing another canoe shortly. Rather you should worry more about the weight of the craft. A 16-foot canoe should not weigh more than 70 to 75 pounds. Many are lighter. You do not want a heavier one. You want a craft that you and your tandem partner can hoist and carry up the riverbank to your car or trailer, even when you are tired. You want to be able to portage (carry) around difficult rapids, often in difficult terrain. Do not accept a heavy canoe.

There are excellent aluminum canoes available. Aluminum can be tough, but some grades of aluminum can be easy to tear or puncture. Royalex/ABS canoes have one-piece plastic hulls noted for their toughness. But there are different grades to that material, too. Rotomolded polyethylene is often used for good overall one-piece plastic hulls. These canoes can weigh in on the heavy side, but the price is usually good. And there are many, many grades of fiberglass reinforced plastic (FRP) canoe hulls on the market. These canoes can range from the ultra lightweight to the battleship built (which are unreasonably heavy).

Some have strong, stiff graphite and Kevlar high-strength woven reinforcement layers, while others have only a minimum amount of fiberglass mat as the structure. Price, weight, strength, and even looks will vary across the board with this type material. So, for now, make sure you are in the weight range you want, then check out the price. After you've been out on the river for a while, you'll learn much more about the make and model canoes that are most suitable for your type paddling.

So let's find a suitable craft. It's time to borrow, build, buy, or rent your canoe. Decide to paddle with a friend and go tandem. Find a 16- or 17-foot canoe, about 34 to 36 inches wide, 14 or 15 inches deep at midships, 22 to 26 inches of end height, with full ends and only a slightly rockered keel line. No keel. Weigh the basic canoe in below 75 pounds.

# Hardware Continued—The Outfitting

First off, tie on two end lines to the canoe, one at each end. These lines, called "painters," are invaluable in handling the craft at water's edge, tying onto the car or trailer, and even aiding in rescuing a pinned canoe. So choose a good synthetic rope material (not cotton clothesline) and securely tie it as near to each end of the canoe as possible. Use a thick enough rope so you will be able to pull hard on it with your bare (probably wet) hands. The painter should be kept somewhat short to keep it from being a hazard in the boat. But it should be long enough to be used as a tie down from atop a car to the car's under-bumper hooks. Eight to twelve feet is about right.

The canoe probably has seats. Make sure they are not too low-slung and that there is enough room under each seat for the legs of a kneeling paddler. Even in flatwater, you should not hesitate to get off the seat and kneel in the bottom of the canoe while paddling. Use the front edge of the seat as a brace to stabilize your body when kneeling. By kneeling, you move your weight to the floor of the canoe. Seats are usually connected to the gunwales so your weight goes to the top of the sidewalls of the canoe when you are seated. The simple act of kicking your feet back under the seat and dropping to your knees increases the stability of the canoe and cargo (you) many times. It is simple to do, and you will soon find that you are much more effective with your paddle strokes from that position. But the floor of the canoe can be uncomfortable when your weight is on your knees. There are many ways to solve this problem. One is to wear knee pads. These range from gardener's to miner's styles in ruggedness. Be careful not to wear a knee pad constructed with open-cell foam, which will absorb water and become uncomfortable in its own right. Another solution is to get the pad off your body and onto the canoe. This is usually done by bonding small sheets of closed-cell foam in the positions where the paddlers will be placing their knees. Not much thickness is required. And, in fact, not much cushioning is needed. Choose a rather firm foam sheeting. It will be more rugged in the normal wear and tear of use. For the first few trips, the sheeting can be placed in the bottom of the canoe without bonding in place while you decide where it is best to place material, and whether you have chosen a suitable foam. Note that some sheeting gets slippery when wet. When you are ready to simplify your life, you can bond the sheeting to the floor of the canoe. A good waterproof contact cement will probably work fine. Make sure you understand how to use solvent based glues if you are bonding to a plastic type hull. Some solvents can eat into various plastic hull materials.

You, of course, need to be wearing a life jacket before setting out on any moving river or large body of water. All paddlers should be wearing life jackets. It is good insurance to provide your canoe with a life jacket, too. Any reputable canoe will have positive buoyancy flotation built-in. But it is a good idea to provide "added flotation" to your canoe. This can be as simple as shoving an inner tube into the center of the canoe under the center thwarts (leaving room for the feet of the bow paddler to stick back into the center area from beneath the bow seat). Tie the tube to the thwarts and then overinflate in place, before you reach the river. This is a heavy solution but quite practical and plenty rugged. It also provides an opening in the center where you can stow some of your gear. For lighter weight and more tailored solutions, there are cylindrical air bags available to use in the center of the canoe. Look for a "split pair," which gives you two tubes, side by side, in the center of your craft. You can use the crack formed between them to stow some of your extra gear. And they don't distort between thwarts, as a single rectangular box-style center bag might. To properly install air bags (which are not as rugged as inner tubes), tie the bag corners to the thwarts and also weave a parachute cord support web from gunwale to gunwale in the open center area of the canoe where the middle of the bags might otherwise pop out when the canoe is awash. Air bags come in vinyl and lightweight coated nylon. Either is rugged enough. But, of course, lightweight costs more. Eventually, you will want to opt for the installed air-bag boat-damage insurance. So watch what others do to their crafts and inquire as to which type bag they prefer, where they got their stainless steel or plastic gunwale fittings, and what web-weaving pattern they use and why.

Keep in mind that some canoes have flotation built into the ends and others have open ends. An end filled with water is heavy. A swamped canoe with open ends will pin easier as it flushes down a shoals. So, when feasible, it is a good idea to find some triangular-end air bags or foam blocks to install in the ends of such a canoe. This installation is not as simple and generally requires the placement of a floor anchor to help hold the end bag down. A floor anchor is usually a D-ring attached to a circular fabric patch that is bonded to the floor using suitable waterproof adhesive.

Now as you get ready to set off down the river, don't forget to carry along a bailing device. Water will splash into the craft, and it is best to keep the canoe as dry as possible. Too much water in the bilge will cause surprising handling problems. So it is best to simply bail out the water shortly after it enters rather than waiting to accumulate enough to paddle to shore to manhandle that loaded canoe as you try to empty it. Find a heavier type plastic jug, such as bleach comes in (not a flimsy milk jug). Make sure the cap is intact, then cut out the bottom with enough sidewall to get all the bottom radius cut away. Tie a string to the handle, and be ready to tie this bail within reach but away from possible entanglement.

Just as you tied in any extra flotation and your bailing bucket, it is good practice to tie in all extra gear. Should the canoe swamp and your gear be untied, some of the stuff will float away, some will sink. All is hard to retrieve. It is easy to tie gear to the thwarts to keep everything together. Only the paddlers and paddles should be independent of the craft.

A few words of caution. Make sure you are careful to preclude possible entanglements when tying gear in. Keep all ties short and do not leave cords or ropes loose in the canoe.

Rescued canoe. There is hidden power in the flow of a river. And paddling mishaps can happen, even on relatively placid streams. Sometimes the canoe can be "stomped" back to shape and the trip continued. But often the picnic-packed fried chicken gets soggy.

And keep in mind these hints on the proper use of painters. Do not leave any knots along the ropes. Always untie any loops and other overhand knots on the painters. And tuck the painters into the canoe when underway. Do not let them stream in the water. Even unknotted, they can catch between rocks and cause surprising changes to the path of the canoe.

So far the outfitting of the canoe has been relatively simple. Tie two painters on the ends, throw in some kneeling material, and shove an inner tube under the center thwarts. Tie in all your gear, grab a bailing bucket, fasten your lifejacket, and get underway.

## Hardware Continued—The Paddle

Well, you won't get very far out down the river without a paddle in your hands. When paddling tandem, each paddler should have one. And an extra paddle should be stowed in the canoe. If, by chance, you are carrying a passenger in the center of your canoe, it is probably best that such a bilge buddy does not try to be helpful by using the extra paddle.

Before getting into the geometry and materials considerations of paddle selection, a basic rule of operation ought to be noted. The primary rule for tandem paddle usage is for the two paddlers to be paddling on opposite sides of the canoe. Although communication between bow (front) and stern (back) is desirable, it remains the ultimate responsibility of the stern paddler to enforce this opposite-side paddling procedure. It is much easier for the stern paddler to view the paddling positions. And if the bow paddler cannot (or will not) hear suggestions to change sides with the paddle, then the stern paddler must do so. When both paddlers are paddling on the same side of the canoe, and leaning to that side, capsize (to that side) is only an unexpected scrape of a barely submerged riverbed rock away. Repeat: tandem paddlers must always paddle on opposite sides of the canoe.

Inherent in this advice is the caution to also avoid changing sides without communication between the paddlers. Hence, it is best to keep to one side and to not switch back and forth. Learn the paddle strokes. You can control your end of the canoe in any direction without switching sides. Drop to your knees, and note how much more control you have with your paddle strokes.

The first consideration of paddle selection generally is length. And there remains much folklore on that subject. However, the matter is actually very simple. The paddle is used to get from you to the water. Its necessary length is a direct function of the particular shape of your upper body. And the easiest measurement to use is to stretch your arms out from your sides, parallel to the ground. Turn palms facing forward and cup your fingers. Fit a paddle to the distance from cupped fingers to cupped fingers. This will be about the same distance as from the floor to your chin. But that height measurement is not as good an indicator for a person who will be sitting and kneeling when using the paddle. If you must grab a paddle from a rack without the opportunity to size it to yourself, take a 60-inch paddle.

For river paddling, a T-grip is preferred. It allows feedback to you about the orientation of the face of the paddle blade while in use. And it allows direct control of that blade orientation. For long-distance cruising, the old-fashioned pear-shaped grip is more comfortable. Generally, the blade should be thin, flat, stiff, and large enough to be effective in the water. Be aware that too large a blade will work the paddler too hard. Bigger is not all that better. There has been a lot of effort in developing effective paddle blade shapes. Pay attention to what paddles are in use on the type water you favor. For general river use, you are seeking a paddle with a blade width of about 7½ inches or so, and about 20 inches long. Narrower widths are good for cruising paddles (the ones with pear-shaped grips). They move less water with each stroke and allow a day-long tempo of stroke, stroke, stroke, keeping the canoe clipping along at cruising speed.

Try not to use a paddle with a shaft diameter that is too small for your hand. It will be fatiguing to your grip. A shaft diameter of 1 inch is too small. A diameter of 1¼ inches is good. Make sure that the part of the shaft under your grip is smooth. Even a small burr will become uncomfortable by the end of a day. You ought to realize that an uncoated aluminum shaft will continually transmit the coldness of the water to the hand gripping that shaft. Even on warm days this body heat drain can become uncomfortable and should be avoided.

Some expert paddlers prefer some spring to the paddle shaft. Some want a rigid shaft and rigid blade. You will find your preferences in time. For now you should be more interested in strength. It is possible to snap a paddle in half during an aggressive paddle stroke or even during an unexpected impact upon a barely submerged rock. So carry a spare and use accepted, proven models. Many rugged paddles use aluminum tubing as the shaft material. Many such shafts are covered in plastic. There are also good fiberglass reinforced plastic (FRP) shafts and some excellent wooden shafts (usually covered with a thin reinforced plastic coating). There are many paddlers who claim that only a wooden paddle (even covered with protective plastic) feels right. And that is true for them. The only catch there is that only the high-end wooden paddles will hold up to river usage. So be prepared to pay for that preference. Many utilitarian river paddles use FRP blades of some sort attached to covered aluminum shafts. And these are good, rugged, serviceable paddles.

# Software—Your Personal Outfitting

This software is not digital. But it does cover your digits. And new revisions are hitting the streets almost as fast as in the computer field. Years ago, the buzzword was "wool." Get cotton out of your wardrobe and wear wool. That still works. Get out of your cottons. Contrary to whatever might be seen in television advertising, jeans are the least desirable type of pants to wear. If you doubt this, go sit in your filled bathtub with your jeans on, then walk around the house for a few hours. Sit down, kneel, jump, run. You will not be comfortable. Things are much worse on the river; within the house you will not be exposed to the chilling effects of such non-drying wet wear. Inexpensive, thin, poly-blend pants are much better. The specialty market is now full of fast-drying poly-wear. And much of it is oriented toward the needs of paddlers. Synthetic underwear is great. Silk underwear works very well. Even wool underwear works if you like that type of thing. Likewise with outerwear. Synthetic outerwear is great. Wool still works well. There is much fleece-wear in use among the paddlers.

A good rule to remember is that your clothing should not be too loose. Should you end up swimming in the river with your clothes on, you do not want clothes that flap out to form an underwater sail taking you along with the current. No ponchos and no long, stylish scarves should be worn. You want mobility in the water.

Your clothing protects your body when you are out in the natural elements. On warm days, many paddlers like to wear shorts. Many others would rather wear the inexpensive, thin, poly-blend pants. These pants better protect your knees when kneeling. They protect the legs when wading through shallow waters. And they protect against sunburn and insect bites.

Also carefully consider your footwear. Those rugged, full-soled, river sandals work well under certain conditions. But when you kneel and kick your legs back under the canoe's seat, the tops of your feet can easily scrape along the floor of the canoe. Before you painfully catch an exposed toenail, it is best to consider just what protection you need and should expect from your footwear. During the trip you will find plenty of opportunities to walk through shallow waters, atop rocks, along gravel bars, and immersed in mudbanks. So you want some traction and a little foot support from your footwear. And most of the time you want some warmth. Neoprene socks with those river sandals work well. Or you might prefer simple, inexpensive canvas shoes and neoprene socks. Generally, the less leather in your footwear, the better. But protect your feet, and realize that they will be wet. You cannot always step directly from a dock to the craft and back again. Before putting on an outer shoe, some people have wrapped their feet in polyethylene bread bag wrappers with a certain degree of water-proofing success. Generally they used the bread bag between two pair of socks within the outer protection of a canvas sneaker.

Gloves can also be a good idea. Again, there are many opportunities to purchase comfort within the specialty marketplace. One inexpensive option is to locate a pair of those green wool hunter's gloves at a surplus outdoor gear provider. Although they look identical, the warmer-when-wet type are made of wool rather than a synthetic. Eventually you'll pay the price and purchase specialty paddling gloves. Half the year you do not need gloves, except for blister avoidance. (Believe it or not, duct tape works just as well . . . simply tape up the tender part of your hand before paddling.) But in the springtime and again in the fall, you'll find excellent paddling opportunities. You'll find good water levels, crisp, clear weather, and cold hands. You can be tough. Or you can be prepared.

Hat, cap, headband, helmet? Yes, one of those. When in an open canoe, a helmet is generally worn on Class III or greater water. Actually, a helmet should be worn whenever the paddler thinks that a head-first rock landing is possible. In Class I or II water, when a canoe overturns, the paddler is usually immersed body first, head last. The open canoe paddler is usually not locked into the craft as severely as a paddler would be in a kayak, so voluntary or involuntary body twisting occurs as the canoe pitches over toward the river surface. A hat is worn to protect the head from the sun, overhanging tree branches, and other environmental hazards external to the river. A wide-brimmed hat or a baseball cap is often preferred for its versatility. Different paddlers want different things from their headgear. In colder weather, a knit cap is often preferred. And the material of preference? Wool!

A helmet should offer protection for the temples on the side of the head, as well as protection to the head's crown. But this temple protection needs to be tempered with some sort of ear-hole perforation to allow the ears to hear and discern direction of sound. It is also common to have other perforations in the top of the helmet to avoid "bucketing" and allow water to pass through the helmet. Many paddlers also add visors to their helmets or wear visored caps under them. Again, shop the specialty shops when buying specialty gear. Not only is there no reason to relearn all the hard (on the head) helmet lessons, but these type of canoe lessons are not particularly practical either.

And now, the "Rule of 100." This is the wetsuit (or drysuit) rule. If the water and air temperatures added together are less than 100, you should wear a wetsuit or drysuit. The Hiwassee near the Appalachia powerhouse can have a dam-release water temperature of 40 degrees. In the springtime, when daytime temperatures can be below 60 degrees, it is wetsuit time there. Probably the most useful wetsuit is a farmer john style, even the "shorty" style with short cut legs. You are looking to keep the core of your body protected, and this style covers the trunk of your body. It also forces you to wear normal protective paddling clothes, such as pants and a synthetic-based sweatshirt (or a wool sweater) over the wetsuit. This is good. Do not simply wear a wetsuit. It does a good job of keeping cold water from draining your finite internal heat reserves, but it can be pretty cool and uncomfortable when sitting in the wind in a dry canoe. So cover your wetsuit with another protective layer. Further, if you think you might be spending a lot of time in the water, then obtain a long-sleeve wetsuit jacket to go over the shorty, or get a full long-legged farmer john style, and so forth. Remember that it's possible to layer wetsuits, too. By the time you are ready to pay the freight for a drysuit, you will have sufficient experience in the cool waters of springtime to be able to make an informed purchase. It is true that a drysuit can offer all the cold-water protection of a wetsuit, but with much more comfort. But drysuits have their own problems, such as the integrity and endurance of the body seals, one-piece versus two-piece designs, ease of wearing, and more. Pay attention to the models that others are wearing. Ask about them. And get ready to obtain your own.

# Training

It is a good idea to get out and paddle. You will learn quickly through direct experience. But there are many paddling skills that are not very intuitive. And you will get wet, many times, trying to figure them all out by yourself. First off, fasten your PFD. Then remember that each member of a tandem team must be paddling on the opposite sides of the canoe. Again, it is the ultimate responsibility of the stern paddler to make sure that opposite-side paddling always occurs. Do not change paddling sides during any particular run through a shoals or chute. This throws overall balance off. It is best to simply learn to shift the canoe to either sideways direction from a single paddling side. The paddle strokes used to move the canoe sideways are called the "pry" and the "draw."

Hold the paddle with one hand on top of the grip of the paddle and the other hand on the shaft of the paddle near the blade. Do not hold the paddle with both hands on the shaft of the paddle. Kneel in the canoe. Keep your hands (and the entire paddle) outboard of the gunwale of the canoe. This means that you will stretch your arms to the side to get them outside the craft. And as you twist and stretch, you will see why kneeling is the preferred paddling position. Use the T-grip to give you feedback as to the orientation of the blade in the water. Sometimes you want to go forward and want the blade facing forward. Sometimes you want to hold the canoe back (backpaddling) with the same blade orientation. Sometimes you want to go sideways and want the blade facing sideways. Stretch that grip-holding hand outboard as far as possible. The objective is to have the paddle perpendicular to the water, outside the canoe.

You need to learn the basic paddle strokes that can give you control in the four major directions: forward, back, draw (sideways to the paddling side), and pry (sideways to the off side). Realize that tandem paddlers are paddling on opposite sides. Hence, if both are doing draws (moving sideways to the respective paddling sides), the canoe will go in a circle. This can be a good maneuver! It is a way to pivot the canoe while moving down the current. Should one paddler be doing a draw and the other doing a pry, the canoe will sideslip and move sideways while still moving down the current. This is good, too. Control is good! Practice these maneuvers.

Beware of "sweepers." These are trees that have fallen from the banks and are resting across the stream at water level. Water flows through these branches and under the trunk. Canoes and people do not flow through the branches, nor usually under the trunk, either. Maneuver away from these obstructions. There is current through that hazard with little or no passage potential. Not a good place to be.

One more major hint. Should you approach some fast water and not know what to do at all, then the safest technique is for both paddlers to backpaddle. The idea is to slow the canoe down. You will want to maneuver some during the run through the fast water to avoid rocks and such. And you have more decision time and maneuvering capability when the canoe is going slower than the current (rather than faster). It's a matter of physics, but a differential between the current and canoe speeds gives more craft response capability from your paddling strokes. So, in this situation, you can either go faster than the current (not a good choice) or go slower than the current. It's a good idea to try to hold the canoe back (contrary to your impulse to speed past the problems).

Winter paddling in the Tennessee Valley—west. Water levels run higher in winter. Some of the small feeder streams offer great get-aways. Indian Creek in Hardin County, a direct tributary of the Tennessee River (west), downstream from Olive Hill. Photograph by Marshall Spencer.

There is much more to learn. And the more you paddle, the better you will get. You will want to learn how to "read the river." At first it looks like a jumble of jumping water. But to a seasoned paddler, there are hidden rocks, chutes, pools, eddies, and more to be seen when looking downstream. A good idea is to look back upstream after going through some shoals. Try to match the upstream view with your previous downstream view. You will eventually learn to read the river, too. Watch others on the water. Follow them. Learn some basics. And you will enjoy your paddling. You really will! Take courses at a local canoe school. There are many good paddling clubs throughout Tennessee. And all the good ones care enough about safety and enjoyment to provide very cost-effective training. Any local outdoor specialty store will know how to find the local clubs. Take their canoe school class. For a one-weekend investment, you will gain the entrance to a healthy and enjoyable lifetime activity.

## Scouting the River

First, buy this book! Find out whatever you can about the river you want to float. Whenever possible, go with someone who has been on this river section before. There are many traps to floating an unknown stream. In some flatwater streams, the channel is not always obvious, and a floater can get lost on dead-end backwaters. There can be streamway obstructions not visible from access points. Many maps do not detail hazards that can affect a paddler.

Canoe School on the Buffalo River. A TSRA club Introductory Canoe School. This class is held along a four-mile section of the Buffalo below Metal Ford. Photograph by Ann Spencer.

Any dam on the river, no matter the size, should always be considered hazardous. The uniform rolling backwash at the foot of a dam can and does trap floating objects for long periods of time. A canoe can roll over and over at the foot of even a small dam for days. The uniformity of the dam and its backwash keeps a swimming paddler from finding an exit in that washing-machine action. Even a small dam can be deadly. Portage around dams. But first you have to know that they are there. The same holds true for other obstructions or significant drops in the streambed. Locate them however you can.

In your search for information, however, you might be somewhat wary of relying literally on local lore concerning the reported wildness to the stream just beyond local fishing patterns. Canoeists are familiar with how a canoe and a stream interacts. Local people fishing probably do not know how a canoe can handle their river's flow. Nor are they particularly tuned in to water levels suitable for floating. They may remember the floods of record and other significant natural riverine events. And generally they will caution you that passage is probably not possible beyond their reach of direct experience with the river.

When studying a section of river, make sure you choose a segment that is feasible to complete during the time you have available. A 5-mile whitewater run with many scout/run/recover rapids might be a full day's trip. A 20-mile flatwater paddle might be an easy day if there is some helpful current. Generally, you are pushing the trip if you plan to paddle more than 12 river miles. Be aware that it is often hard to get to the river site, arrange the shuttle set up, assemble all the gear on the riverbank, and get everyone underway in any expeditious fashion. Good daylight time is always lost on the front end of the trip. Pay attention to the available light during the time of year you are paddling. You want to get to your "take out" a couple of hours before dusk. If you are on the river from 11 A.M. until 5 P.M., that is 6 hours. At an overall average pace of 2 miles per hour, you will just cover those 12 miles.

## Determine a Car Shuttle

Your map scouting will be oriented toward finding suitable put in and take out points. You have to determine both your river segment needs and the suitability of a connecting road system. You do not need any particular built-up ramp to get your canoe to or from the river. But you will need a pull-off area for unloading from the car and some sort of rudimentary staging area at the riverbank. Often, when a map shows a roadway closely adjacent to a stream, there will not actually be an access point. The road will be atop a bluff using the streamway cut to get passage through rugged terrain. Do not choose access points by simple map reading. Scout the potential access spots firsthand. And, of course, be aware of a land-owner's rights to the streambank. Some roads are privately owned and may be gated. You have no rights to other people's properties. In some cases, only the flowing waters within the streamway remain in a public easement. Even the riverbottom can be privately owned. Get permission whenever there is any question as to private landownership of an access you want to use. Generally a highway crossing a stream provides public easement under and closely alongside its bridge. However, many bridges have long guard-railed approaches that do not provide any pull-off areas. And there are bridges that span off bluffs to cross the streams. These have little or no suitable accesses to the streams, even on their public right-of-ways. Wherever you find your access points, respect the rights of passage of others. Do not block the roads during off-loading, and do not block tracks to the river when parking your shuttle car. These tracks are in more use than you probably suspect; otherwise, they would be more overgrown and not particularly usable by you.

## The Paddling Party

For river floating, the general rule is to have a minimum party size of three craft. Many trips are made with only two craft, and even solo excursions are not uncommon. But the three-canoe rule came about through a lot of experience based on the need to meet extreme conditions. If one of the canoes becomes unusable, it is possible to continue to the take out by carrying one person each in the remaining two craft. Or if a canoe is pinned and help needs to remain on site, there is still a craft available to continue to the take-out to obtain further aid. A party of three canoes also provides people to effect a certain amount of on-site effort.

To set up a shuttle almost always requires a minimum of two cars or some other external shuttle help. There are river loops that allow a walking shuttle across a narrow neck of land forming the loop. And there are even upstream paddling segments that allow to-and-fro floats. But most of the time a car is needed at the take out and the paddlers must be also transported to the put in. A shuttle is needed for both the paddlers and the craft. The only trick, then, other than to maintain some sort of geographical understanding or communication between the drivers, is for the shuttle cars to be outfitted with double canoe racks. A shuttle becomes simpler if all craft can be transported at the same time as the paddlers are moved. And three canoes can be carried atop a double car rack on a single shuttle vehicle. So, even if you only own or borrow a single canoe, you should provide a double canoe rack atop your vehicle.

## Let's Go Paddling

That is all there is to getting out on the water. Find a good 16-foot canoe, tie on painters, grab a 60-inch paddle, fasten your life jacket, pull on your long pants, find a good tandem partner, join a party of two other canoes, do your map scouting, set up your shuttle, make sure you have enough daylight, and push off into the current. With a little preparation, you will enjoy the experience. And you will be back. You will improve. And you will enjoy the experience even more. Your life will change.

See you on the river!

Let's Go Paddling. After aggressively performing an excellent "draw" stroke at just the right time, the life-long joy of self-directed adventure has just been successfully passed to the next generation amidst the sparkling flow of a small clear-water riffle.

*Part 2*

# River Descriptions

# Mountains, Ridges, and Valleys

## Doe River

The name Doe River Gorge makes it sound both friendly and rugged. A better description would be rough and rugged. This used to be a relatively unknown river run. A few decades ago, some sharp-eyed mapwork revealed that the companionable Doe River, which faithfully accompanies US 19E down the Tennessee side of Roan Mountain abandons that vehicle roadbed outside Blevins, chops its narrow way into the rugged overlapping mountains and leaves the roadway to find its own way to Hampton. Actually, many people had witnessed the riverine wonders of the Doe River Gorge long before those two adventuresome map-reading women decided to canoe the unseen. Indeed, although the way is tight through the gorge, an earlier era antique narrow-gauge railroad had made the grade to traverse the area following the river's cut. That railbed was later used to haul sightseers through that remote terrain. So even today, while paddling and portaging the steep drops of the gorge, the paddler is accompanied by an exit lane out.

Doe River Gorge. Here the author notes a juxtaposition of natural rock wall and fast-dropping waterflow and ponders (quickly) the meaning of the universe and his place in the greater scheme of things. Photograph by Monte Smith.

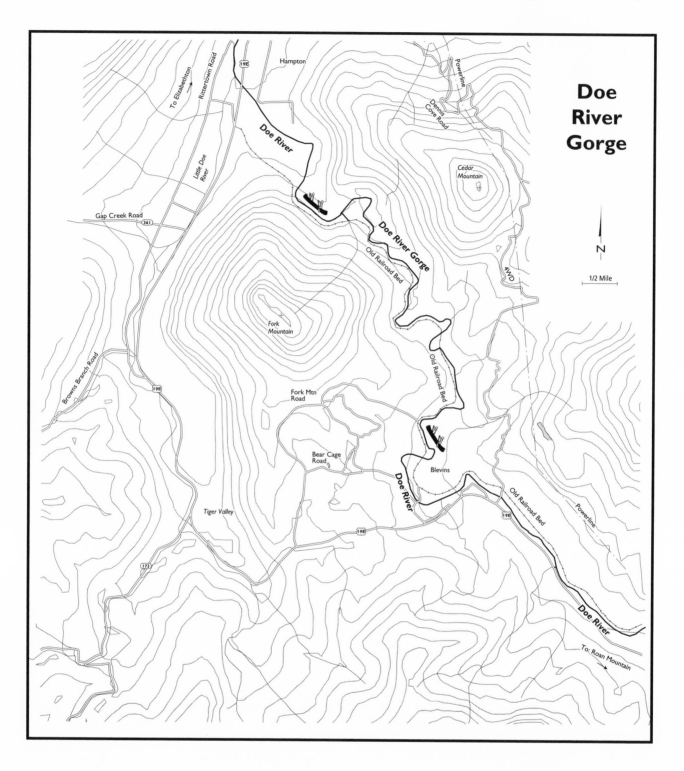

Scenery on the Doe is extremely spectacular with the steep rock and evergreen facade of Fork Mountain on the west and Cedar Mountain on the east scrambling skyward almost 1,100 feet from the water's edge. Indeed, it appears from the shady depths of the gorge that only this narrow ribbon of dancing water keeps the respective mountain giants apart.

Originating high on Roan Mountain near the North Carolina state line, the Doe River rumbles through the town of Roan Mountain and along US 19E before disappearing into the gorge. Emerging from the gorge south of Hampton, the stream continues north through Elizabethton before reaching its mouth at the Watauga.

The Doe is runnable from near the town of Roan Mountain to its mouth. Between Roan Mountain and Crabtree the stream is narrow and rocky but fairly straightforward with a level of difficulty of Class II. Scenery here is pleasant with a good cross-sectional view of Tennessee mountain culture. Below Crabtree, the Doe becomes challenging, with the gradient reaching 60 feet per mile and two Class III (or IV) rapids one-half mile downstream of the confluence with Roaring Creek. Both of these rapids are very technical, congested, and have a tendency to catch deadfalls. Under no circumstances should they be run without prior scouting.

At the tiny town of Blevins, the paralleling highway (US 19E) cuts sharply west while the Doe continues down and out of sight into the gorge. Civilization follows the stream for a couple of miles with a number of small farms at streamside. Several put-ins are available for the gorge run, since the road running out of Blevins crosses the Doe in three places.

The gorge section is rated Class III–IV. Narrow, boulder clogged, and congested, with limited visibility (because of rocks in the stream and occlusion of direct sunlight by surrounding mountains), the river's volume is accelerated through tight passages and over drops of up to seven feet. In general the best advice is to give yourself plenty of time to make the run and be prepared to do a lot of scouting. If there is nobody in your group who is familiar with the river, spend a day scouting from the road and the railroad tracks. Particular spots to watch out for include a sharp turning four-foot drop to the left just above the first railroad bridge (Class III–IV); a boulder garden on a river curve to the right approximately one mile downstream from the first railroad bridge where the flow is diverted around and under the obstructing rocks to the extent that no navigable channel remains. Carry on the left. Next comes Tennessee's version of Seven-Foot Falls (at the downstream end of the obstructed channel). Carry left or run right. Human-made rock walls constructed to prevent the river from eroding the base of the railroad track are landmarks of the next two danger spots. At the first rock wall there is a Class IV series of diagonal drops with some particularly capricious converging currents. At the second wall the flow splits, with the main current crunching through a horrendous and unrunnable Class VI rapid on the left. The right, which unfortunately is also unrunnable, consists of a boulder maze that can (with difficulty) be carried or lined through. From here to the take-out at Hampton there are at least three additional rapids that require scouting and at least that many more where boulders and curves in the river inhibit the paddler's downstream view. While the latter are not rated above Class III, they should be scouted nonetheless to ensure that the passage is clear of deadfalls or other obstructions. Though the entire gorge run is only six miles or less in length (depending on where you put in), it is incredibly exhausting and depleting and requires, on average, an hour and fifteen minutes for a group of four advanced, decked boaters to run each mile. Expressed differently, do not be lulled by the brevity of the run; the Doe Gorge is not the run to catch real quick on Sunday morning before you drive home.

From the US 19E bridge south of Hampton to its mouth at the Watauga in downtown Elizabethton, the Doe River widens slightly and calms down a lot. Whitewater is still continuous but primarily Class II in difficulty; there is one solid Class III area where the river makes a tight loop beneath rock cliffs after passing under the first US 19E bridge north of Hampton. Emerging from the loop, the Doe passes under US 19E again before running over a wide, technical succession of ledges that are somewhat difficult to scout from the bank. At moderate to lower water levels, there is usually a route to the right of the center. However, the nature of the rapid is such that perhaps the best approach is to scout from the water by ferrying from eddy to eddy at the top of the rapid. Scenery on this section is not as inspiring as in the gorge because of the population explosion along the stream, but the stretch between North Hampton and Valley Forge is quite beautiful.

The Doe is primarily a wet-weather stream, but it can be run from December to late April in many years. Oddly enough, some of the upper sections (Roan Mountain to Crabtree) can be run into midsummer in years of average rainfall. Hazards to navigation other than rapids and deadfalls mentioned above include a dam in Elizabethton three hundred yards downstream from the covered bridge. Access to the river is readily available and good (except, of course, in the gorge).

# Watauga River

Mention the Watauga River to any experienced boater in the Southeast and the awesome Watauga Gorge which starts in North Carolina will come to mind. The Watauga Gorge is a Class II–IV, experts-only run with drops of up to 16 feet, truck-sized boulders clogging the stream, and a gradient that approaches 200 feet per mile in some stretches. That section is not covered in this text. And, in any event, such a notorious run should not be attempted without the immediate guidance from others in the party who are already experienced with this intensive, hazardous run.

However, the lower Watauga below Wilbur Dam also has much to recommend it. Dropping out of the mountains north of the lake, the Watauga winds through a fertile farm plain west of Elizabethton in Carter County. The level of difficulty between the dam and Elizabethton is Class I with sufficient ripples and small shoals to keep the paddling lively. The banks are sparsely vegetated and thus allow a panoramic view of the receding mountains (and also, alas, of countless small houses and sheds that dot the riverside). After passing through Elizabethton, the Watauga once again enters a beautiful gorge with 150-foot vertical rock walls and numerous islands (some suitable for camping) in midstream. Level of difficulty for the scenic lower gorge is Class I and II, with one borderline Class III area about a half mile upstream of the Dungans Ford (Watauga Road) bridge where the river splits around an island. To run the rapid, go to the right around the island. This lower gorge is a happy surprise in a remote northeastern corner of Tennessee. Intimate, secluded, and well shaded with both hardwoods and evergreens, the lower Watauga is a delightful run.

Emerging from the lower gorge just northwest of Watauga in Washington County, the river flows through the valley terrain of the Watauga Flats before emptying into the Boone Reservoir where the Watauga joins the Holston River. Dangers to navigation between Wilbur Dam and the mouth of the Watauga are limited to small rapids (as described) and to occasional deadfalls, especially around bridge pilings. Access is good throughout.

# Holston River

The Holston River, with its two main forks, ranks with the Clinch as one of eastern Tennessee's most important yet most polluted industrial rivers. The North Fork of the Holston originates in Smyth County, Virginia, and flows southwestward to cross into Tennessee just north

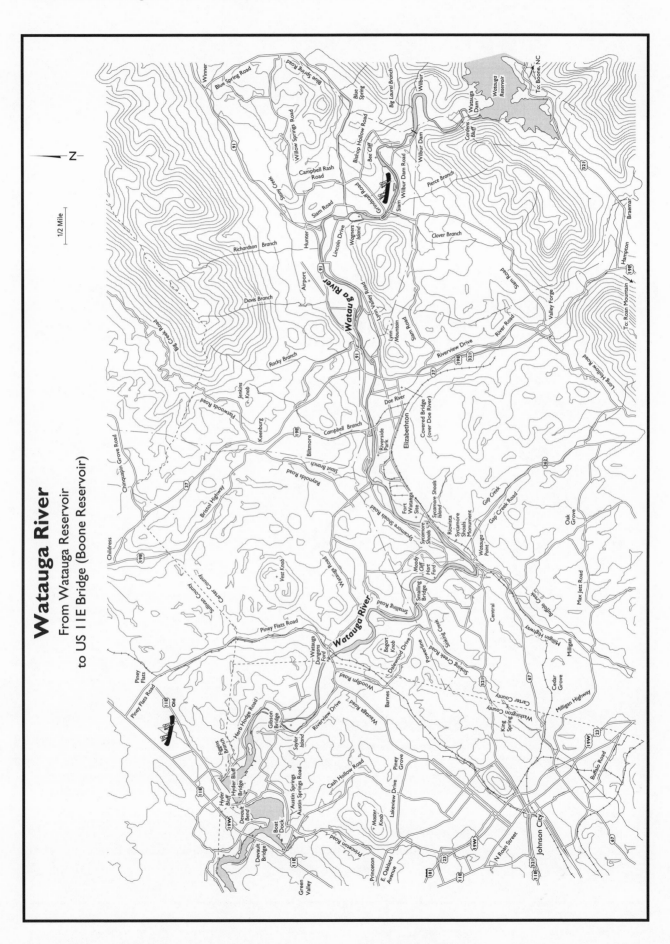

# Watauga River
## From Watauga Reservoir
## to US 11E Bridge (Boone Reservoir)

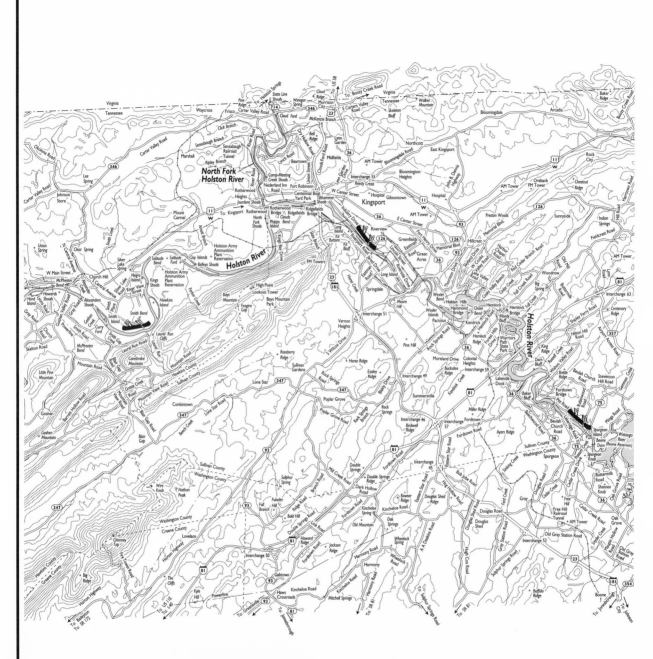

# Holston River

From: Cherokee Lake

Through: John Sevier Reservoir

South Fork Holston River

North Fork Holston River

Through: Fort Patrick Henry Reservoir

Through: Boone Reservoir (including mouth of Watauga River)

To: South Holston Reservoir

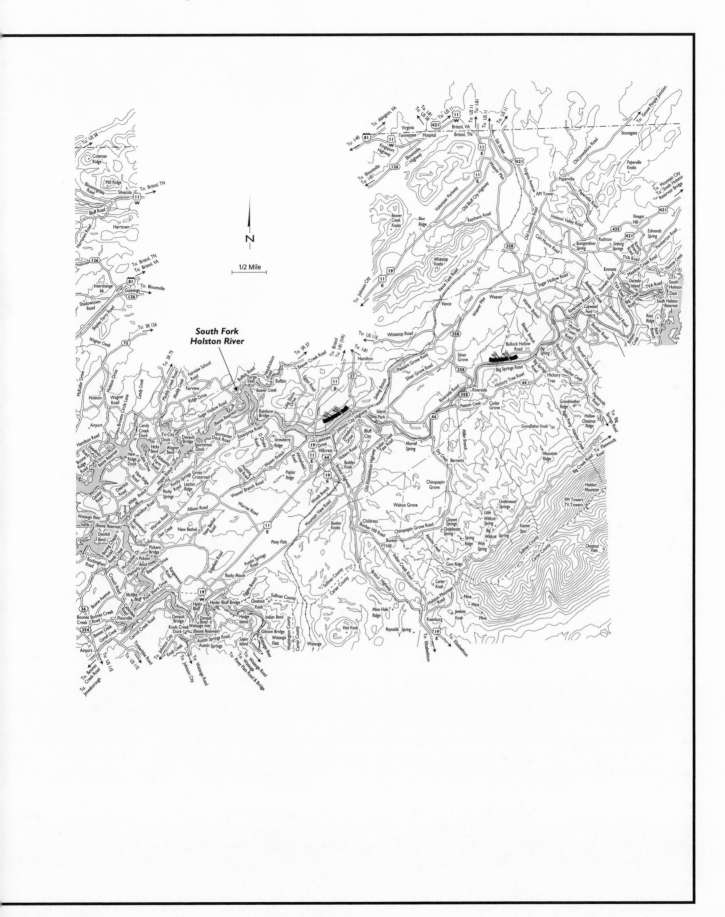

*South Fork
Holston River*

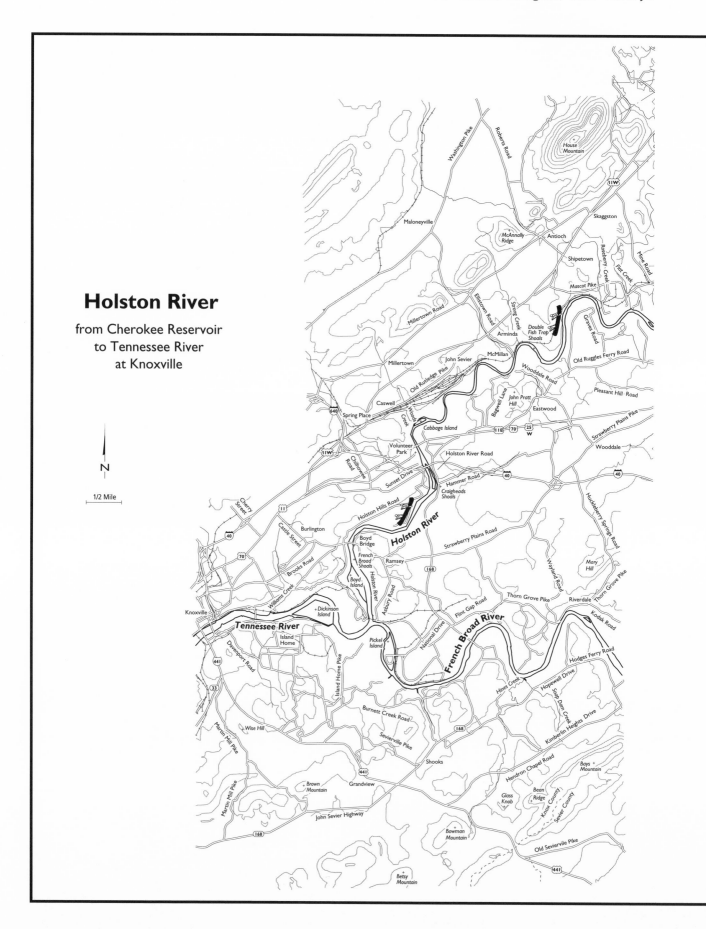

# Holston River

from Cherokee Reservoir
to Tennessee River
at Knoxville

N

1/2 Mile

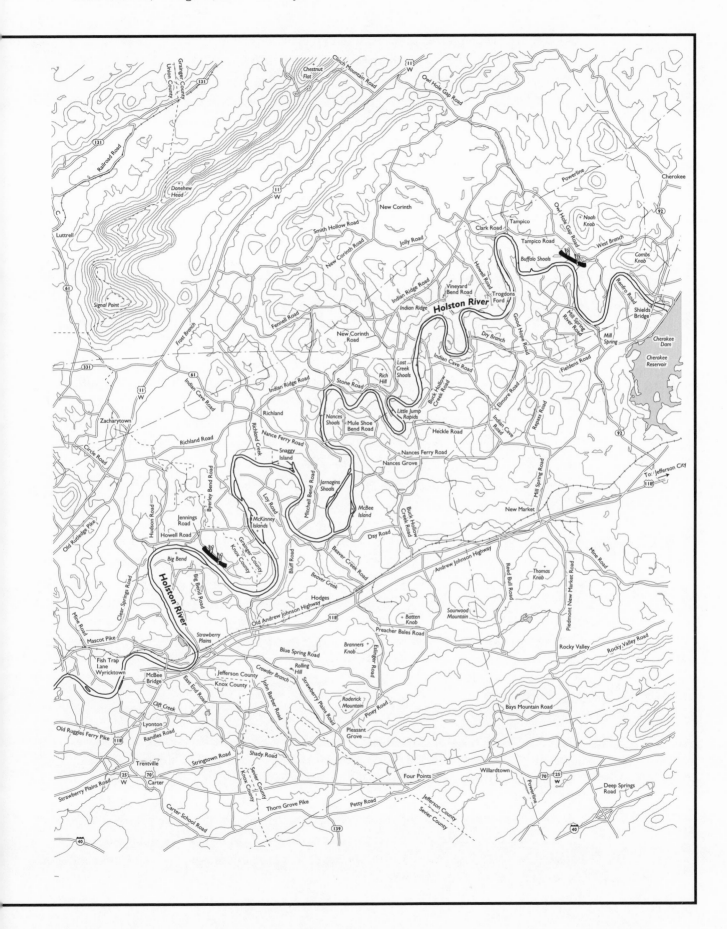

of Kingsport. The South Fork of the Holston is born in Smyth County, Virginia, also, and it is impounded immediately in South Holston Lake as it crosses into Tennessee east of Bristol. Below the South Holston Dam, the South Fork is allowed to flow freely for approximately ten miles before encountering the backwater of the next impoundment, Boone Lake. Below Boone Dam, the South Fork cuts north for about a mile before it is again impounded, this time in Fort Patrick Henry Lake, and then it drifts up to its confluence with the North Fork after passing over a series of dams as it flows through Kingsport. Above Fort Patrick Henry Lake, the water quality remains questionable for direct contact. Hence, floating on the Holston is best confined to the section below the Patrick Henry Dam.

Downstream of the confluence of the North and South forks, the Holston River snakes towards Cherokee Lake in great sweeping loops, some of which are three miles in length. Averaging three hundred feet or more in width, the river flows through a broad expanse of bottomland dotted with agriculture and industry. In the distance to the north and south stand the Clinch Mountains and the Bays Mountains, respectively. The Holston, as it drags through the intervening valley, is characterized by the absence of trees along its banks and by numerous large islands midstream. In general the vistas are pastoral. Runnable all year, this section of the Holston can accommodate both canoe camping and day cruising. The stream's level of difficulty is Class I, with a collapsed bridge just upstream from the Holston Ordnance Works and the dam at the John Sevier Steam Plant being the only hazards to navigation. Once the Holston drops into Cherokee Lake, the scenery improves immensely, with tall, wooded, cone-shaped hills rising from the water. Unfortunately, access is poor in the lake area, and, of course, there is no current (except in the cold-weather months when the lake pool is lowered). The Holston once again sets on its way at Cherokee Dam near Buffalo Springs. From here the river flows without further damming until it joins the French Broad to form the Tennessee River in southeastern Knoxville. Until the Holston approaches the outskirts of Knoxville, it is vastly improved from what was observed above Cherokee Lake. Averaging 110 feet in width, the river moves within tall, steep, mud banks surrounded by an abundantly fertile, modern farm valley. Water quality remains poor, but vegetation once more becomes evident along the stream. The level of difficulty remains Class I although several easily negotiable, riverwide shoals are encountered. Dangers to navigation include powerboats and gusty head winds.

# French Broad River

By far the most popular section of the French Broad River is the Barnard to Hot Springs, Class III–IV whitewater run in North Carolina. Paddlers interested in this beautiful and exciting run should consult *Carolina Whitewater*, Bob Benner's classic book on the whitewater of western North Carolina. Below Hot Springs the French Broad River parallels US 25 and US 70 until it crosses into Tennessee. In this stretch, the mountains gradually dissolve into foothills, and the boulder-strewn rapids so characteristic of the river above Hot Springs are replaced by small shoals and occasional Class II ledges. Sycamore, poplar, and sweetgum trees line the steep, 8- to 12-foot banks.

Moving downstream, the road veers away from the river but signs of civilization continue to be frequent along the French Broad's course. Near Bridgeport the river widens to more than three hundred feet and runs along under spectacular exposed rock cliffs. Small shoals and islands make the paddling interesting as the river meanders through the rich farming valley near Newport. At Newport the French Broad constricts to about 180 feet before fanning out as it approaches Douglas Lake four miles farther downstream.

While not pristine, the French Broad River above Douglas Lake is nevertheless pleasantly scenic while providing a panoramic glimpse of eastern Tennessee industry and culture. Access is adequate. Below Douglas Lake the French Broad rambles as a wide, lazy river through the farms of northern Sevier and southeastern Knox counties. Less foliage is in evidence at streamside, and signs of habitation, including some industry, are present throughout. Difficulty is Class I. While primarily suitable for day cruising, a number of large islands downstream from the TN 66 bridge in Sevier County allow for some canoe-camping opportunities. Below Knoxville the French Broad splits around the sizable Pickel Island just before joining the Holston River to form the Tennessee River.

# Abrams Creek

The trail to Abrams Falls is one of the most popular hikes in the Great Smoky Mountains National Park. Abrams Creek flows through the heart of Cades Cove, then carves its way into and through the surrounding mountains. For thousands of years the powerful current of Abrams Creek has been working hard to change that cove into "Cades Gulf," or maybe "Cades Box Canyon." Thousands of people each year hike over the ridge from the cove to see the water in this beautiful creek do its carving at the Falls.

Abrams Creek is a spectacular, clear, rock-bottom, boulder-strewn stream as it makes its "gulf" cut. It is wider than would be expected for its normal flow. Hence, it is usually too shallow to paddle. By the time the creek leaves the cove, feeder streams have brought in waters from the ridges on all sides of the cove. And when the water levels are sufficient, the stream has been paddled out of the cove (usually below Mill Creek at the Falls trailhead, which brings in the last block of water from the surrounding ridges). This is wilderness canoeing in Class III whitewater. There are hazards to navigation. Blowdowns and sweepers drop off the forested riverbanks and can block the entire streamway anywhere along the entire run of the stream. Of course, there is the noteworthy and permanent obstruction at Abrams Falls. Portage is mandatory. Take out and portage well above the Falls. The terrain at the Falls site is rugged. Fishing trails are on river right, but portage is difficult. Portage at the edge of the Falls is even more difficult. Below the falls, the stream continues to drop at a quick rate until the NPS Abrams Creek Campground site near the Park's boundary. There is no access to the stream between the Cove and the campground except for wilderness hiking trails. Hence the Class III rating requires extreme caution in paddling. Beyond the campground, the creek flattens out, but turns and maintains its position within the park to continue to provide a wilderness (no access) setting for a whitewater trip all the way to Chilhowee Reservoir. Here the stream can braid to several possible channels and dangerous sweepers can block any of the

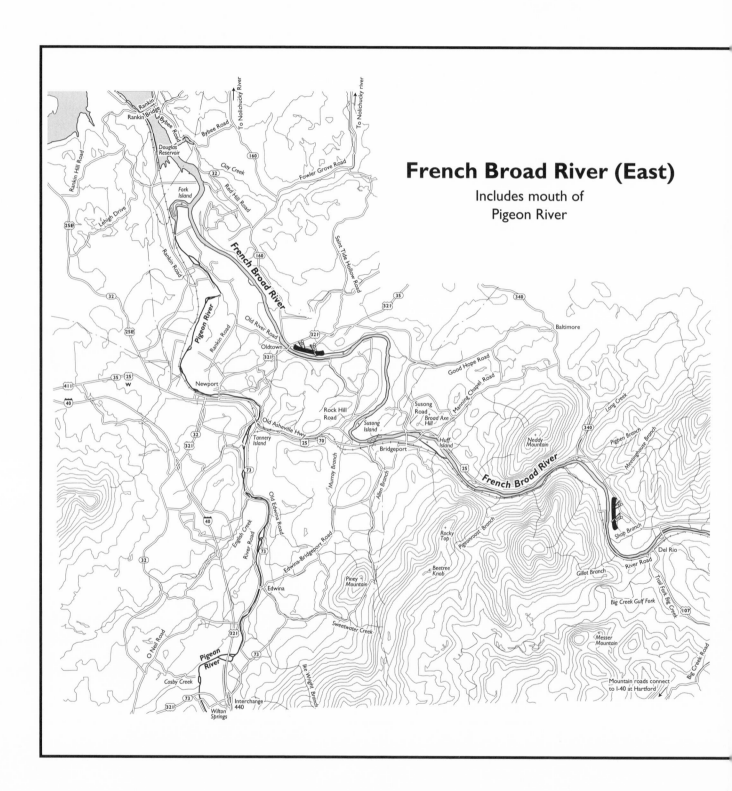

**French Broad River (East)**
Includes mouth of
Pigeon River

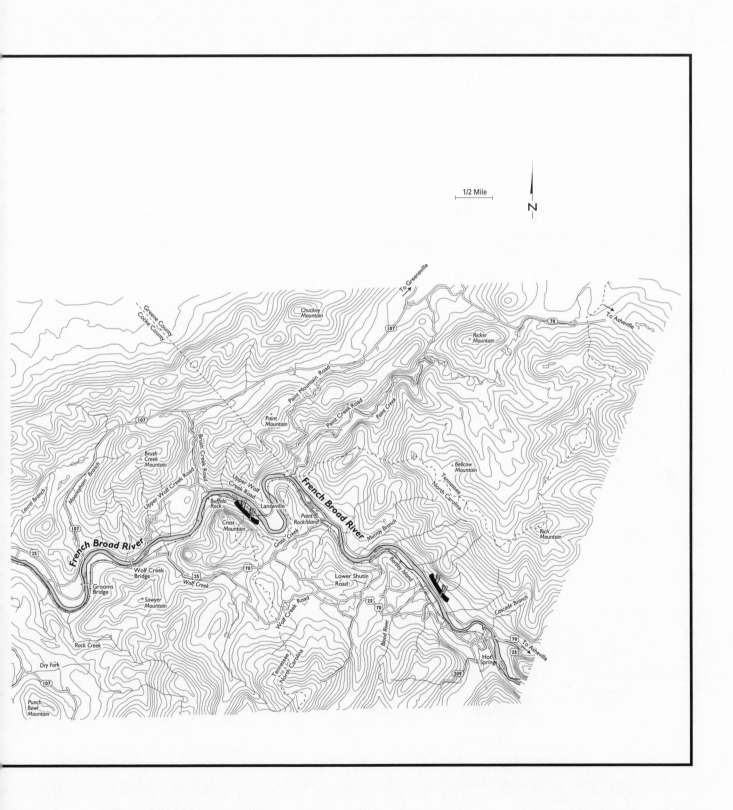

# French Broad River (West)
## Douglas Reservoir to Holston River at Knoxville
## Includes mouth of Little Pigeon River

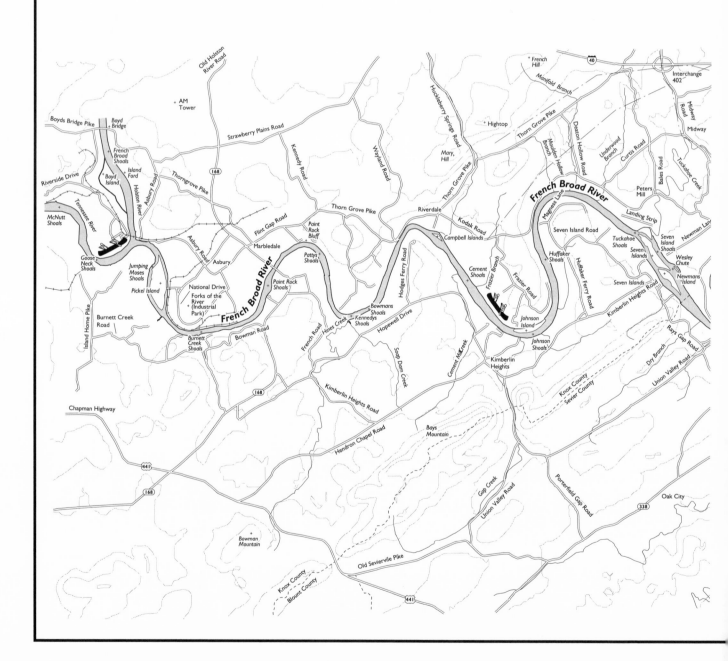

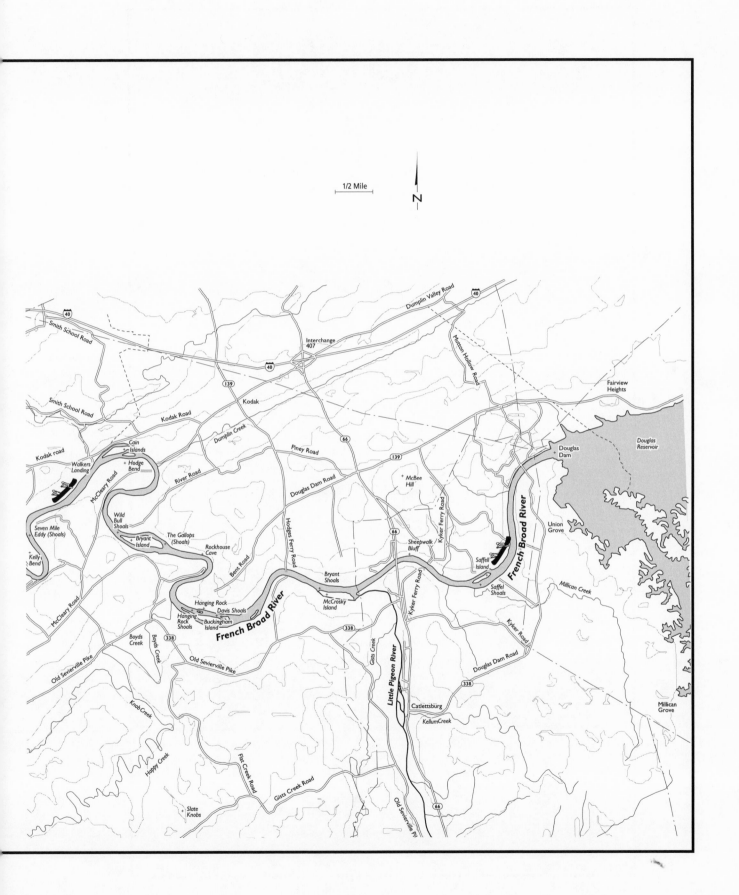

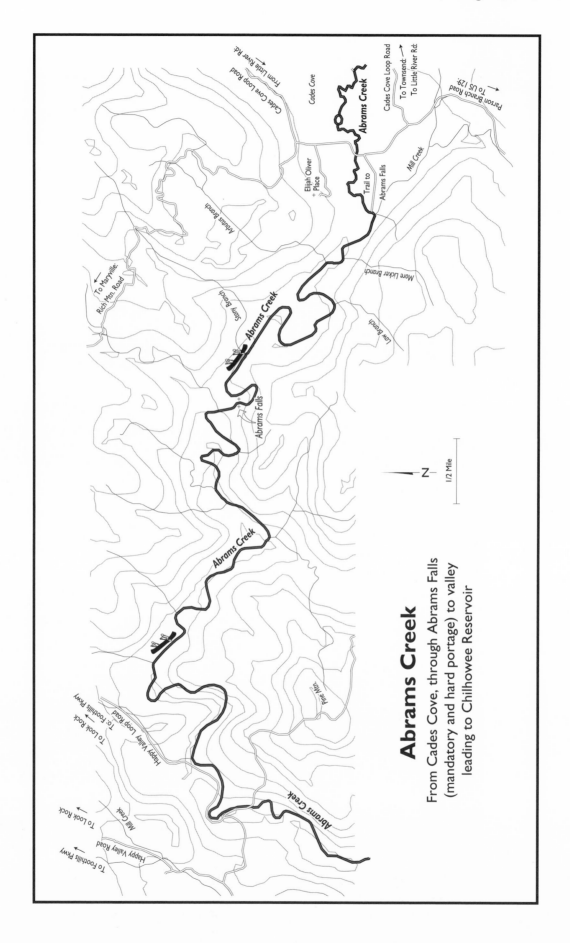

**Abrams Creek**

From Cades Cove, through Abrams Falls
(mandatory and hard portage) to valley
leading to Chilhowee Reservoir

otherwise passable streamways. The water is at least a solid Class II. Abrams Creek is a mountain stream completely within the Great Smoky Mountains National Park. That means that the scenery and water quality are superb, but access is difficult and mostly nonexistent. And you must paddle out on the Abrams Creek embayment of Chilhowee Reservoir to get to the Highway 129 access area. Make sure your trip is self-contained. Have the necessary equipment and skills and do your river map and shuttle scouting.

## Citico Creek

Citico Creek is a small, crystal-clear mountain stream draining the Cherokee National Forest just south of the Great Smoky Mountains National Park. The creek originates in the Unicoi Mountains of the Smokies in eastern Monroe County and flows northward before emptying into the Little Tennessee River at Tallassee at the Blount County line. A road runs along

Try Citico Creek if there is too much water on the Tellico. But it will be wintertime and the rapids will be nonstop. It features beautiful and exciting whitewater tucked deep in Tennessee's eastern mountains. Photograph by Julie Keller.

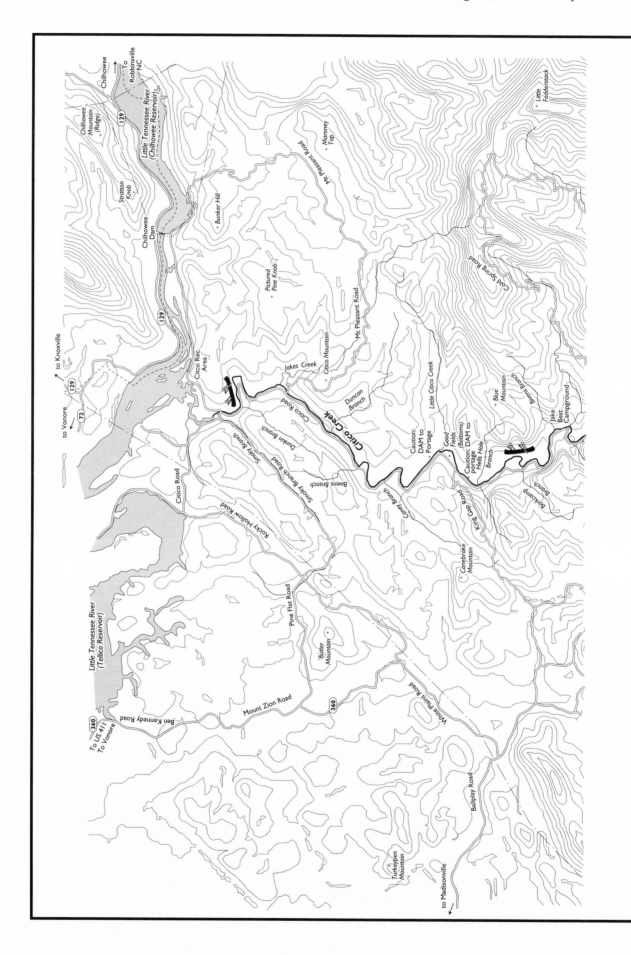

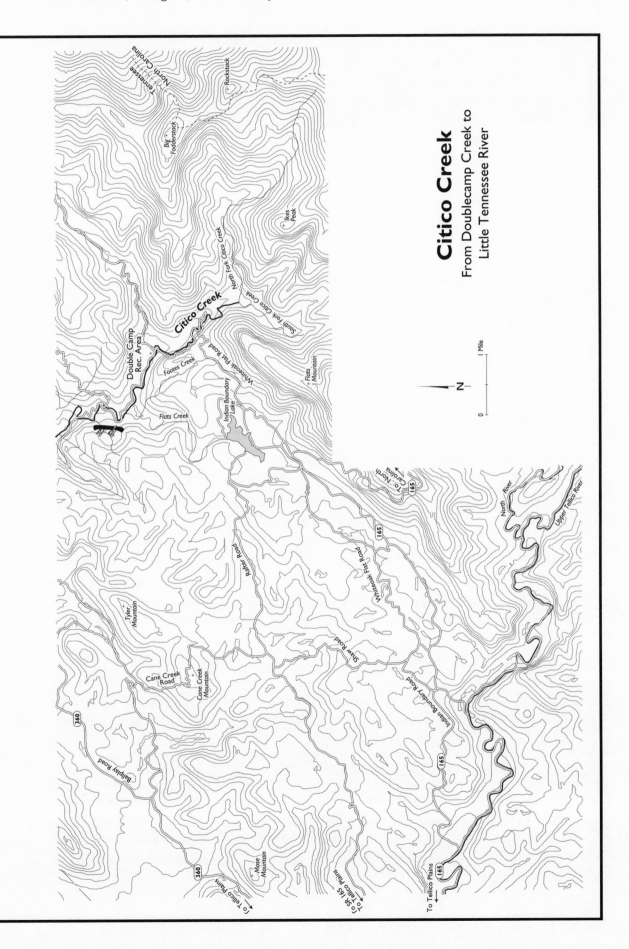

**Citico Creek**
From Doublecamp Creek to
Little Tennessee River

this creek and the gradient is moderate. The upper section contains some Class III rapids, but the lower part is relatively flat and has few technical difficulties.

The major problem with Citico Creek is the water level. There usually is not enough water; when it does flow well, it is usually late in the winter and the water and weather are cold. Your best guide to the Citico water level is to gauge the Tellico. When canoeists can happily float the upper sections of the Tellico, the lower sections of Citico are generally runnable. When these same canoeists are being blown off the upper Tellico by high water (which does not happen too often), then the upper Citico run is probably a good, continuous Class III. Again, this generally occurs only during cold weather. There are two potentially dangerous human-made dams on Citico Creek. The first is about 300 yards below the mouth of Hells Hole Branch. Both are six feet high and should be portaged. Be aware of the dangers of cold-water canoeing and how it can affect your stamina if you choose to try Citico Creek. But being hard against the Smoky Mountains, the scenery is hard to beat.

# Upper Tellico River

The word "Tellico" has meaning as a well-known and well-appreciated area for outdoor activity in East Tennessee. To some it means unusual hunting of formidable wildlife; to others it suggests exceptional and challenging hiking; to the paddlers it brings forth images of clean, clear, cascading waters. The watershed of the Tellico is the scenic Cherokee National Forest, hard against the Citico Wilderness in Tennessee and the Kilmer/Slickrock Wilderness in North Carolina. The Tellico drains God's own watershed, and the quality of the water tumbling over the streambed boulders is unmatched anywhere in the East.

The upper reaches of the Tellico River bear little resemblance to the slow pastoral stream it becomes through its "plains." The upper Tellico is a raging whitewater river with many Class II, III, and IV rapids. The Tellico River, in general, is a trout stream, noted for its clear woodlands drainage, with only the indigenous Tellico hogs and bears to muddy the flow (along with an occasional flatlander who might dislodge a riverbed rock or two on his careening trip downstream). Generally the water level on the upper Tellico is too low to float, but in the winter or early spring this free-flowing little gem jumps up in cfs while the eager boaters follow the flow down the 100-foot-per-mile rapids. Canoeists look for 250 cubic feet per second (cfs) on TVA's Tellico gauge as optimum for an upper Tellico run. A level of 100 to 150 cfs is considered low, and, above 500 cfs, good boaters like to take nature hikes to erase the ominous-looking, Class V traps from their minds. A road follows the stream and nerve-shattering scouting is possible all the way to the put in.

The upper Tellico is somewhat arbitrarily divided into two parts with the bridge below Bald River Falls marking the dividing point. At 350 cfs on the Tellico gauge, the floatable upstream portion, known by the unimaginative name Upper Upper Tellico, begins at the trout hatchery operated by the Tennessee Wildlife Resources Agency (here up to 140,000 rainbow trout are penned, fed, and grown to keeper size each year. You may look but not touch).

Action on the river starts quickly with a pair of ledges 3 feet in height (Class III). For the next 2.5 miles the river presents numerous Class II chutes and a few rock gardens requiring good water-reading skills and a strong pry stroke. Less than a mile below the private Green Cove Campground, visible from the river, there is a 4-foot ledge, followed in 400 yards by another series of 4-foot ledges. All are runnable but scouting is advised. After these ledges the river flows past Panther Branch Picnic Area (USFS) and becomes again an exercise in water reading and Class II chutes. Just below here the North River joins the flow from river right. (Look for 200 cfs for a minimum flow for the rest of the Upper Upper Tellico.)

Unless you want to run Class IV ledges of 4 to 8 feet each, take out at the next bridge (3 miles below North River.) For the next 2.5 miles, you will be in the "Ledges" section of the Upper Upper Tellico. This small section can be a full day's effort to scout and run the technical rapids. Refer to Monte Smith's *Southeastern Whitewater* (Boise, Idaho: Pahsimeroi Press, 1995) for a good drop-by-drop description of this short section of river. If you're confident and decide to run these drops, be aware that the 14-foot, Class V Baby Falls is just around the corner. A boat and paddler inadvertently encountering this straight-down-drop are in for a bruising encounter. Portage Baby Falls on the left and watch for cars. From just below Baby Falls to Bald River, the Tellico is nonstop Class III–IV, expect-no-rest technical paddling. This segment of river has devoured more than its share of plastic boats. The 0.8-mile run from Bald River Falls to the bridge contains "Jerrods Knee" rapid, which is extremely difficult and hard on equipment. A convenient put in right in the teeth of a Class III rapid occurs at the bridge. This is the common Upper Tellico put in. It's also a convenient place to use your four-wheel-drive traction to pull wrapped boats off the rocks 20 feet into the trip. (That has been done!) The normal upper Tellico run at optimum water levels is from this put in to the Ranger Station Road bridge 5.5 miles downstream. It's short, but there's a lot of bubbling water. This is not a trip for beginners, nor is it for those who overrate their abilities or those who have to depend on luck. The water remains cold through the springtime, so wetsuits are an excellent precaution.

Should you complete the Class III, put-in rapid under the bridge intact, you will find a good recovery pool just below that signals another Class III shelf system close ahead. The river is rather wide at this point and an early overturn in this rapid could present rescue problems. It is suggested that you not overturn at the beginning of this rapid. One-half mile from the put-in bridge you will make a straight approach toward an enormous boulder. A powerful right turn is needed. This could be a dangerous place in the event of an upset, since the boulder is undercut and can snare partially submerged debris. If you do overturn, get away from your craft and keep your feet on the surface. Avoid that boulder if at all possible.

At 1.5 miles below the put-in bridge, you'll come to the Turkey Creek access area. At high water levels, this is a prudent put in for open craft. The next four miles are Class II with occasional Class III drops. Three-foot drops, shelves, and souse holes all enliven the run. The drop in this run averages 60 feet per mile, but it hits 110 feet per mile above the put-in bridge.

As Dick Wooten, a Nashville canoeist, has been known to observe: "The Tellico is a fun run on beautiful water, especially when the mountain laurel is at its height of bloom." He looks at the flowers?

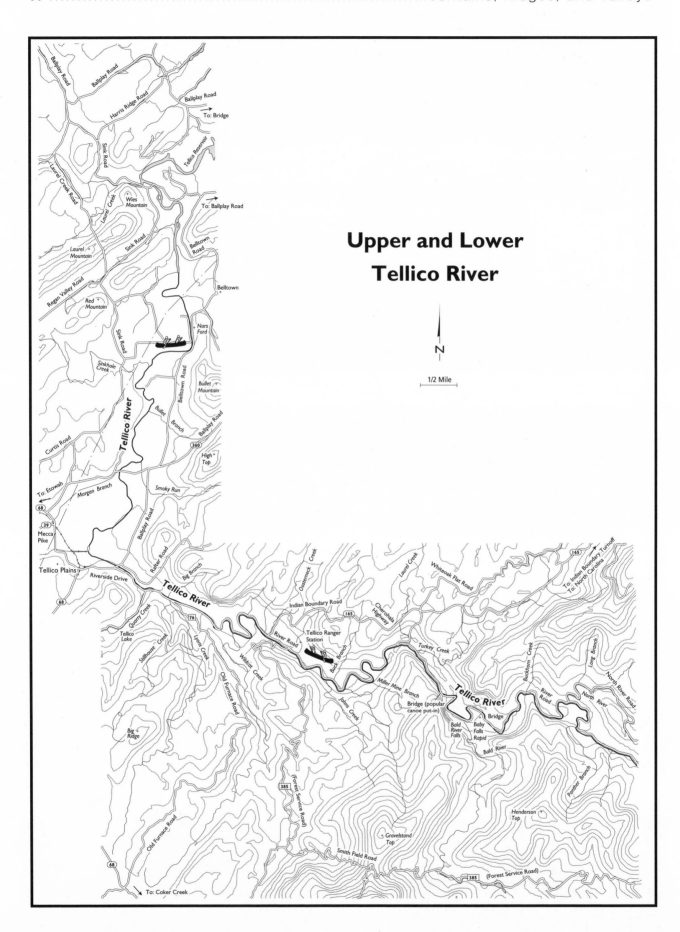

# Upper and Lower
# Tellico River

1/2 Mile

Tellico River. Think ledges and clean, clear, fast-moving whitewater. When the water is up, this is the state's premier run. Photograph by Julie Keller.

# Lower Tellico River

The lower Tellico becomes a pastoral stream as it works its way across the foothills into the heart of the great Tennessee Valley. Below the Ranger Station Road bridge and for the next four miles to Tellico Plains, the river widens, flattens, but still gathers together time and again to provide strong Class II shoals. At lower water levels there are two wide, rocky shoal areas above Tellico Plains that are hard to completely navigate. You'll probably get your feet wet dragging the canoe. Below Tellico Plains the stream still retains its beauty and appeal but it begins to meander. The Cherokee National Forest is on one bank and agricultural land is on the other. Similar minimum water levels are needed for the lower Tellico as for the upper whitewater stretches, but optimum flow occurs at about 1,000 cfs. Excessive flow creates trouble typical of pastoral streams. It is best to stay off when the river is muddy and out of its banks. There are many alternate access points along the lower Tellico, or a take-out on the Tellico Reservoir can be used.

The lower Tellico makes for a pleasant, pastoral, family float trip through the rural countryside of the historical Little Tennessee valley lands. Unfortunately, most of the time the water level will be too low or marginal.

# Powell River

The Powell River is one of Tennessee's mystery rivers. Flowing out of southwestern Virginia, it crosses into Tennessee and winds beneath Waller Ridge in the valley between Cumberland Mountain to the north and Powell Mountain to the south. It is a mystery only because few have ever been inclined to paddle it and even fewer have produced any record of their floats. Slipping lazily through a farm valley bordered by mountains that alternately converge on and recede from the river, the Powell River forms the major drainage for this historic Cumberland Gap area of Hancock and Claiborne counties. Its level of difficulty is Class I all the way from the Virginia border to where the Powell becomes part of Norris Lake in southwestern Claiborne County. There are sufficient ripples, small waves, and fast-moving water to keep the paddler awake, but nothing serious enough to distract from the scenery. For the most part, the Powell runs over a mudbed between well-formed, steep mudbanks eight to twenty feet in height. From the Virginia line to just below River View forestation is spotty, with hardwoods lining the bank in some areas but completely absent in others. In the region of the Virginia border the Powell flows through a relatively flat valley that gives way to rolling hills by the time the river reaches Riverside, downstream. Habitation and farm roads are common all along this stretch. Toward River View, the bottom hills increase in size and continue to do so almost incrementally all the way to Norris Lake. Between River View (south of Cumberland Gap) and the Virginia line, almost all the land along the river is cultivated. Downstream from River View, the hills turn into knobs and ultimately, near Norris Lake, into veritable mountains.

As the topography becomes more rugged, signs of habitation are seen less frequently until the river slips off by itself into a steep, forested wilderness east of the lake. Here, for almost twenty miles, the Powell winds in a convoluted fashion at the base of immense hardwood-covered gumdrop-shaped mountains. As it crosses the state line, the Powell River averages 40 feet in width, but it expands to 70 feet at Riverside and to almost 85 feet by the time it reaches the lake. Hazards to navigation are limited to deadfalls and a low-water bridge at an access point that collects debris. The Powell is suitable for day cruising upstream of River View and for both day cruising and canoe camping between River View and the lake. Access is readily available via unimproved roads except in the Norris Lake area, where few roads approach the river. In years of average rainfall the Powell is runnable almost all year. Within Norris Lake the Powell merges with the Clinch River, which continues below Norris Dam to be one of the major tributaries of the Tennessee River.

# Clinch River

Like so many of the major rivers of northeast Tennessee, the Clinch is a Virginia native. Flowing out of Tazewell County, Virginia, the Clinch has already meandered more than 70 miles to the southwest before crossing into Tennessee. Thus the Clinch is a big, well-developed river from the moment it flows over the Tennessee state line. Averaging 70 feet in width within well-defined 45-degree mudbanks that are 12 to 15 feet high, the river flows in and out among steep, hardwood-covered, gumdrop-shaped mountains. The Clinch River is runnable

Brushing the Canoe. A canoe can be an effective wildlife blind. Sam Venable of Knoxville shows how he can disappear even while floating down the streamway. Sam has a well-developed wilderness ethic. He takes only photographs and eats all he shoots (or something like that). Photograph by Barbara Stagg.

all year (for our purposes) downstream from Clinchport, Virginia. Unimproved farm roads parallel the Clinch practically all the way to the backwaters of Norris Lake and provide access almost anywhere. Some shade trees remain along the banks, but much of the flora has been reduced to scrub vegetation as the bottomland adjacent to the river has been cultivated. With few exceptions there is cultivated land interspersed between the mountains and the stream all along its course. Ironically, despite the advanced state of cultivation, few dwellings, barns, or outbuildings are in evidence along the Clinch. The level of difficulty is Class I throughout, with the exception of some very mild Class II water where the river loops back on itself

# Lower Holston River
# Powell River
# Clinch River

Virginia Line to Norris Reservoir

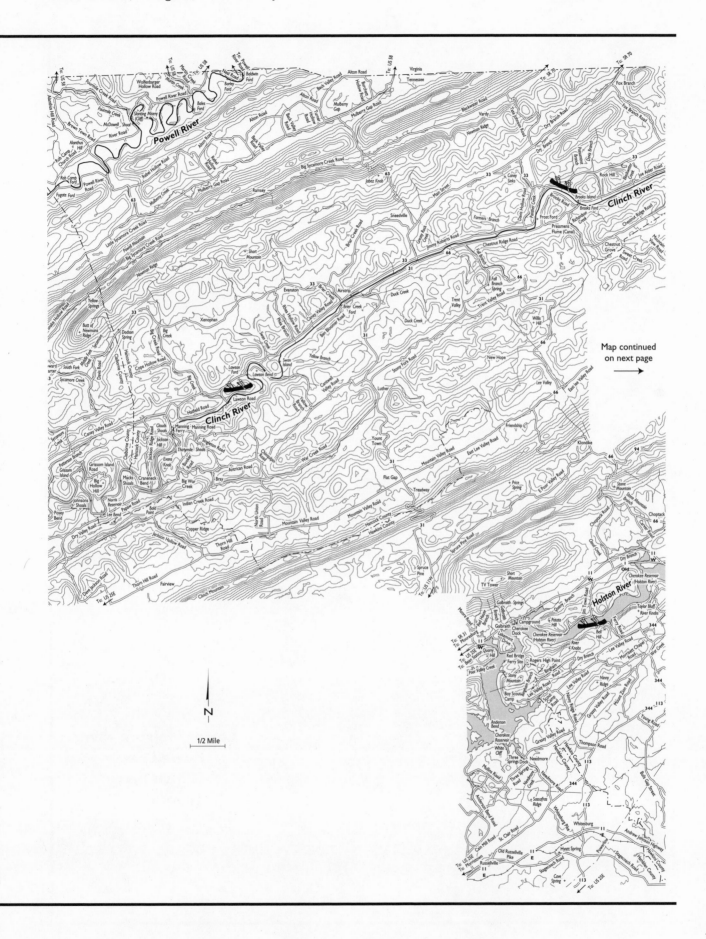

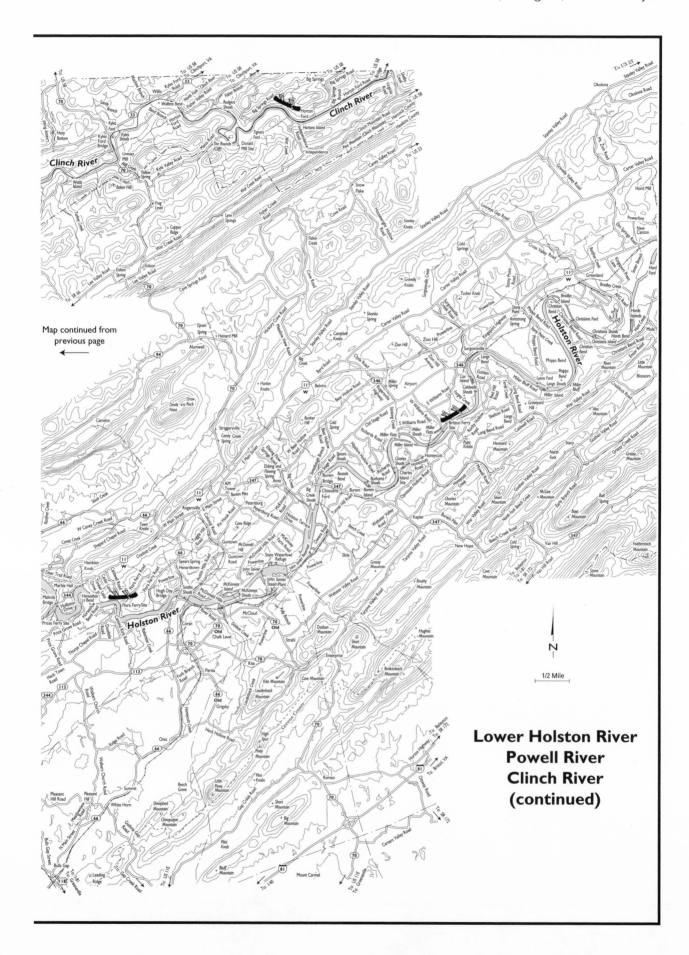

Map continued from
previous page

**Lower Holston River
Powell River
Clinch River
(continued)**

## The Darter and the Dam

Figuratively speaking, opponents of TVA's Tellico Dam project were always a day late and a dollar short.

Had this issue reached the halls of Congress in the 1990s, it surely would have been machine-gunned as a prime example of government waste. During the free-spending fifties, sixties, and seventies, however, it was a different story. Just like Lola, TVA got whatever it wanted. In this case, it was a dam that flooded thousands of acres of productive farmlands, wiped out nearly thirty-three miles of blue-ribbon trout stream, and polarized the nation around a three-inch fish called the snail darter.

Despite what news reports of that era indicated to the contrary, the snail darter and its endangered-species implications were not at the heart of this matter. Even before University of Tennessee zoologist David Etnier discovered the new species, the destruction of the Little Tennessee River valley was an archetypical example of fiscal foolishness and government intrusion into private property rights.

But old habits die hard. Not even the loss of the Cherokee Indian nation's birthplace and sacred burial grounds was enough to stop TVA. The snail darter put a temporary hold on the project, but in August 1979, when U.S. Rep. John Duncan Sr. (R-Tenn.) engineered an eleventh-hour legislative end-around that exempted Tellico from the Endangered Species Act, the fate of the river was sealed.

Tellico was a pivotal point in TVA's history. Long hailed as a benevolent overseer of the valley's economic and environmental interests, the agency's luster was tarnished greatly over Tellico, and its credibility was seriously damaged. This was, indeed, the beginning of the end of the "old" Tennessee Valley Authority.

True, Tellico Lake is a picturesque body of water that supports a popular fishery for bass, walleye, and crappie, as well as powerboating and skiing. But the price of this reservoir—in real dollars, loss to the environment, and erosion of support for the agency—was clearly too high. Canoeists, trout anglers, and other lovers of the river are left with another "lake" in a region of the country where human-made impoundments are a dime a dozen. After Tellico was finished (at untold expense), TVA did develop the tail-waters below Norris Dam into a decent trout fishery, but it will never match the shallow, fast-flowing, rubbly-bottomed, insect-rich cornucopia of the Little Tennessee.

Ah, progress!

—Sam Venable, columnist
*Knoxville News-Sentinel*

between Independence and Kyles Ford. Near Kyles Ford and up on the nearby ridges lie the Melungeon settlements. Ancestors unknown, the Melungeons were removed from the fertile Holston valley by the early settlers. If you get interested in their history, browse around Sneedville for more information.

Generally speaking, the stream itself is not so mysterious, although the surrounding terrain, is pleasing.

For 12 miles below Norris Dam, floatability of the Clinch depends largely upon the needs of TVA's hydroelectric system. When one or both generators at Norris Dam are in operation, one may enjoy a pastoral float on the cold waters, which offer some fine trout fishing. (the Tennessee Wildlife Resources Agency stocks brown and rainbow trout at several locations between Norris Dam and Clinton.) At the highway 61 bridge (location of TWRA's

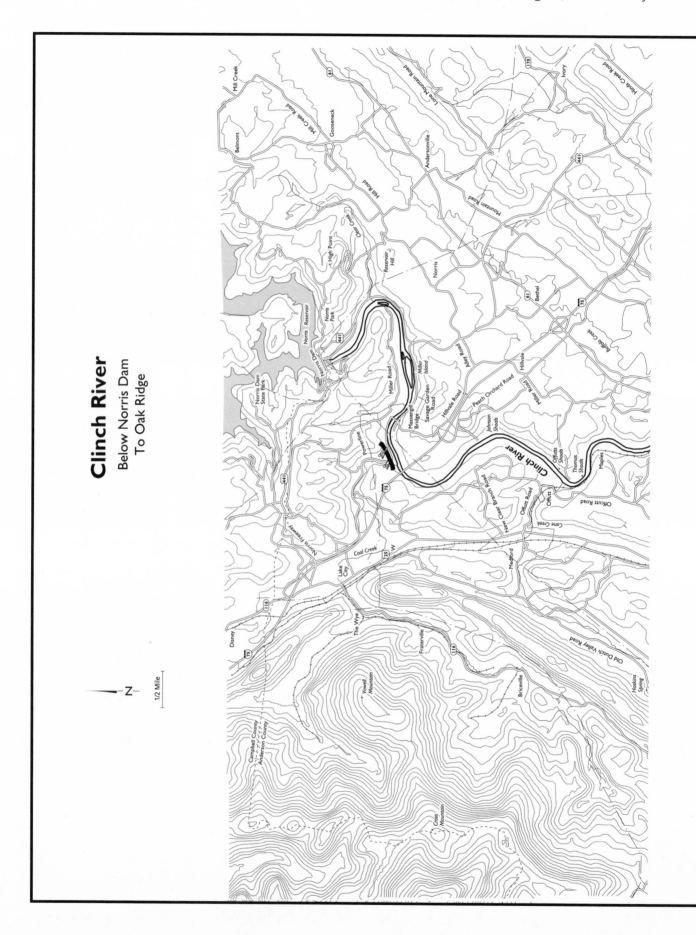

## Clinch River
### Below Norris Dam
### To Oak Ridge

1/2 Mile

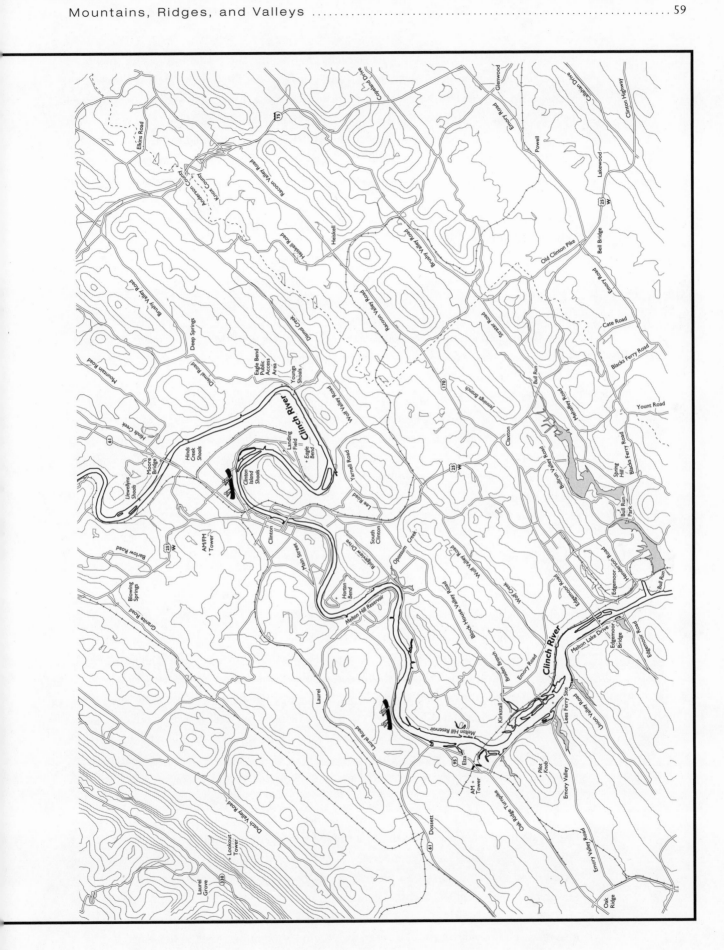

Eagle Bend Fish Hatchery), the flow slackens slightly, and the floatability of the stream no longer depends upon hydroelectric demands. It is here that the Clinch enters the impoundment called Melton Hill Reservoir. Though it retains the appearance of a river until well below Clinton, the channel depth is consistently maintained to allow barge traffic to reach Clinton. Thus industrial development of the Clinch River is a notable feature from Clinton and downstream. Below Melton Hill Dam the river flows for a scant two miles before dropping into Watts Bar Lake, the final connecting link to its mouth at the Tennessee. Hazards in these lower sections of the Clinch include powerboat traffic and strong headwinds. Though the scenery is anything but pristine, an interesting behind-the-scenes glimpse of eastern Tennessee industry is available for those interested.

# Nolichucky River

From the highest point in the entire Appalachian chain (Mt. Mitchell in North Carolina) water careens, crashes, and cascades downhill, acquiring enough volume and momentum to kick a paddler through the 900-foot Nolichucky gorge cut, all the way into Tennessee.

The Nolichucky River erupts into being at the confluence of the Toe and Cane Rivers in North Carolina. Throwing everything it's got at you right at the beginning, the Nolichucky foams and rattles down an awe-inspiring gorge cut through the Bald and Unaka mountains below Poplar, North Carolina. The Nolichucky roars into the gorge in North Carolina like the proverbial lion, calms somewhat, then exits at Erwin, Tennessee, like a feisty and not-so-proverbial lamb.

# Nolichucky Gorge

So what is there to see in this gorge? Excerpts from other descriptions of this spectacular whitewater adventure might give you an idea of what is in store:

"For those who would like to enjoy the rugged grandeur of the gorge and the river to the fullest, hiking is the way. The paddler can only enjoy the river, for it gives one little opportunity to view the magnificent scenery above" (Bob Benner in *Carolina Whitewater*).

"The difficulty of the float trip through the gorge will depend on the water level, however, this trip is difficult at any water level" (Rick Phelps in the *Tennessee Eastman* bulletin).

"The Nolichucky Gorge is spectacularly wild in spite of the Clinchfield Railroad which follows the river. However, most boaters will be too busy with the challenge of the technical, powerful rapids to see much scenery" (Don Bodley in the *Tennessee Valley Canoe Club* bulletin).

The Nolichucky Gorge is a respected, challenging piece of whitewater found where this big drainageway forces itself through rugged Appalachian mountains along the spine-like border of North Carolina and Tennessee. The Clinchfield Railroad is a small connector line across those saw-toothed ridges; the line is one of the few consistently profitable railroads purely because its builders had the foresight to note that there were almost no passageways across the rugged highlands. So years ago they hacked out a bench along the Nolichucky to lock up that cross-ridge traffic. Heavy traffic continues along that track to this day.

The gorge run (for both train and paddler) is 8.5 miles long. The U.S. Forest Service has provided a rustic access and parking area at the village of Poplar in North Carolina. Poplar is in a scenic little cove on the North Carolina side of the mountain that does not quite qualify as even a crossroads on the map. There are no crossroads there, just a gathering of dwellings called Poplar. Erwin, Tennessee, at the take-out, is a healthy railroad town, although it is still relatively remote. And between these two points on the map lie parts of the Cherokee National Forest, the border mountains, and the superb Nolichucky whitewater. The TVA-monitored gauge at Embreeville (downstream from the gorge) gives an accurate reference point for the gorge canoeist. Open canoes are advised to outfit with extra flotation at any level. Levels on the gauge above 500 cfs are suitable for open canoes. Optimum flow is found at 1,000 cfs. The stream is dangerously difficult and almost too pushy at 1,500 cfs. All knowledgeable area canoe clubs cancel their trips if the flow is above 2,000 cfs. (Take that hint as these people are experienced with this river and know what they are doing.)

The entrance set of rapids is a good test for your particular boating skills for any given day. It is a long, technical drop requiring movement from one side of the river to the center, judicious use of eddies, and hole-avoidance maneuvers. Should you experience difficulty maintaining control in these initial rapids, it is suggested that the long, arduous, brush-beating portage back to the shuttle car be undertaken (as has been done many times) to avoid an even longer, more difficult, enforced mid-run take-out when the going gets considerably harder. You still must face Riverboat Rapids, Big Mother, and other complex drops. The river drops an average of almost 60 feet per mile in the early part of the run, which is a powerful stream in the heavy flow above 1,000 cfs. Rapids rate from II to IV below 1,000 cfs, and from III to V above 1,000 cfs.

To summarize, the Nolichucky Gorge begins and ends with a railroad trestle. Most of the heavier-duty rapids are packed into the first third of the run. At higher water levels, multiple routes are available. At moderate to lower levels, the gorge can become a technical maze. Specific hazards include On-the-Rocks Rapid in the early part of the run, where the main current splits around a large boulder that has eaten its share of boats. Quarter Mile Rapid (because it is a quarter of a mile long) sports large, jagged fragments of old iron railroad canisters. Immediately below Quarter Mile Rapid, just when you think the worst is over, a river-wide hydraulic materializes to grab the complacent. This should be run far right. Several more of these riverwide holes crop up throughout the run. At practically all levels, these holes should be run to the extreme left or right.

Commercial rafting companies have service on this section of the river. The water quality suffers from heavy, sandy/silty loads derived from mining higher in the North Carolina watershed. Newly formed sandbars are evident wherever the water slows down. But the scenery and excitement of the whitewater are spectacular.

# Lower Nolichucky River

After the Nolichucky Gorge, between Erwin and Embreeville, the Nolichucky assumes the characteristics of a typical Smoky Mountains valley stream; it has a broad, rocky bottom, frequent ripples and small waves, and an occasional big surprise. Scenery is beautiful in spite of paralleling highways and considerable industrial development. Exposed rock bluffs rise and

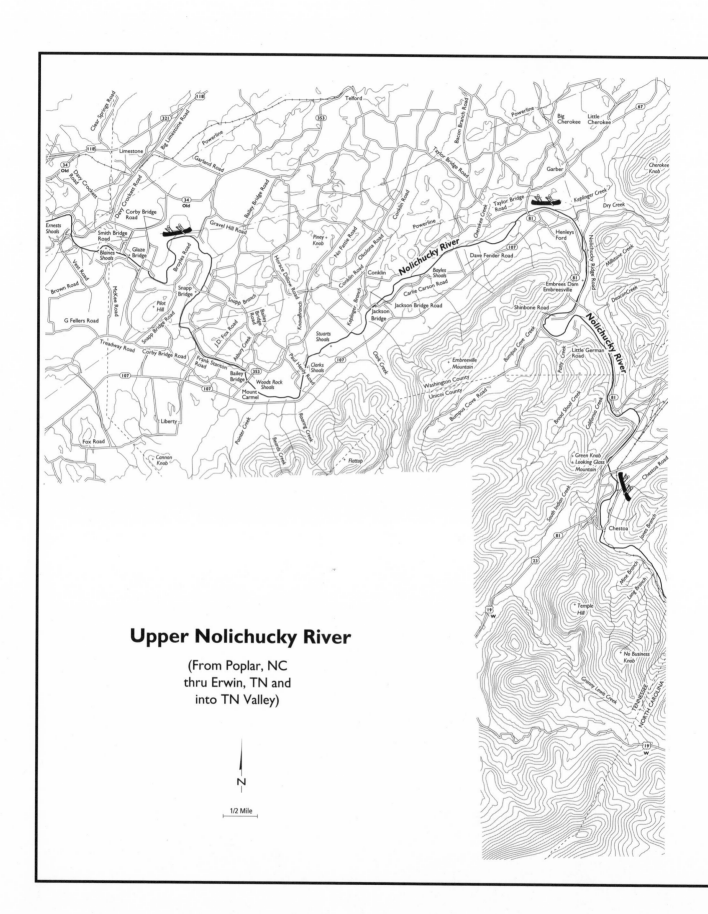

# Upper Nolichucky River

(From Poplar, NC
thru Erwin, TN and
into TN Valley)

N

1/2 Mile

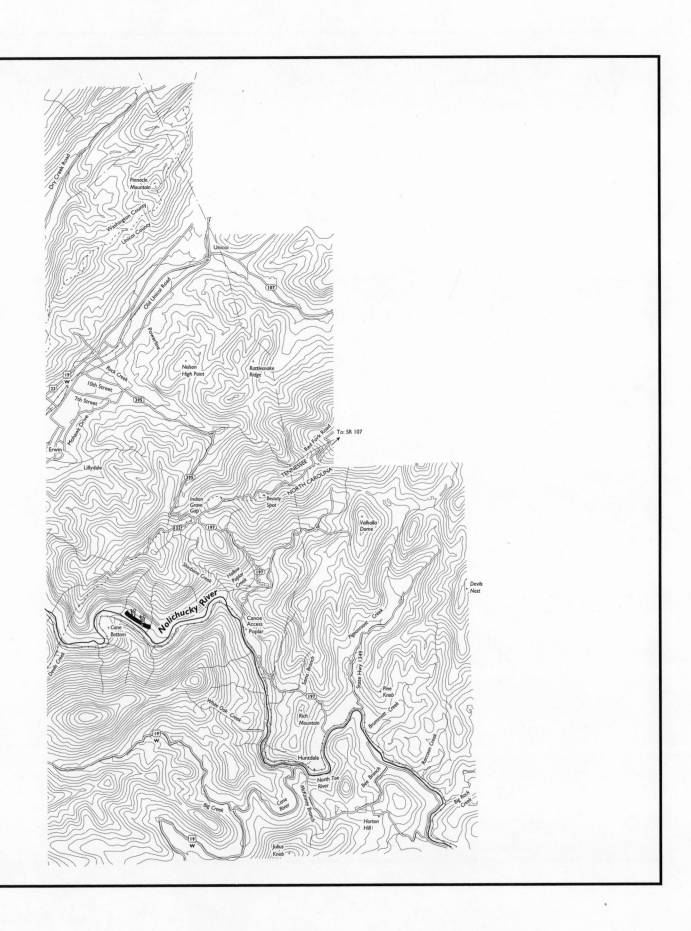

# Lower Nolichucky River

(Davy Crockett Reservoir
and near Tusculum and
Greeneville)

N

1/2 Mile

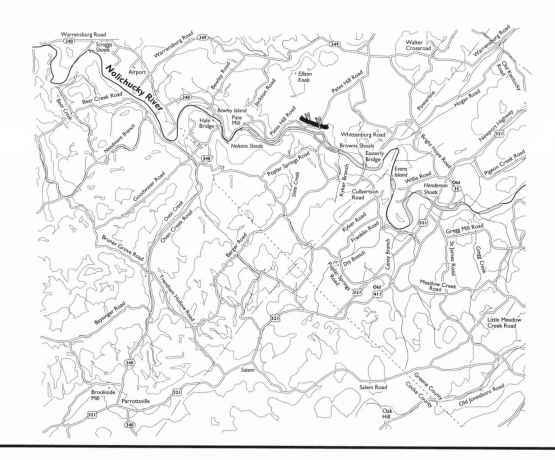

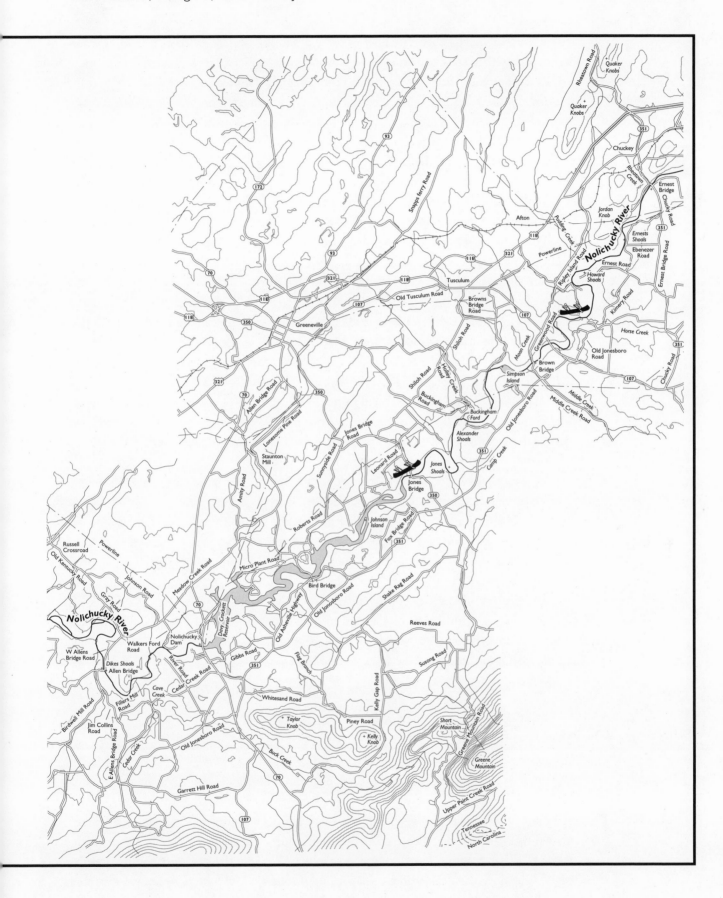

recede from the river's edge. The level of difficulty of this section is Class II, with one bor-derline Class III rapid a half mile downstream from the TN 81 bridge as the river loops around a mammoth rocky pinnacle just upstream from Embreeville. Access is fair to good and dangers to navigation are limited essentially to the one larger rapid mentioned above. Runnable from late November through early June in most years, this section makes a good practice run for the novice whitewater paddler. River width varies from 65 to over 90 feet.

Below Embreeville, the Nolichucky continues to flow through mountain terrain for five miles and then exits into the rolling hills of Washington, Greene, and Hamblen Counties before emptying into the French Broad River at the headwaters of Douglas Reservoir south of Morris-town. This section offers numerous paddle trip opportunities since it has plentiful access, lively, Class I or higher water, and pleasant scenery. Upstream from Davy Crockett Reservoir in Greene County, the Nolichucky is characterized by high banks and some exposed rock walls rising from the river. Hardwoods shade the stream, which now averages 70 feet in width. While almost all property along the river is privately owned, an exception is the Davy Crockett Birthplace Historical Park just downstream of the Washington–Greene County line. Camping is allowed here, thus making canoe camping practical on this section. Four hundred yards below Davy Crockett Birthplace Historical Park, watch for a 50 yard long series of Class II ledges. This rapid can easily be run on far right or portaged on the right bank. Hazards to navigation for the remainder of the section are limited primarily to deadfalls. The Nolichucky from Embree-ville to Davy Crockett Reservoir can be run from mid-November through mid-July in most years. Though certainly not a wilderness stream, the farms bordering the river are usually not visible from the water, and the atmosphere of natural solitude remains largely intact.

Below Greeneville Dam on Davy Crockett Reservoir the Nolichucky River meanders through rolling, rich farmland and is guarded by sharply inclined banks 15 feet in height. Small shoals and ripples keep the paddling busy as the stream threads through bottomland at the base of tall, curving hills, and islands appear frequently in midstream. As the Noli-chucky approaches its confluence with the French Broad River, it widens perceptibly from 80 to 100 and finally to almost 300 feet. The dense hardwoods of the upstream reaches are here replaced by intermittent foliage and short scrub vegetation. The level of difficulty is Class I or greater, with few or no dangers to navigation. Access is fair and signs of human habitation are frequent. The Nolichucky can be run from Davy Crockett Reservoir to its mouth whenever the Greeneville Dam is releasing.

# Pigeon River

There is a severe and serious water quality problem with the Pigeon River. And I, person-ally, will not paddle on those waters. I'm not a fan of the water quality of the Ocoee River either, but at least there the water is not toxic. It has been widely reported and well docu-mented that carcinogenic dioxin has been found in Tennessee in the Pigeon River down-stream of the paper mill outfall in North Carolina. Certainly the cast to the water and the smell of the flow attest to decades of paper mill discharge. And I am personally acquainted with an Ocoee raft outfitter who is trained in the medical field and will not extend his

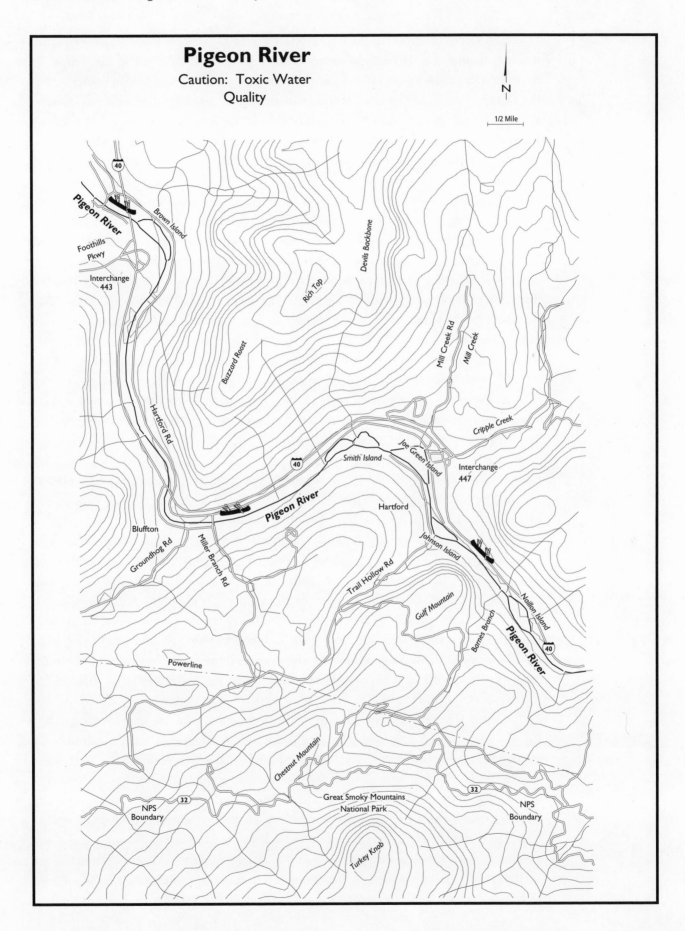

**Pigeon River**

Caution: Toxic Water
Quality

successful Ocoee operation to the Pigeon River due to his concern that his raft guides not have any regular contact with the waters of the Pigeon. A careful cruising canoeist could float through the area with little actual personal exposure, but normal whitewater activities by rafts, kayaks, and even whitewater canoes include many possible incidents of water contact and ingestion. Currently, races and "rodeos" are being promoted and held on the Pigeon River within its toxic reaches. I am sure that many participants have not been alerted to their exposure and risk. And I am concerned for them.

Supposedly the paper mill has seen a new light and the discharges are changing. Well, they didn't seem to see this revealing light for many, many years (actually, for many, many decades), and the legacy of their outfalls will exist in the little stream's riverbed for longer than I will be interested in paddling. So in anyone's lifetime, there are some things that just won't get done, and I guess there are some whitewater runs that I just won't ever make.

The following description was written by Bob Sehlinger for the previous edition of this book and was written before the public documentation of water-borne toxics. Take my advice and leave the Pigeon to the North Carolina politicians and Tennessee lawyers. Go paddle the Nolichucky.

As in the case of the French Broad River, much of the better paddling water of the Pigeon River is situated on the North Carolina side of the state line. (For a description of the area, see *Carolina Whitewater* by Bob Benner.) The Pigeon nevertheless does provide one good whitewater run and several miles of tranquil, pastoral cruising in Tennessee before emptying into the French Broad River north of Newport.

The whitewater run commences at the Walters (North Carolina) Power and Light Plant just over the state line. Like the Hiwassee, the Pigeon is runnable when the power plant is releasing water through its generators. The level of difficulty for the run from the power plant to Denton is Class II–III for readings of 30,000–10,000 kW at the Walters plant, and Class III and higher for readings over 30,000 kW; 50,000 kW is the maximum for open boats. At lower water the run is essentially a straightforward Class II with easily recognizable routes. At higher levels, the Pigeon is big and pushy and has numerous large holes and standing waves. Most of the intimidating water lies between the power plant and Hartford, and it can be scouted from the highway. Though the water quality is poor (sometimes even smelly), the scenery is excellent, with high rock walls and gumdrop-shaped mountains rising from the river's edge. Where the exposed rock gives way to more gently inclined slopes, sweet-gum, maple, hemlock, and poplar trees overhang the stream. And from the river, the bustle of I-40 paralleling the stream halfway up the ridge, is hardly noticeable.

Below Hartford, the Pigeon emerges from the mountains into a wide farm valley with the rapids decreasing in size and frequency as the river flows past Denton. Beyond Denton, the Pigeon flows between eight-foot, shaded banks of varying steepness and ripples over small shoals from time to time. By the time the Pigeon reaches Newport, it has widened from 65 feet at the power plant to more than 110 feet. From Denton to its mouth, signs of human habitation increase markedly, particularly as the stream passes through Newport. From one end of the Pigeon to the other, islands of various sizes and vegetation are encountered midstream. Access is fair to good throughout, and hazards to navigation below Denton are limited to a Class II rapid one mile downstream from the I-40 bridge near Pleasant Grove and some deadfalls above Newport.

# Little Pigeon River, Middle Prong

When the bumper sticker appeared saying, "SAVE THE MIDDLE PRONG," it caused much amusing comment by noncanoeing folks. Frog gigs, pitchforks, tableware, and other handy utensils were all, at times, brought to mind, with a general dismissal of yet another kooky cult displaying their message. But the sticker-displayers knew the Middle Prong to be a mountain-born, free-flowing, clean-water stream, and "STMP" was an unusual coalition of riverside landowners and whitewater canoeists who were determined to keep it that way when the town of Gatlinburg proposed piping in water from the Middle Prong and returning it after using it. Those who knew the Middle Prong did not believe the stream would be enhanced by all this and preferred to have the stream left alone. The STMP campaign succeeded, and the canoeist may still enjoy this free-flowing, clear-water stream in the Smokies.

The Middle Prong of the Little Pigeon River begins in the Smoky Mountains in Sevier County near the Tennessee border and runs north through Pittman Center before joining the East Fork east of Sevierville. A run on the Middle Prong can actually start just inside the Great Smoky Mountains National Park near the Greenbrier Ranger Station. An intimate, wooded, Class II run goes to the park's boundary. Cross under US 321 and civilization appears. (On a nice, bright spring day, the riverside sunbathers will make you feel overdressed in your PFD.) Unsolicited advice is always freely given you about the reportedly terrible turn to the river just downstream and out of sight. You, in turn, can amaze the onlookers with your expertise as you run simple straightforward four-foot drops (at low flow) in the stair-step area where many bathers congregate. With luck, no one will witness your run of the surprisingly complex Class III rapid on downstream. There are cabins along the banks, and the flow is brisk. The many Class III drops can take their toll. Downstream, the pace slackens and the press of the bankside civilization begins to degrade the water quality. The stream loses appeal as it approaches Sevierville and the mills. Taking out above this industrial area is recommended.

To judge water level in the Middle Prong, use the same gauge and same flow rates as for canoeing the upper stretches of the Little River.

# Little Pigeon River, West Prong

The Little Pigeon River, like the song for Davy Crockett says, is born high on a mountaintop in Tennessee. Actually several mountains in the Smokies are drained by the three "prongs" of the Little Pigeon. The south side of English Mountain in northeastern Sevier County is drained by the East Fork of the Little Pigeon. The Middle Prong, along with Porter's Creek and False Gap Prong, forms the drainage for the northern slopes of Mount Guyot, Mount Sequoyah, Laurel Top, and the northeastern slopes of Mount Le Conte. The West Prong of the Little Pigeon carries the run-off from the northwestern face of Mount Le Conte and the northeastern face of Clingmans Dome.

Of the three prongs, the West and Middle Prongs are the most often paddled. The West Prong is best known to most tourists visiting the Smokies because the main highway (US 441) across the mountains into Tennessee from North Carolina follows the West Prong's

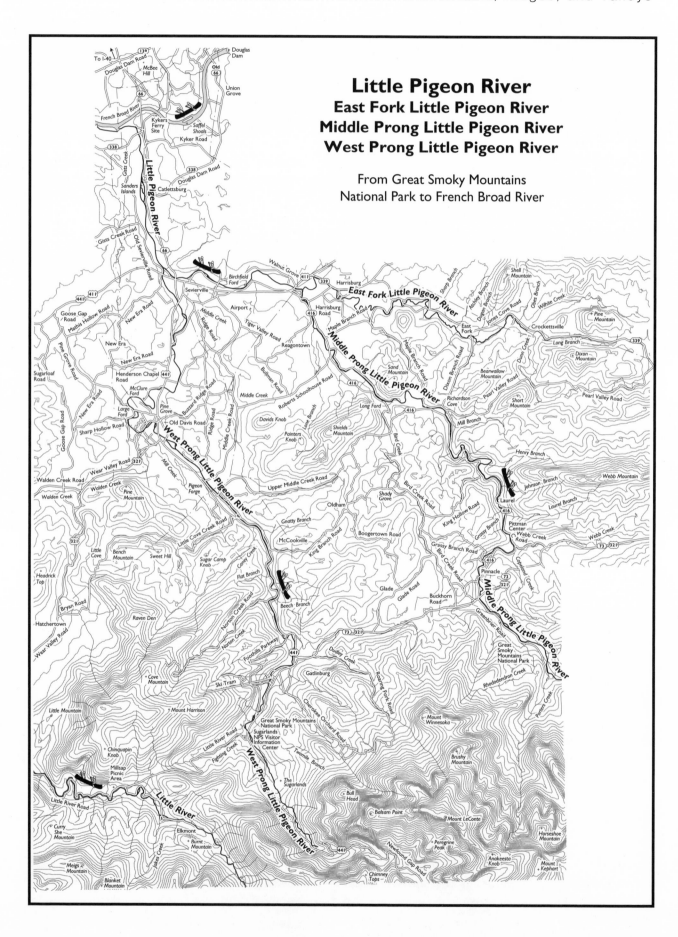

**Little Pigeon River**
**East Fork Little Pigeon River**
**Middle Prong Little Pigeon River**
**West Prong Little Pigeon River**

From Great Smoky Mountains
National Park to French Broad River

tumultuous course down the mountains into Gatlinburg. All along the road park visitors can be observed hopping out of their vans and campers to pose for photographs along this scenic stream's bank. It is not, however, until the West Prong drops into the narrow valley southwest of Gatlinburg that the stream settles down sufficiently (and picks up enough volume) to be runnable.

Beginning at the park facility located on the park boundary near the Gatlinburg by-pass, the run qualifies as Tennessee's ultimate "hot dog" whitewater run. The West Prong rips right through the middle of wining, dining, honeymooning Gatlinburg. Nowhere else can the oft-forgotten whitewater paddler gain such instant recognition and attention. Think of it . . . surfing waves beneath the balconies of the Howard Johnson Motel, blasting through playful Class II rapids to the enthusiastic cheers of hundreds of tourists watching from the sidewalks, or making a neat eddy turn under the noses of the free-spending elite as they sip French onion soup in one of Gatlinburg's riverside restaurants.

Fortunately for the paddler, this run's toughest rapid, a borderline Class III, occurs at the beginning of the trip before the course runs in front of the grandstand. This rapid, which involves a tricky slanting drop, can be scouted from the left. Tactics differ somewhat with varying water conditions. Proceeding downstream, the West Prong is typical of most Smoky Mountain streams—it flows over a rock and sand bed liberally sprinkled with small- and medium-sized rocks. Rapids are Class II separated by short pools. Hazards include two dams just as the stream enters Gatlinburg. The large dam is a little over four feet high, and the small one is approximately two feet—portage both. In the middle of the run, the stream splits around Motel Island after passing under the Greystone Hotel bridge. The best route here is on the right. Just beyond Motel Island are some of the longest and most interesting rapids encountered. They remain, however, Class II with the best routes easily identifiable. As the stream exits from Gatlinburg, the paddler can take out at the Gatlinburg water plant or continue on toward Pigeon Forge for a little longer trip of more of the same (but without an audience). Paddlers are advised, however, to avoid the McCookville/Pigeon Forge area downstream where there is a series of dams.

The West Prong is runnable after heavy rains. Paddlers should use extra caution at higher water levels since the stream is channeled with twelve-foot vertical concrete walls through much of Gatlinburg, which makes it almost impossible for a paddler out of a boat to escape the river.

# Little River of Sevier and Blount Counties

Another cascading waterway spilling off the front range of the Smokies, the Little River has made a magical impression in the minds of many quick paddlers in East Tennessee. Containing exceptional water quality, delicate water quantity, and sections of difficulty that can only be adequately described around campfires (usually the night before a descent on the river), the Little River cascades precipitously down from the heights of the Smoky Mountains to become, between Elkmont and Townsend, one of the most difficult whitewater runs in Tennessee. Firing down the mountainside at a furious pace, the Little River squeezes its

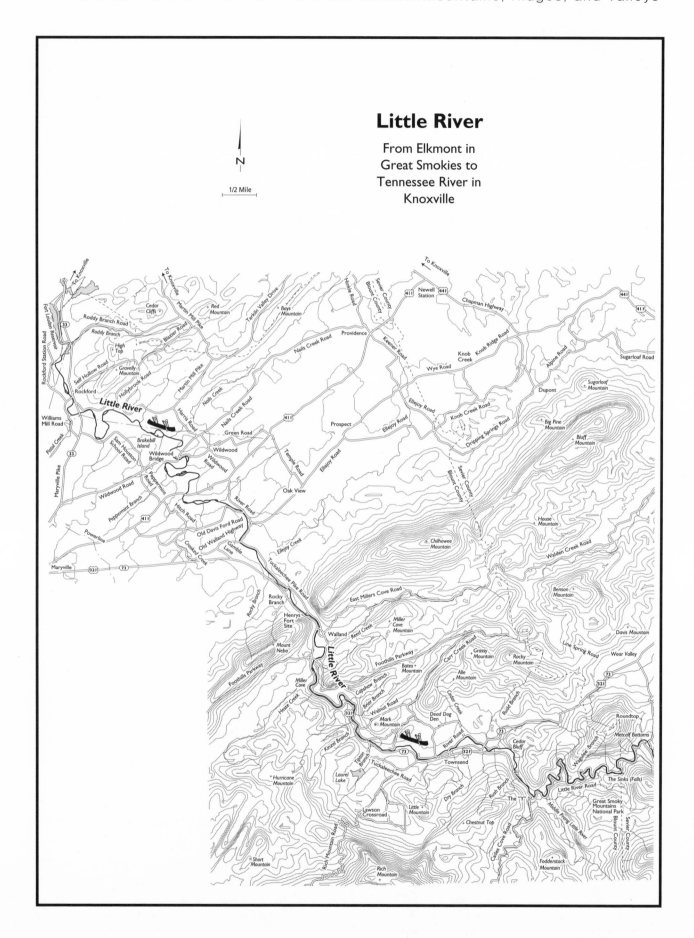

# Little River

## From Elkmont in Great Smokies to Tennessee River in Knoxville

N

1/2 Mile

flow through a continuously narrow, boulder-infested bed with an average gradient of 70 or more feet per mile. Technical in the extreme, and almost devoid of eddies for long stretches at a time, the Little River is stuffed mile after mile with successive Class III and IV rapids, disguised by exploding foam and mined with boat-crunching rocks. To say the least, it is a run for experts only.

For most of us, catching the Little River with sufficient water for a run is almost as tricky as getting home with boat and limbs in one piece. Definitely a wet-weather stream with tremendously quick runoff in the upper sections, the Little River draws most of its following from the Knoxville/Oak Ridge/Maryville area, where local paddlers are within striking distance when they hear that the water is up. For the rest of us, it's catch-as-catch-can. The Little River is usually considered to be runnable downstream from the Millsap Picnic Grounds near Elkmont. From the put-in the rapids are continuous and come at the paddler with alarming speed; pools just do not exist. Drops are frequent and often severe (three or more feet), rapids are long and technical. As the river passes under the Little River Road (Alt. TN 73) bridge near the mouth of the Poplar Branch, three Class IV rapids occur within two hundred yards; scout from the left bank.

After the river passes under the bridge leading to Little Greenbrier School, it tames down somewhat (Class II–III) as it parallels Alt. TN 73 along the left bank. Following a half loop to the left, the river curves right and flows relatively straight for about a third of a mile before beginning a large loop to the left. This loop, containing some particularly fierce water, forms the entrance rapids for the ten-foot vertical drop of the Sinks of the Little at the end of the loop and just under the Alt. TN 73 bridge crossing. This entire segment should be scouted carefully before running, and the Sinks probably should be portaged.

Below the Sinks, to the next downstream crossing of Alt. TN 73, the Little River continues true to form with several Class IV, long, technical rapids interspersed with lots of challenging Class III and long Class II rapids. Past the Alt. TN 73 bridge, the Little calms down somewhat in what is sometimes called the Elbow section. Unlike the Sinks section, which is normally regarded as suitable for decked-boat experts only, the Elbow section is considered a good run for open- and decked-boat intermediates. The rapids persist in being long and technical, but pools are more frequently encountered here and the gradient flattens out to a mere fifty feet per mile.

Do not relax prematurely, however, for one of the most dangerous rapids on the Little River rears its seething head right in the middle of the run. It is the namesake of this section, Elbow Rapid. It consists of a tricky approach on the right, followed by a drop, and a sharp left turn (the latter in a crashing boil of falling, converging currents). An alternate route down the middle is possible at certain water levels, but it carries the paddler into and sometimes under a head-crunching overhanging rock at the bottom of the drop. Except at lower levels, it is heartily recommended that this rapid be portaged. It is reported that this rapid was formerly known as the 90 Percent Rapid; i.e., no matter how good the paddler or what technique was used in the run, he would be chewed to pieces about 90 percent of the time. Enough said. Elbow is Class IV at moderate levels when there is a good collection pool below. A good take-out for this section is at the tourist parking area just inside the park boundary, two miles upstream from Townsend. Because the characteristics of the Little River from Elkmont to the park boundary vary considerably with changing water levels, paddlers should avail themselves of the paralleling road network and carefully scout their proposed run in its entirety before putting in. Due to the narrow, rocky nature of the Little River and the distinct absence of alternative routes in some of the more difficult rapids, deadfalls lodged across the stream can be lethal. Paddlers, therefore, should take extra pains while scouting to ensure that the channel is clear of obstructions.

From the park boundary to Melrose the river increases in width, and long pools separate the playful Class II rapids and rock gardens. This section is appropriate for well-schooled beginners in both decked and open boats. This section also marks the descent of the river into a gorge with tall cliffs alternately rising up beside the water and receding from its edge. Signs of civilization are common in this area with resort property dotting the water's edge wherever the precipitous terrain permits.

Downstream from Melrose the Little River flows almost tranquilly through foothills and farm country before emptying into the Tennessee River near Singleton. Here the Little drifts quietly beneath tree-shaded mudbanks. The fishing is not bad, and anglers in john-boats are encountered frequently. The level of difficulty is Class I with deadfalls and dams at Melrose being the only hazards to navigation. Access to this lower section is adequate.

# Ocoee River (Whitewater Section)

Before the Olympics visited Tennessee, more people knew about "that river with the wooden box running along side it," than knew its name: the Ocoee. And not long before that, no one even knew that the Ocoee River was a premier whitewater run. Why? Well, it is true that there were whitewater canoes and experienced whitewater canoeists before the Ocoee was discovered. And there were lots of whitewater paddling activities on nearby mountain streams. But there was no water flowing down the Ocoee streambed, just upwardly angled rockbed seams and dry boulders down there alongside the adjacent roadway. For years, paddlers traveling the Old Copper Road (US 64) in southeastern Polk County would marvel and conjecture about potential souse holes, rapids, and falls. But high on the mountainside, also beside that stretch of roadway, that leaky sixty-five-year-old wooden flume carried the river's entire flow to a powerhouse seven miles downstream. One day that old wooden boxway could carry the liquid load no more; seventeen megawatts of generated power was transformed back into 1,000 cfs of river flow. The paddlers would conjecture no more. Double Trouble, Diamond Splitter, Table Saw, and Hell's Hole were exciting manifestations of the newly found, fifty-seven-foot-drop-per-mile water. Even before the shutdown for repair, during a temporary flow diversion away from the box for flume inspection purposes, the paddlers gathered at the face of Ocoee #2 dam to catch the new flow downstream. There were no names to the rapids then, but we "entered" the stream at that damsite, and "Grumpy" (as it later became known) promptly ate our inner-tube-flotation-equipped open canoes and discharged us all at various points downstream. A southeastern paddler, Murray Johnson, who was destined to later move to Oregon to open up the greater northwest to open canoe paddling, was the only one to complete that day's run. I was portaging up the bank when he blew by me. "Don't take out," he yelled.

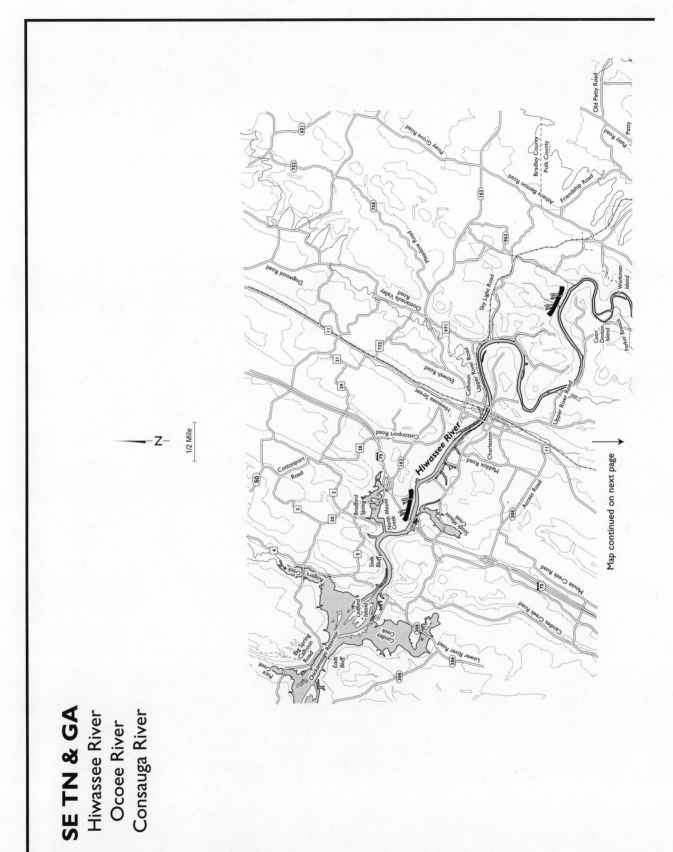

**SE TN & GA**
Hiwassee River
Ocoee River
Consauga River

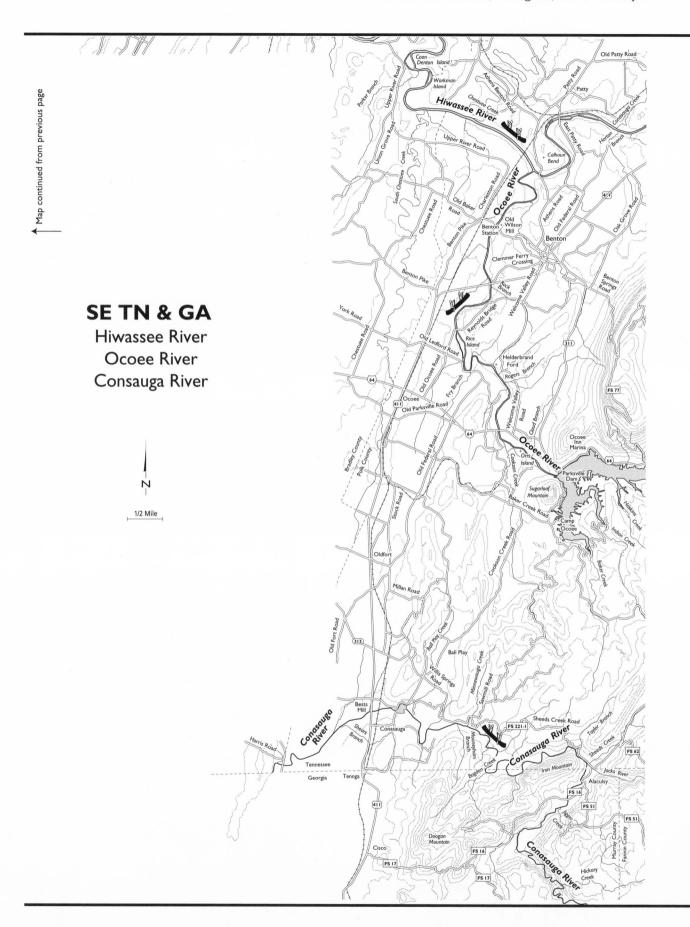

Map continued from previous page

## SE TN & GA
Hiwassee River
Ocoee River
Consauga River

N

1/2 Mile

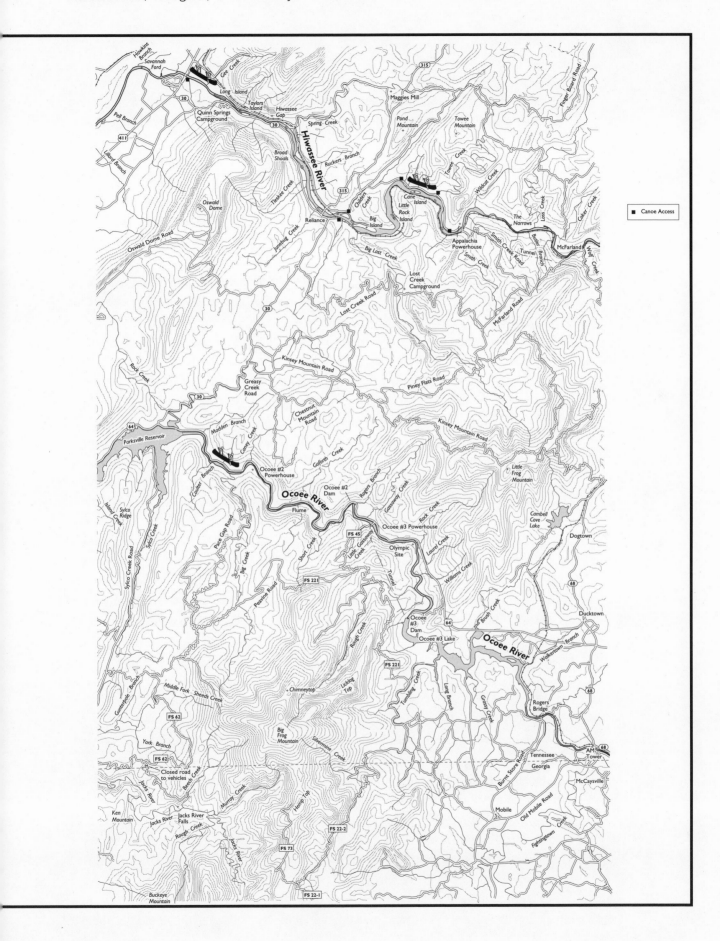

Canoe Access

"Follow me, we'll take the chicken routes." "How do you think I got this far?" I yelled back as I stumbled on up to the roadway.

The Ocoee gained instant notoriety as river runners learned how various flow levels affected their craft on this new-found whitewater. Commercial raft outfitters sprang up. National decked-boat championship races appeared. With their typical bureaucratic insensitivity to changing times, uses, and needs, the TVA continued to aggressively pursue its Ocoee wooden-flume rejuvenation project (claiming a desperate need for the pitifully few kilowatts to be sluiced from that antique generating plant, while TVA itself simultaneously abandoned multi-thousands of kilowatt capacities in other generating-plant construction projects elsewhere in the Tennessee Valley.) This flimflam flume reconstruction included pouring concrete over the antique wooden dam (a wooden dam!) and changing some of the run of their river as needed for the project. The Ocoee outfitters have done all they can to educate TVA to the true values of this river as a nationally significant whitewater flow. But TVA remains hidebound to its traditions from the 1930s. Don't kid yourself. TVA does not care for the concerns of the paddlers no matter what its press releases say. TVA does care that it gets a cut from the Outfitters for every hour that the river runs free of their old wood box. But TVA sets the release schedules and is ill-concerned about actual paddling problems with those schedules.

For the time being, one of the most "taxing" whitewater streams in the southeast exists along seven miles of the Old Copper Road from Ocoee No. 2 Dam to Ocoee No. 2 Powerhouse. This run is marginal for open boats. Only whitewater canoes rigged with extra flotation should attempt the run, and the paddler should be a confident expert. Damage reports from the Ocoee are legendary. Know your advanced paddling techniques or stay off. The Ocoee whitewater is not for general recreational canoeing. It is solid Class III and IV. (However, the road runs nearby along the entire run, so you can walk out if the whitewater becomes too strenuous.)

The Ocoee is Tennessee's portion of Georgia's Toccoa River, an attractive mountain stream skirting the southern reaches of the Smokies. Unfortunately, at the Georgia–Tennessee border, the Copperhill mining basin fouls the water quality. Sulfuric acid leached from forty years of mining and smelting has completely sterilized the Ocoee tributaries coming out of the great copper basin. Years of airborne acid have also denuded the forested hillsides in the basin. (This little red dot amid the sea of Smoky green, along with the Great Wall of China, is one of the few human-made earth modifications visible to the orbiting astronauts.) The bare hillsides of the basin also choke the same dead Ocoee tributaries with fine-grained red silt. Water quality coming down this premier whitewater run is somewhere between repulsive and lethal. Keep your mouth closed!

Hazards on this run begin before you even get your boat in the water. The only safe loading and parking area is upstream of the put-in on the lake side of the Ocoee No. 2 dam. This parking area is preferable to the challenge of unloading amid the dizzying fumes of speeding diesels and the careening autos of rubbernecking tourists on US 64. Here, with nothing more at risk than your life, you can park on a constricted ribbon of road shoulder near the put-in (but below the major boat-swamping "Entrance" rapid) and attempt feverishly to unload your gear, a little at a time, when breaks in the traffic allow. This type of river access for private boaters is not encouraged.

Once in the water, the paddler will find the Ocoee to be synonymous with continuous action. The pace is intense and the eddies are not always where you would like them to be. Below the put-in, Class II and III rapids follow one upon the other and consist primarily of big waves and some respectable holes. These rapids are agreeably straightforward for the most part and have recognizable routes. Following this stretch of warm-up rapids, however, the river broadens and runs shallow over a long series of wide, shallow ledges known as Gonzo Shoals. Route selection is anything but obvious, and the going (particularly at minimal flow) is extremely technical.

Below the wide, shallow stretch, the river begins to narrow slightly and bend to the right. This is the approach to Broken Nose (alternately known as Veg-O-Matic), a potentially lethal series of three drops in rapid succession. The drops are near the right bank. Powerful crosscurrents surge between each of the drops and a keeper hydraulic lurks at the base of the final drop. There is a "cheat route" along the far left for those who prefer not to encounter the main activity in Broken Nose Rapid.

Action continues and bears back to the left on through a Class II–III series that includes Second Helping and Moon Chute. When the river begins to turn back toward the right, prepare for Double Suck. Double Suck gets its name from two closely spaced souse holes. You will recognize the rapid by the large granite boulders thrusting up and blocking the center one-third of the stream. Go just to the right of these boulders and over a four-foot drop into the first hole. Don't relax after this one, however, because the second hole follows immediately, and it will eat the unwary. Eddy out behind the large boulders in the center if you need time to recover your composure or bail the water from your boat.

Continuing downstream, the river swings away from paralleling US 64. Here the paddler should move to the far right for Double Trouble, a double set of holes and waves. Below Double Trouble, a number of smaller rapids lead into a long pool known as the Doldrums. This, the longest pool on the river, signals the presence of Class IV Table Saw about three-fourths of a mile ahead. At the end of the Doldrums the stream broadens conspicuously and laps playfully over the shallows with little riffles and waves. Protruding from the right bank, a large rock shelf or boulder beach funnels the water to the left.

The river narrows and the current deepens and picks up speed as it enters the most formidable rapid on the Ocoee. Table Saw is named for a large rock situated in the middle of a chute that splits the current and sends up an impressive rooster tail. Below the rock is a violent diagonal hole that fortunately is not a keeper. Table Saw can be scouted from the boulder beach on the right or from eddies on the left. In either case, key on the rooster tail and run just to its left, bracing hard as you hit the hole at the bottom. Rescue can be set on the river right just below the hole, where there is a nice, if not overly spacious eddy. Speedy rescue of people and equipment is important here due to the proximity of Diamond Splitter just downstream.

Consisting of yet another river-dividing boulder, Diamond Splitter rises ponderously out of the water, presenting the potential for broaching or entrapment. The generally preferred route is to the right of the boulder. From here Class II and III rapids rampage more or less continuously, with only one significant intervening pool as the Ocoee approaches the powerhouse. A quarter of a mile upstream of the powerhouse is Torpedo, a long, confusing, technical rapid with several powerful holes. Frequently omitted in descriptions of the Ocoee, this rapid can be very rough on a boater who chooses the wrong route. Most easily scouted from the road while running the shuttle, Torpedo should be of particular interest to first-timers.

Torpedo is separated from Hell's Hole, an enormous, deep, aerated, river-dominating hole by a pool just upstream of the powerhouse and bridge. Situated toward the right bank of the river at the new powerhouse bridge, Hell's Hole can be played, surfed, or punched with the happy prospect of being flushed out in case of an upset. While Hell's Hole monopolizes the channel, a technical run skirting the hole on the left is possible (and generally advisable for open boats). Hell's Hole, however, is only the first part of a double rapid. Not twenty yards beyond the fearsome hole itself is the drop known as Powerhouse Rapid. Powerhouse consists of a four-foot vertical ledge and nasty hydraulic spanning the left two-thirds of the stream, with a more manageable tongue spilling down on the right.

Arriving safely at the bottom of all this requires making it through or around Hell's Hole, fighting the current at the bottom of the hole, which tries to carry you left, and working hard to the right to line up for the tongue through Powerhouse. Have a good roll if you try to play Hell's Hole, and anticipate that the current will kick you left as you wash out. When the water is high (1,800 cfs or more), Hell's Hole washes out while the Powerhouse hydraulic becomes lethal. In this situation, run close to the right bank to avoid being carried too far left as you approach the bridge. Scout this complex stretch either while running the shuttle or from the TVA plant bridge.

If you make it this far you can drift for a while (a quarter mile) to the raft take-out shortly downstream. Continuing past this study in (un)organized human activity and milling about, the stream flows through some shoals to the new, private boater take-out another half-mile downstream.

# Lower Ocoee River

There's plenty of action on the waters of the Ocoee above the Parksville impoundment. As noted above, the upper Ocoee waters are more or less biologically dead. But after settling out the Copper Basin silt load below the still waters of Parksville Reservoir, the waters flowing below that Dam become much more supportive of riverine life forms again. And where the lesser forms exist, the higher forms congregate, too. Fish, herons, and occasional paddlers can be found in the "wildlife" areas of the lower Ocoee. The Ocoee is on its way to the Hiwassee. Parksville Dam anchored in Sugarloaf Mountain is positioned at the edge of Chilhowee Ridge, the last ridge of the Unaka mountain range. The dam releases the river from those mountains into the historic Overhill Indian territories, where the river bottoms provided village sites and their farm and game lands. It's a placid river, but steeped in history and prehistory. There is even a livery on this stretch of the river, renting tandem canoes on the Ocoee.

# Hiwassee River

Do you live in Tennessee? Did you take any basic whitewater canoe training? Then you probably floated the Hiwassee. And, if not, then you should have; it is not too late. The Hiwassee continues to be a superb training and recreational stream. This stream has successfully introduced more people to the joys of river paddling than any other in the state. The Hiwassee has it all: clean and cold water, fast current, rock ledges, great scenery—it is an ideal habitat for whitewater canoeing or put-and-take trout fishing: you'll find both on the Hiwassee, a Tennessee State Scenic River. The trout supply is stocked, and so the canoeists seem to be when the water rises. In northeastern Polk County, near the North Carolina border, the Appalachia Dam impounds this major drainageway of the southern Blue Ridge mountains. The Hiwassee begins on a ridge near the Appalachian Trail, high above Helen, Georgia, and meanders northward through some highland patch-farm, north Georgia country. It rests in an impoundment or two, masquerades under the more Indian-sounding "Hiawassee" spelling, and then cuts across the forested foot of a couple of North Carolina peaks and plunges into Tennessee via the Appalachia powerhouse release. It's a big watershed and an equally large riverbed for this Tennessee portion of the river. For a different type of experience on the Hiwassee, take a look at the interesting and scenic fifteen-mile section of the river between the dam and the powerhouse. This bed is now mostly dry and carries water only during periods of extremely high natural flow from heavy rainfall. Hiking access is via the railroad tracks (still in regular use) on river right or the John Muir trail on river left. The scenery is beautiful, with mountains on both sides and unusual rock formations. There are high trestles crossing over brooks, and at one point the track rather famously crosses over itself. The railroad makes more than a complete circle, known as the Hiwassee Loop, to gain altitude. Nearer the powerhouse is the abandoned townsite of McFarland and the Narrows, where the river is constricted between the tracks and high rocks of unusual formation.

Hiwassee River. The Hiwassee River is a fun feast of mountain scenery, clean water, and friendly flow. This is Tennessee's best introduction to river canoeing. Photograph by Jim Robertson.

Downstream from the powerhouse, where the river is again canoeable, the water is extremely cold. Releases come from deep in the impoundment. It is rather unusual to find such cold water in a wide, shallow stream. Trout thrive; dunked canoeists shiver.

After all its mountain meandering, this river still has one ridge left to clear in its surge toward the Tennessee River. And it is a beautiful, scenic setting as the clear-water, bouncing river makes a dramatic horseshoe bend at the foot of Tennessee's Hood Mountain. It is truly a worthy member of the state's scenic river system.

Anglers and canoeists have almost learned to coexist on this stretch of rockbound water. When there's no dam release, the waders line the rocky outcroppings in the riverbed, hunting the pooled-up fish. When the 1,500 cfs dam release comes along, tubers, rafters, and paddlers of all types follow it, plunging over those same rock ledges and recovering in those same fished-out pools. The first five miles of the Hiwassee below the powerhouse are Class I and II with a couple of rapids rating a strong Class II. It's a fun ride, and the Hiwassee is a forgiving stream, but one that accelerates a desire to hone your skills. Swift current and the wide reach across the river can often make recovery a difficult, chilly experience. The put-in is at the powerhouse access ramp (about a quarter mile below the powerhouse). Two miles downstream is the Big Bend parking lot, hidden in the trees at the foot of a series of ledges. If rain, cold, or mishap creates a need to take out early, you should know how to find that access—there isn't another one until the ramp at Reliance. Between the powerhouse and Reliance, you'll encounter a mixed bag of paddling possibilities: swift current and bouncy waves at Cabin Bend; big, unstable drops at No. 2 Rapids and Oblique Falls; tricky cross-currents at Bigneys Rock and follow-the-flow, water-reading exercises at the Ledges and the Stairsteps; peel-off and eddy-turn practice at the Needles; and big swamper waves at Devils Shoals. Below Reliance, the river flattens out as it makes its final run out of the mountains. Six miles downstream you'll find the U.S. Forest Service Quinn Springs fee campground across TN 30 from the fishing access on river left and the Tennessee State Park's Gee Creek campground along the river just below. The Gee Creek ramp is up the creek a few yards, and its entrance is marked by an old Indian-built fishtrap of V-shaped shallow rock shoals just below the mouth of the creek in the Hiwassee.

# Conasauga River

Big Frog is the best; the gem of the Cohuttas. Crystalline, clean, cold, free-flowing waters supporting native trout. A pristine, clear Tennessee State Scenic River, and Georgia claims it! The Conasauga River is born deep in Georgia's Cohutta Wilderness, where it falls off the slopes of those north Georgia mountains. The waters drain only national forest lands as they gather together as a streamway. The upper Conasauga, this little crystal clear gem of the woodlands, then flows north through steep and almost inaccessible terrain until the highland Alaculsy Valley is reached near the Georgia–Tennessee border. As the stream works its way north stepping across from Georgia's Cohutta Wilderness into Tennessee's Big Frog Wilderness, the westbound Jacks River joins the Conasauga and doubles its flow.

It is there, also, that the stream become canoeable. And it is there that the newly combined flow enters Tennessee (with its official State Scenic River designation). But natural

# In Celebration of Scenic Rivers

[Editor's note: Rivers run through almost every major and many minor cities in Tennessee. The following contemplation of the many gifts our rivers bring all of us was read by Ed Young at a special Tennessee Scenic Rivers Association meeting. The TSRA was celebrating the twentieth anniversary of both the state and national Scenic Rivers Acts. Aptly, Ed was chosen as the TSRA Conservationist of the Year of 1988, earlier that month.]

Some of my best friends are rivers. Rivers provide drinking water for all living things. They nourish animal and bird life along their banks. They provide a home for fish, turtles, and other forms of life.

Rivers are wonderful places to spend sultry summer afternoons fishing on a shady bank or cooling down in a swimming hole. They provide exciting whitewater paddling or leisurely floats in an inner tube. Rivers make sweet music to sleep by.

Rivers can be lively and bubbling in the spring but also serenely beautiful beneath their coats of ice and snow on a gray, cold wintry day. They are ever changing and endlessly fascinating. Rivers are paths of exploration through the mountains and forests of our imaginations. They offer scenery and vistas that lift our spirits and touch our hearts.

We form deep emotional attachments to rivers. They hold precious memories of friends and loved ones who have shared them with us. They remind us of the old homeplace, of our growing up and of our deepest roots. Rivers are the places where our fathers taught us how to fish, and where our children splashed and played when they were young.

Perhaps best of all, they are places of solitude in a world that is moving too fast. If we will only look, rivers will teach us much about the incredible, fascinating, and altogether wonderful world we live in. And, in considering the passage of a river through the seasons, from its source to its end, we come to a deeper understanding and acceptance of our own course through life.

How we use rivers—how we treat them—is a true measure of our values, for rivers are ever and always both fragile and eternal. Tonight is for celebration, but when tonight has passed, let us gather at the river. You will love it. And you will always come back.

—Ed Young
Nashville, Tennessee

boundaries and political boundaries don't always agree. Twice in the next five miles of flow, the Conasauga, a Tennessee State Scenic River, leaves Tennessee and drops back into Georgia, only to reenter soon after. Eventually it makes a permanent southern plunge into Georgia about fifteen miles from where it first enters Tennessee. But your float will remain uninterrupted by those political boundaries. No matter where you are, your concern will be only with the rocks and rapids, the flowers, trees, and trout. This is a naturally flowing stream that drains mostly forest lands in southeastern Polk County. The only sustained season of floatable water is during winter and early spring—during this time of year, however, the water is cold; cold enough, in fact, to support native trout. Even at the high levels needed for floating, the water remains clear and clean—clean enough to drink.

This is an absolutely superb river run. In his normal manner of understatement, Don Hixson of Chattanooga once observed in a past newsletter of the Tennessee Scenic Rivers

Association: "The Conasauga is among the most beautiful rivers you will ever paddle." Many of the rapids require intricate Class II maneuvering—excellent waters for skill sharpening. But the river isn't pushy or threatening. Put in near the Jacks River confluence for the ten-mile run. This gives you a half mile warm-up for the Class II or better shoal, Taylor Branch Rapid. There's good primitive camping and river access just above the rapid if you think warm-ups are superfluous. A mile and a half downstream, you'll find The Falls, a Class III three-foot drop following a difficult, technical approach. This is the most difficult rapid on the river, but there's a convenient recovery pool below. A fishing camp on river's right is often used for lunch while the dunked boaters drag their canoes back up to run this approach and drop time and again until success smiles on their grim, wet, cold, determined faces. Success usually happens soon after the boater realizes that there is a tricky, strategic cross-current that has a tendency to push the bow of the otherwise perfectly aligned canoe to the right just before entering the drop.

About four miles down river, in a deceptively swift shoals stands the infamous "fiberglass-covered rock." Beware this innocent, rounded menace. You're lulled to inattention by the scenery and your past rapid-running successes. You see the river valley opening up and know the whitewater is playing out. Yet this final kiss goodbye from the river has claimed more canoes than any of the upper rapids you've encountered. It's simple. All the recently accelerated river currents converge on this rock. By the time you realize your impending impact, the shallow, swift shoals allow no purchase, no matter how hard you stab the slick-rock riverbed with your paddle. And you regain your normal river-running alertness to the sound of a crunching canoe and the feel of a chilling dunking. Beyond fiberglass rock, the river settles into an agricultural valley and the float becomes more leisurely. The current remains helpful until the take-out on river right about one-half mile upstream of US 411 bridge.

It should be noted that an old logging road, a 6.5-mile hiking trail, exists along the river from Taylor Branch Camp until the river leaves the mountains for the agricultural valley. The trail starts on river's right and crosses the river twice. (Canoe assists for the hikers might be needed.) One crossing is near the Georgia–Tennessee border, where the river again reenters Tennessee below Taylor Branch Camp, about two miles below The Falls rapid. The second crossing is near where the trail terminates. It crosses back from the river's left to its right, then shortly heads away from the river to intersect the shuttle road 4.3 miles west of Taylor Branch Camp.

Whether canoeing the whitewater or hiking through the well-watered forest, the clean and clear Conasauga is a beautiful springtime expression of nature's bounty.

# Cumberland Plateau

## Stinking Creek, Hickory Creek, and Clear Fork of Campbell County

Stinking Creek is a misnamed Cumberland Plateau stream that drains northwestern Campbell County before flowing into Hickory Creek, which, in turn, empties into the Clear Fork, which runs north into the North Fork of the Cumberland River in Kentucky. Most have never heard of these streams, because they are the headwaters of Kentucky rivers and drain a relatively remote northern part of Tennessee's Cumberland Plateau. Flowing northeast on the south side of Pine Mountain, this stream network is runnable in the late winter and spring and following heavy rains. Tremendously scenic, the network is surrounded by massive, forested mountain terrain. Along the banks, particularly in the section that parallels TN 2526, development and habitation are common. West of the town of Habersham, Stinking Creek joins Hickory Creek and cuts north alongside TN 9. From here to the spot north of Morley where Hickory Creek meets the Clear Fork, and beyond to Highcliff near the Kentucky state line, the stream enters a rock-walled canyon with the highway on the left and the L&N railroad tracks on the right. Scenery here is more rugged and pristine and the paddling more interesting as Class II rapids increase in frequency and become almost continuous in certain sections around Morley and south of Highcliff. Tall bluffs overhang the water in this section as the stream tumbles along over small ledges and among rocks. Paddle routes are fairly straightforward and only in one or two spots does the going become technical. Scouting, though not mandatory, can be easily accomplished from paralleling roads. Both on the Stinking Creek section and below in the canyon, the primary danger in these thirty- to forty-foot-wide streams is deadfalls. In a high-water situation, particularly in the canyon where the river comes at the paddler pretty quick, strainers become an important factor to consider.

In the upper sections of Stinking Creek the stream is tree-lined. Banks are uniformly steep until the stream network emerges from the mountains in southern Kentucky. Hazards to navigation in all sections consist of strainers in narrow passages and brush or logjams at bridge pilings. Good access is limited to the Stinking Creek and Highcliff areas, although a put-in or take-out could be forced at almost any point by negotiating the steep brushy bank from the adjoining highway.

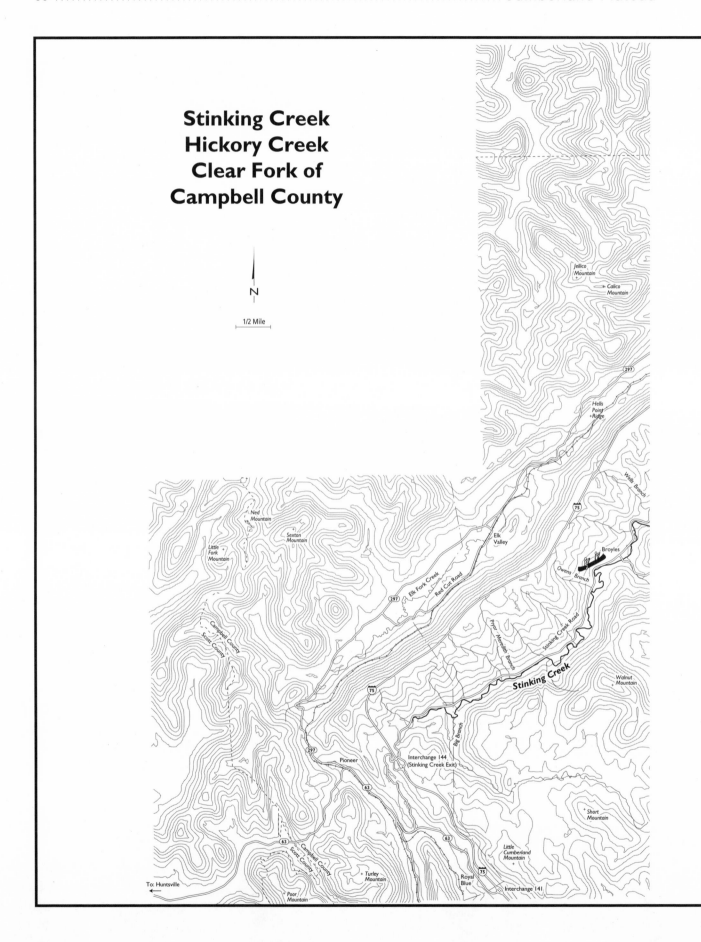

**Stinking Creek
Hickory Creek
Clear Fork of
Campbell County**

N

1/2 Mile

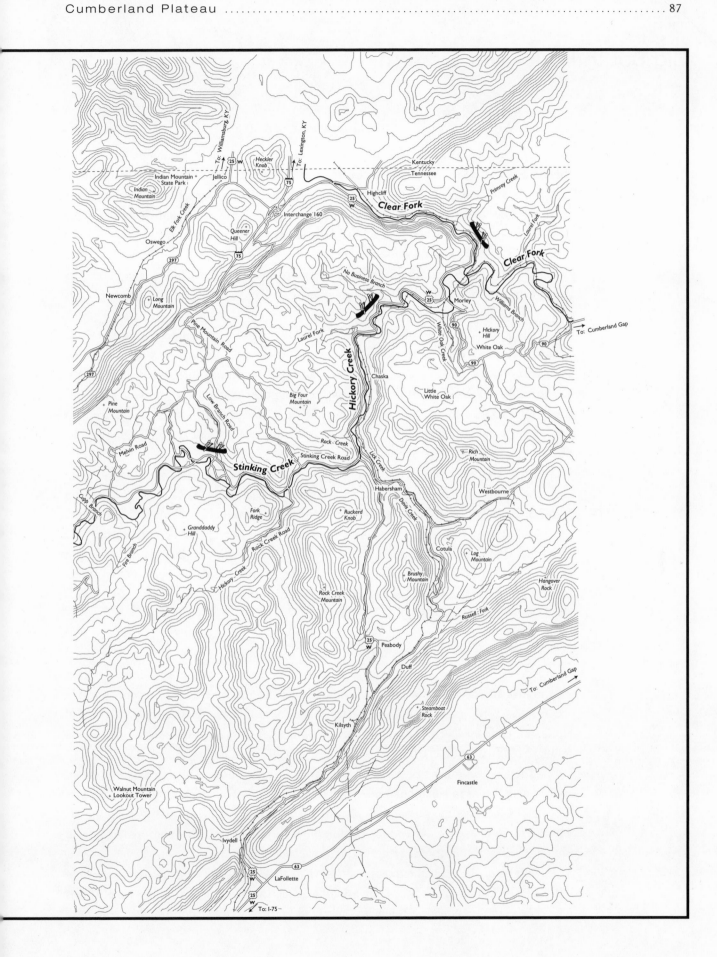

# Big South Fork River System

## Clear Fork River

Clear Fork River is the quiet side of the Big South Fork. As its name implies, Clear Fork is a fresh, crisp, clean-water run through a rural part of the Cumberland Plateau. In fact, it is so rural that much of the river serves as the time-line break between Eastern and Central times. "Fast Time" over on river right. "Slow Time" on river left. Clear Fork begins on the upland borders between Fentress and Morgan Counties and eventually flows into the core of the Big South Fork National River and Recreational Area, those special lands managed by the National Park Service. After twenty-six canoeable miles, Clear Fork finally joins with Tennessee's often muddy New River to form the better-known Big South Fork of the Cumberland River. This major tributary to that featured Park river offers excellent canoeing potential through this part of the remote, rural plateau.

Clear Fork has free-flowing, clear water, wild country, and gorgeous scenery. Clear Fork is a remote, scenic experience, a rural escape from familiar urban pressures. However, Clear Fork is not a wild, crashing, thrashing, hair-raising mountainside cascade. Rather, it is a remarkably well-behaved cruising waterway, cutting deeper and deeper into the old sandstone plateau as it completes the descending river miles heading toward its confluence with the New River. In fact, that is the appeal of this river. You cruise, at ease, simply enjoying the flow of the water and the surrounding beauty.

From Gatewood bridge to Burnt Mill bridge, Clear Fork is a Class I and II stream with only one rapid of significant note: the aptly named Decapitation Rock. Here, on the run below Brewster bridge, you will remember this Class III brainbuster if you do not note the whole streamway swinging under an overhanging rock. If prepared, you can maneuver along the outer edge of this undercut so as to keep your skull intact, but—surprise!— you may also maneuver into a sure-shot line-up for the swamper hole below a sudden three-foot drop just beyond the headknocker. You can't seem to win—so that particular rapid is rated almost Class III.

Clear Fork is favored for canoe camping as well as for day floats. Starting at Gatewood bridge, the placid stream immediately sets forth its streamside greenery of thickset laurel and rhododendron to screen you from any nonriver concerns. Shoals and occasional boulders start to hint at a deeper penetration into the plateau. By the time you get to about a mile above Peters Ford bridge, you will be hard at the foot of sheer, massive rockface sidewall bluffs, but engrossed in maneuvering through the solid Class II whitewater caused by the resultant bluff-cut rockfalls. It's an exciting end to a short, scenic six-mile run.

The next six miles to Brewster bridge contain more shoals, small drops, and enjoyable scenery. Large indentations under the riverside bluffs (called "rockhouses") contain remnants of Indian encampments and provide shelter to this day for knowledgeable trippers who know how to seek water and comfort under these primitive conditions. And from Brewster bridge to Burnt Mill bridge, conditions keep improving.

Just before you pass the mouth of White Oak Creek, you will pass through a couple of still-water, rock-bottomed pools, known locally as the Gentlemen's Swimming Hole. This is where the English residents of Rugby frolicked (and probably bathed) during that interesting late-1800s European community experiment. It's worth your time to visit the restored Rugby while in the area. Beyond Rugby, at "The Meeting of the Waters," White Oak Creek adds considerably to the flow, and the stream becomes bigger and slightly more placid. Should you stop at the rock shelf on river right on the upstream side at the mouth of White Oak Creek to have a lunch break, you will be continuing a 120-year-old picnic tradition at that spot. The founders of Rugby favored that particular getaway, and their 1.5-mile trail from town can easily be found nearby. Twenty-two miles downstream from Gatewood is the quiet pool (and old gauging station) at Burnt Mill bridge, an old, one-lane steel truss. This is the final take-out for the enjoyable and scenic Clear Fork float. No novices or campers should plan to float below this bridge. Clear Fork changes considerably below Burnt Mill. It uses its final three and a half miles to whip the whitewater wanderer into shape for tackling the Big South Fork Gorge of the Cumberland River just below the confluence with the New River. It is serious, technical whitewater below Burnt Mill bridge and should only be attempted by experienced teams of experts who know what they are doing, have all the proper equipment, and know and understand exactly what the present river flow reading will mean to their trip. External rescue is next to impossible below Burnt Mill bridge. Any party in there should be able to handle any condition or emergency as a self-contained unit. Knowledge, equipment, skill, and endurance are all necessary by those who will float below this bridge. No reason for alarm, but Clear Fork paddlers should definitely realize that Burnt Mill bridge marks a boundary for casual floating experiences.

## New River

Not of the size, scope, or reputation of its namesake river in West Virginia, the New River in Tennessee, however, does have some of the same features. It is a primary drainage for a large coal-mining region; thus, the water quality of the New still carries a legacy from past coal-mining abuse. And strip-mining activities still occur in the watershed. Current regulations help keep things from getting worse, and there are even efforts to remediate some of the legacy. But the New still adds the negative component to the Big South Fork water quality equation when it joins up with Clear Fork.

The New drains most of Scott County in northern Tennessee as it flows west to join the Clear Fork River, which forms the Big South Fork of the Cumberland River. Runnable below the US 27 bridge from mid-November to late May, the New River winds placidly through a deep, wooded valley, working its way around rocks or over small ledges and shoals for the first 5.5 miles. Then, as the New begins to drop down to its confluence with the Clear Fork, the gradient picks up, and several Class II and III ledges are encountered in quick succession. The kicker for this run is that it is part of a package deal; when you run the New River, you get the Class III and IV Big South Fork Gorge thrown in at no extra charge. When you reach the mouth of the New, there is no place to go except on down the gorge. This turns the reasonably friendly little eight-mile zip down the New into a rowdy, sixteen-mile expedition on one of the toughest stretches of whitewater in Tennessee.

If your interest is primarily in the Big South Fork Gorge, an alternative way of getting there is down the Clear Fork River from the Burnt Mill bridge put-in. Many veterans of both routes prefer the Clear Fork since they wish to avoid the silt and the acid-mine drainage that pollute the New.

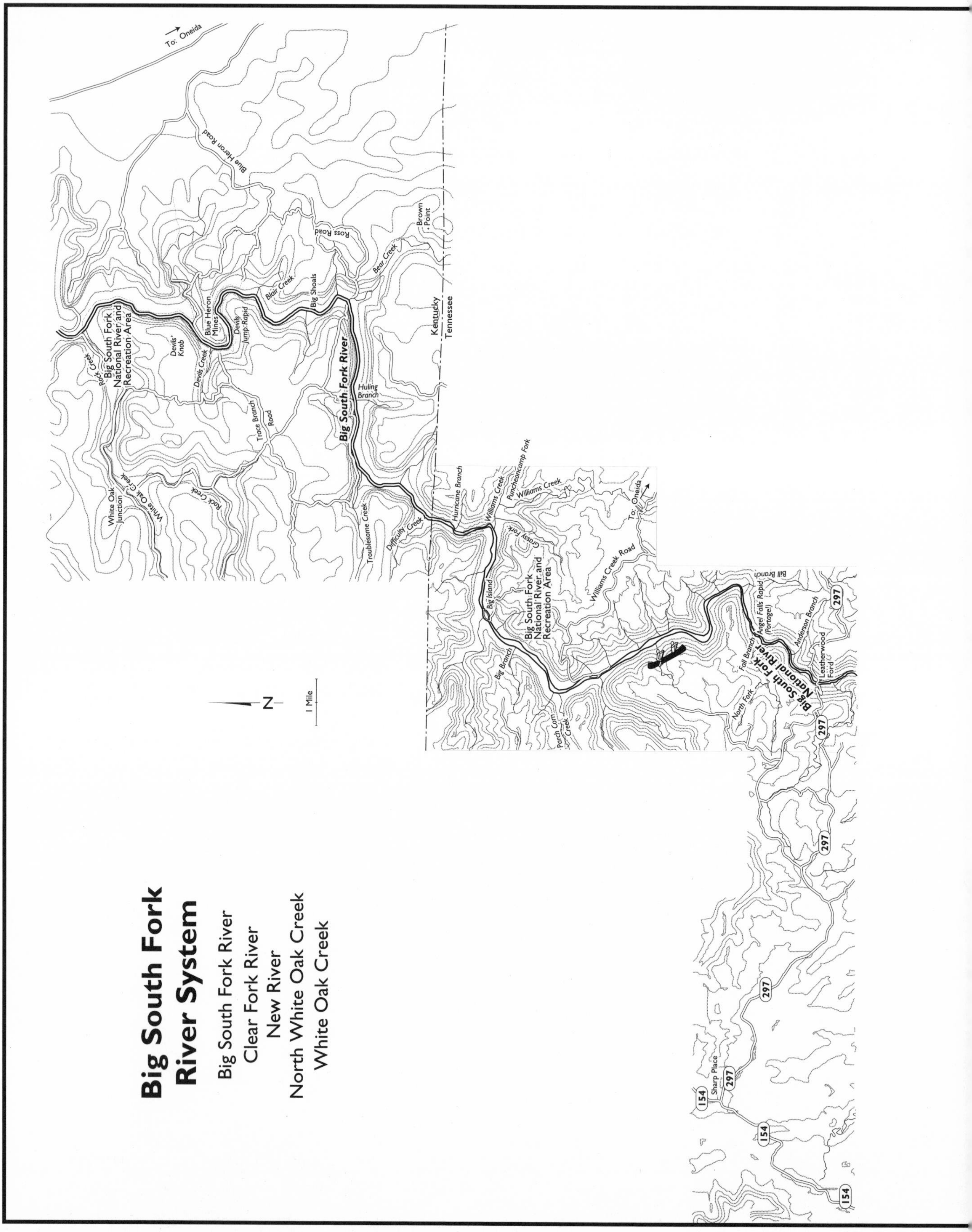

Big South Fork
River System
Big South Fork River
Clear Fork River
New River
North White Oak Creek
White Oak Creek
To: Oneida
Blue Heron Road
Ross Road
Brown Point
Bear Creek
Blair Creek
Big Shoals
Kentucky
Tennessee
Big South Fork National River and Recreation Area
Blue Heron Mines
Devils Jump Rapid
Devils' Knob
Devils Creek
Rock Creek
Big South Fork River
Huling Branch
Trace Branch Road
White Oak Junction
White Oak Creek
Troublesome Creek
Difficulty Creek
Hurricane Branch
Williams Creek
Puncheoncamp Fork
Grassy Fork
Williams Creek Road
Big Island
Big Branch
Porch Corn Creek
North Fork
Fall Branch
Angel Falls Rapid (Portage!)
Bill Branch
Anderson Branch
Leatherwood Ford
Big South Fork National River
Sharp Place
297
154
N
1 Mile

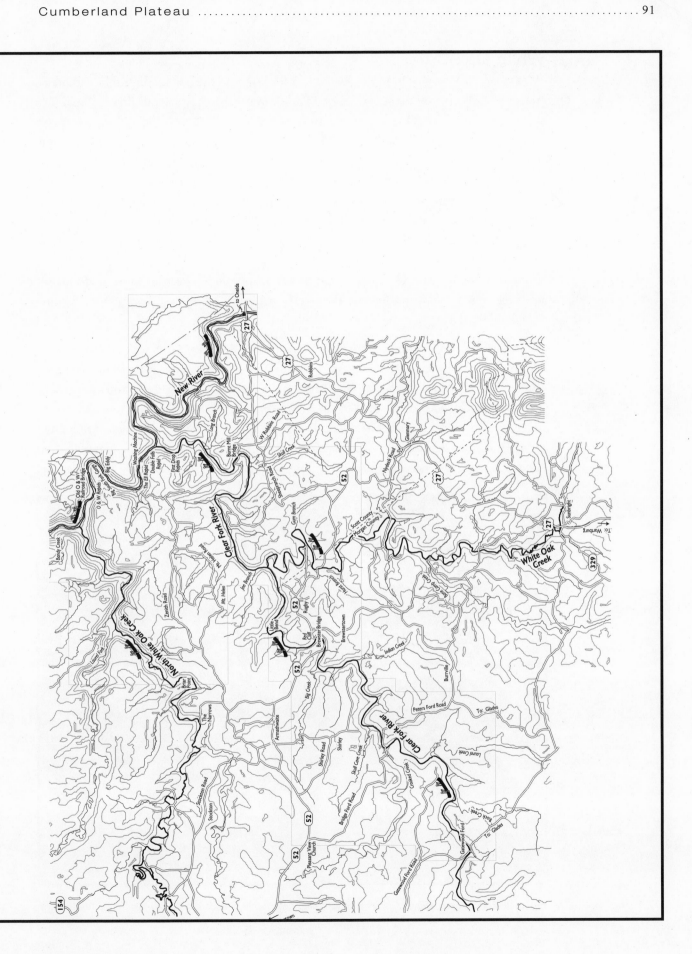

## White Oak Creek

White Oak Creek begins in Morgan County a few miles to the east of Sunbright and drains from the flanks of the Tennessee Valley Divide toward the Cumberland River system. The stream becomes canoeable at the twin culverts under Burrville Road bridge. Expect a scratchy, narrow, brushy float until the waters of Bone Camp Creek double the flow about halfway toward Nydeck bridge. This part of White Oak Creek drains pastoral farmlands and rolling bottomlands, with the rising boundary hills visible in the background. Shallow shoals add burble to the stream waters. It's best to keep your canoe burbling along, too. Slow up and the deer flies will home in on your position and call in their buddies.

Above Nydeck bridge, some interesting streamside stonework warns that you are approaching an old breached dam. No particular pool backs up, but it's best to scout before trying to run—it could be lethal at high flows. Below there you tour more bottomlands for a few miles but you will note the stream seems to be cutting deeper into the surrounding plateau.

Past the new, curving concrete bridge on TN 52, the stream gets serious. You are now skirting the historic English settlement of Rugby (now a restoration district) and you have entered the Big South Fork National River and Recreation Area. Bluffs and rockhouses increase, the woods become thicker, the water drops faster, and the deer flies are left far behind. The first two miles below the 52 bridge are relatively flat as you paddle around historic "Horseshoe Bend" and past the abandoned SunnySide, an original Rugby home. Then the drops and ledges become technical and the high bluffs begin to dominate at streamside.

Big South Fork in early spring. Get all your paddling gear ready because the water is waiting. Photograph by Julie Keller.

Midway down this run a bank-to-bank angled hydraulic appears that ought to be scouted before committing to the rapid. This awesome wave has not proven to be a keeper. But it is also not a straightforward shot. Take this drop with care (left side advised) and you should be able to enjoy the rest of the historic sheer bluff scenery as you continue along the backside of the Rugby historic district. You are heading for "The Meeting of the Waters"—the confluence of White Oak Creek with the Clear Fork River. The English settlers of years past built a trail from Rugby to this confluence just to view the scene and meditate upon its meaning. The meaning for you is that you can play in some nice Class II water on the last half mile of White Oak Creek then float out on five and a half miles of the bigger Clear Fork River to an access point at the Burnt Mill bridge.

## North White Oak Creek

Contrary to the similarity in names and location (in Scott and Fentress Counties), this little stream bears no direct relationship to its bigger neighbor in the same watershed, White Oak Creek. North White Oak is a sparkling, intimate tributary to the mainstem of the Big South Fork of the Cumberland River, joining that bigger river in the heart of the Big South Fork National River and Recreation Area about a mile above Leatherwood Ford.

This creek is a springtime-only float; the rest of the time it is hikeable. Only one section is floatable, and before National Park Service attention the access to the put-in was extremely tenuous and difficult. The float is from Zenith Mines to Leatherwood Ford (on the Big South Fork). Zenith is in a deep, round canyon formed by the creek and Camp Branch. Zenith Mines is the site of an old creekside deep mine, the attendant coal-mining camp, and a railroad coal-loading tipple. In the early twentieth century, the miners went on strike and had a shoot-out with the sheriff's men, who were on the cliffs above them. Reports vary, but it seems that the miners learned that it is easier to shoot fish in a barrel than vice versa. Zenith was finally abandoned when the access road got too bad to bring the mule supply train over. It deteriorated even more as the early canoeists ran their shuttles. Canoeists would often portage their canoes down this two-mile "road" for their first run on North White Oak. (After seeing the abandoned junk cars at streamside, the less ecological paddlers considered banding together to purchase one-way clunkers to haul their craft to the creek.) But they still felt that when the water was up, North White Oak Creek was worth the considerable effort. It is still well worth it, but the effort to get there is now less, thanks to the efforts by the Big South Fork Park Service.

North White Oak Creek seems to float in the heart of the sandstone canyonlands. It features a close, narrow creek in a four-hundred-foot gorge; Class II paddling; an occasional undercut rock to dodge; and mountain laurel and rhododendron reaching out for the banks. In short, North White Oak Creek provides a beautiful river experience. Be sure to look back upstream now and again to get full impact of the impressive rock and tree scenery. A hike along the old O&W railbed is just as rewarding as the North White Oak float, so bring the nonpaddlers in the family, too.

This area is also interesting for history buffs. The old Zenith mines can be found just upstream from the put-in. And you can follow traces of that narrow-gauge railroad bed on the left bank all along the creekway. Two miles downstream, if you beat the bushes, you will find the long-forgotten lumbering and mining village of Gernt. Gernt was a German settlement noted for its cheese. It's hard to imagine life at the foot of the bluff along that narrow creekside.

If there is enough water to float on North White Oak Creek, you will be amazed at the "big water" that'll propel you the last mile to Leatherwood after you reach the Big South Fork. Hang on!

## Big South Fork Gorge

The waters flowing through the Big South Fork gorge are the combined waters from two major rivers. The gorge is considered the headwaters of the Big South Fork of the Cumberland River, but don't think that the use of "headwaters" here means "creek boating." This is a major river run consisting of almost continuous Class III (and IV?) whitewater. The water can be big, and the enforced mid-rapid bailing to avoid swamping out can be furious. Extra flotation, helmets, and all the other precautions for big water whitewater are needed by open boat paddlers. The same is true for decked boaters. Do not run a kayak through the BSF gorge without air bags or any that leak.

The run begins on the Clear Fork (which will soon combine with New River to form the Big South Fork), about twelve miles southwest of Oneida and ends at Leatherwood Ford, west of Oneida. In all there are thirteen major rapids and several dozen smaller ones. Considered by many to be a decked-boat-only river, the Big South Fork gorge has frequently been run successfully by both solo and tandem open boaters. The nature of the run varies incredibly with water level. It is extremely technical at lower water and big and pushy (much like the New River gorge in West Virginia) when flowing high. At moderate levels the paddler gets a taste of both worlds with quick, technical water on the Clear Fork and bigger, less-technical water below the confluence of the Clear Fork and the New River. Scenery is magnificent, when you have time to notice it, with boulders lining the banks and canyon walls rising on both sides. For a Class III (IV) river, the Big South Fork gorge is surprisingly free of dangers; deadfalls and logjams are infrequent, and the holes are washouts at almost all levels. However, equipment damage is a very real possibility. The drops are huge (several exceeding four feet), and helmets are a must for all paddlers. Also, some of the rapids are extremely long, making rescue difficult (especially at higher water levels). Extra flotation is essential for open canoes and a good roll is definitely recommended for decked boaters. Access at the river is good at both put-in and take-out, but connecting roads are sometimes muddy and slippery. The Big South Fork gorge is runnable from late fall to mid-May in years of average rainfall. If you want to see the terrain of the Big South Fork gorge, hike out to the Honey Creek overlook. It is high on the bluff, overlooking the heart of that gorge run. You won't be able to scout rapids from there, but you will get an idea of why you want to complete the trip and not be forced to leave damaged equipment and walk out from there.

## Big South Fork of the Cumberland River
## (Leatherwood Ford to Lake Cumberland)

Leatherwood Ford bridge marks a strange changing of the guard. From upstream, the small-boated whitewater warriors come flushing in wearing the latest in rescue-aiding PFDs, helmets, drysuits, spray skirts, carabiniers, and more. They dock beside the downstream-bound campers stowing plastic camping buckets with tents, stoves, freeze-dried foods, and more into their more spacious boats.

Big South Fork Gorge. The Big South Fork Gorge features big boulders and heavy water. Here, these wet paddlers properly brace their way while threading a good route down the turbulent flow.

After leaving this mid-Park bridge, the Big South Fork of the Cumberland River continues north, flowing out of Scott County (Tennessee), and into McCreary County (Kentucky) before emptying into Lake Cumberland. One of the most popular canoe-camping runs in the southeastern United States, the Big South Fork continues to wind through the heart of National River and Recreational Area. An exceptionally beautiful river that flows swiftly below stately exposed rock pinnacles, the Big South Fork is dotted with huge boulders both midstream and along the banks, and it is padded along either side by steep hillsides of hardwoods and evergreens. Wildflowers brighten the vista in the spring, and wildlife is plentiful.

Paddling is interesting with as many as five legitimate (and six borderline) Class II rapids (some of which are quite long), consisting primarily of nontechnical small ledges and standing waves. The main channel is easily discerned in these rapids, and scouting is normally not required. At moderate to low water, all the Class II's can be run with a loaded boat. At higher water, loaded, open boats can avail themselves of sneak routes to avoid swamping.

Two Class III to IV rapids are encountered on this section of the Big South Fork. Both are technical, complex, high-velocity chutes that are dangerous at certain water levels. The first is Angel Falls, 1.5 miles into the run, where the river takes an eight-foot drop in closely spaced one- and two-foot increments, with the main flow being forced between two large rocks toward the right of the river. After the first two ledges (normally run from the left), converging smaller chutes of water join the main flow from the right, further aerating the water and causing the current to impact a large boulder to the left. A smaller boulder at the bottom of the rapid, in conjunction with the converging currents from the right, causes the

# Devils Jump Dam, Howard Baker, and the Big South Fork

The towering bluffs and deep coves could be just another shoreline for a huge lake created to produce hydropower and control flood waters. This was the plan the U.S. Army Corps of Engineers had been investigating over a thirty-year period. During the 1960s, the Senate passed several authorization bills. But each time the House of Representatives refused to go along. Public concern for the environment in general and the fate of the Big South Fork specifically, which was building during the 1960s, was imbued in two organizations: the Big South Fork Coalition and the Tennessee Citizens for Wilderness Planning.

Their fight to save this remote and beautifully scenic area from becoming another Lake Cumberland bore fruit when John Sherman Cooper of Kentucky and Howard Baker Jr. of Tennessee sponsored authorization in 1974 to create the 113,000-acre Big South Fork National River and Recreational Area. The legislation was unique and quite specific. Two distinct areas were created: the gorge area and the plateau or upland area. The gorge includes the river from bluff rim to bluff rim. This sensitive environment is more restrictively protected to preserve its plants and animals and to promote a wilderness recreational experience. Motorized vehicles are not allowed in the gorge, except at designated river access points. The law directed the U.S. Army Corps of Engineers to acquire the land and plan the development, then transfer it to the National Park Service (NPS), which would be responsible for operation and maintenance.

Development of the National Area spanned fourteen years. About $108,000,000 was used to acquire the land and mineral rights, build two major recreation sites (Bandy Creek and Blue Heron), establish seven river access points, build

Leatherwood Ford bridge and road, and create 170 miles of hiking and 102 miles of horse or bike trails. Now, facilities enhance opportunities for camping, hiking, picnicking, fishing, canoeing, horseback riding, sightseeing, swimming, boating, hunting, and other outdoor recreation pursuits.

[Editor's note: Susan Neff was a project manager within the Corps of Engineers and had a direct influence upon the corps's sensitivities to providing compatible enhancements to the outdoor environment at the Big South Fork—a type of planning the organization has not particularly been noted for.]

Although much was done, full acquisition and development as indicated in the law and embodied in the corps's master plan was not accomplished as funds were frozen during the Reagan administration. The corps officially turned the National Area over to NPS in 1990.

This wonderful resource, now protected and sympathetically developed, is preserved for our public enjoyment because private citizens took the initiative and constructively worked with elected officials. Planners and designers were careful that facilities would tread as lightly as possible on the land yet provide long-lasting structures for future generations to enjoy.

The National Area's purpose is best stated in the law that created it: "To Conserve and Interpret unique cultural, historic, geologic, fish and wildlife, archaeologic, scenic and recreational values ... and to preserve the Big South Fork of the Cumberland River and certain tributaries as natural free-flowing streams ... for the benefit and enjoyment of present and future generations."

—Susan Neff
Banner Springs, Tennessee

current to turn left at the end of the rapid before pooling out. This rapid must be scouted and different strategies for dealing with it are appropriate at different water levels (though, as a point of departure, Angel Falls is usually run far left to left center to right center). Regardless of water level, boats should be emptied of all gear before attempting the run. Portage is possible via a trail on the right, fifty yards upstream of the rapid, and is recommended at all water levels except for competent, experienced boaters. Canoes have been wedged for weeks at that 90-degree lefthand turn within the Angel Falls chute due to small miscalculations by even expert canoeists. Most expert canoeists choose to portage.

Devils Jump, a difficult Class IV rapid, is closer to the end of the run, upstream from the Blue Heron Mine. Here current flows into a house-sized boulder, from which it is diverted at an angle through a high-velocity chute. The trick is to align your boat for the chute by riding the pillow off the left of that boulder. This is done at low to moderate water levels by practically setting your bow on a collision course for the giant boulder and then allowing the pillow to divert your bow into the top of the chute. The route to the right of the giant boulder is usually avoided because of a mean hydraulic at the bottom. Once again, all boats should be run without gear and after careful scouting (if you do not understand the dynamics of converging currents, leave this rapid alone). Portage is possible and is recommended at all water levels except for competent, experienced boaters.

The Big South Fork is runnable from late fall through early June in this section. Because of the scouting and preparation required, it is not recommended that the Big South Fork from Leatherwood Ford downstream be attempted in one day. Several nice camping locations are available along the run (which can be lengthened to three or more days by continuing on down into Lake Cumberland). Between Leatherwood and Devils Jump, the river averages eighty to one hundred feet and settles down conspicuously with fewer rapids in evidence. Downstream from Yamacraw the current comes to a halt as it reaches the lake pool. Dangers to navigation are as described above; in addition, a damaged concrete ford between Blue Heron and Yamacraw must be portaged on the right, and the river has the potential to rise at an alarming rate after heavy rains (remember this when you set up camp). Because of the remoteness of the Big South Fork, access points are few and far between, with connecting roads often unpaved and rugged, but generally passable in a passenger car.

# Wolf River of Fentress and Pickett Counties

The Wolf River is born among the small streams dropping off the edge of the Cumberland Plateau north of Jamestown in Fentress County. It flows northwest, draining central Pickett County before being impounded in Dale Hollow Lake. Runnable in winter, spring, and during wet weather, the Wolf River at first runs through typical Cumberland Plateau terrain, as the stream meanders in a narrow farm valley surrounded by knobby and wooded, tall hills. From just north of Red Hill, the Wolf descends into a beautiful, exposed-rock gorge with vertical walls rising in alternating fashion on both sides of the river. The level of difficulty is Class I above Red Hill and a lively Class II with frequent, uncomplicated rapids downstream from just north of Red Hill to just above the backwaters of the lake. Hazards in the

# Wolf River

(Cumberland Plateau)
From US 127 at
Pall Mall to
Dale Hollow Reservoir

N

1/2 Mile

Kentucky
Tennessee

Falling Water Creek

Rocky Creek

Stoker Creek

Buck House Mountain

Jim Creek

Bud Creek

Little Jack Creek

Blue Ridge

Upchurch Road

Dale Creek

Flat Rock Ridge

Statehouse Ridge

Wolf River

Steve Pile Mountain

Little Dry Creek

Big Dry Creek

Sawmill Ridge

Pickett County
Fentress County

Baylor Knob

Tater Hill

Ratten Fork Wolf River

Pall Mall

Mill Dam

Reed Creek Road

Sergeant Alvin York Mill State Historic Area

Frogge Mountain

Reed Creek

127

Arion Mountain

Shellotte Branch

Forbus

127

Honey Spring Mountain

Travisville

Caney Creek Road

Riley Mountain

Riley Ford

Reed Creek Road

Buck Mountain

Davidson

Littoral Mountain

Golman Mountain

395

Red Hill

Buck Mountain Road

395

Chapman Branch

Adkins Ridge

Dry Creek Road

Kroger Mountain Road

Holbert Creek

Cedar Grove

Cedar Grove Road

Sulphur Springs

Wolf River

Dry Creek

Double Top Road

127

Chanute

Asbury

South Lick Creek Branch

Bagley Branch

Wright Branch

Mount Airy

Moodyville

Moody Road

Double Top Mountain

Step Gap Road

Pickett County
Fentress County

Sextic

127

42

Red Hill

Hildreth Knob

Parker

Poore Knob

Nicholas Road

395

Ford Road

Molly Larry Road

395

Robbins Fork Road

Lick Creek

Dry Cleaners Road

Etter

Widow Creek

335

Regan Knob

Huddleston Knob

Kentucky
Tennessee

Young Road

Okra

Green Brier

Mullins Road

Wolf River

Brimstone Creek

Main Street

Clark Mountain Road

Byrdstown

Town Branch

42

135

Smyrna

Love Lady

Jones Chapel Road

42

Dale Hollow Reservoir

Dale Hollow Reservoir

Boom

42

upper section consist of deadfalls and a dam below the US 127 bridge. Dangers downstream consist primarily of deadfalls and occasional logjams on bridge pilings. Access is good at most points.

# Obey River, East Fork

The East Fork of the Obey River is born high on the Cumberland Plateau in northern Cumberland County. Picking up momentum with a rapidly increasing gradient as it crosses through the tip of Putnam County, the East Fork descends into the veritable bowels of the plateau. Dropping as fast as 125 feet per mile in some stretches, the fork runs between timbered walls that rise at a sharp angle from the compressed river corridor. Remote as any spot in the eastern United States, the East Obey Gorge is completely without access for almost fifteen miles. Needless to say, the wooded folds of the gorge hide a fair torrent of serious whitewater.

Rated conservatively as Class III–V (VI), the East Obey is characterized by boulder jumbles, large drops, and a narrow channel where fifty cfs one way or the other makes a big difference in the run. Because of its nearly impenetrable inaccessibility, the East Obey Gorge is classified as an "experts only" run, i.e., when you tackle the gorge, the only way out is on the river—no mistakes allowed. If you have never met anyone who has run the East Obey Gorge, you are in the majority. Not only is the river difficult and dangerous, but it is also frustratingly hard to catch at a runnable level. In summary, it takes a lot of persistence to run the East Obey Gorge.

The middle section, below the TN 85 bridge, is somewhat more tame (Class II–III), but almost equally remote and difficult to catch with adequate flow. Most of the more challenging rapids are crammed into the first mile and a half of this fourteen-mile run; the remainder of the trip is Class II and Class I. Scenery here remains spectacular, with the stream running even deeper in the gorge. At the lower end of the run an unimproved farm road snakes its way upstream from TN 52, providing a possible early take-out.

The lower section is a short Class I run as the East Fork finally passes out of Fentress County and into Pickett County, where it joins the Wolf and the West Fork of the Obey in forming Dale Hollow Lake. A pleasant float trip with imposing Cumberland Plateau vistas surrounding the river, the lower East Fork runs through steep mudbanks and attains a width of 60 feet before it flows into the lake. Access in this section is fair to good.

Because of the narrow, constricted nature of the East Fork all along its course, deadfalls, brush jams, and logjams rank even ahead of its formidable rapids as navigational dangers. As intimated above, the East Fork is runnable (particularly in upper section) only following wet weather.

# Obey River, West Fork

The West Fork of the Obey River flows north, cutting an intimate, forested gorge in the Cumberland Plateau. Confined exclusively to Overton County, except where it drops into Dale Hollow Lake in Pickett County, the West Fork is a wet-weather stream. Runnable

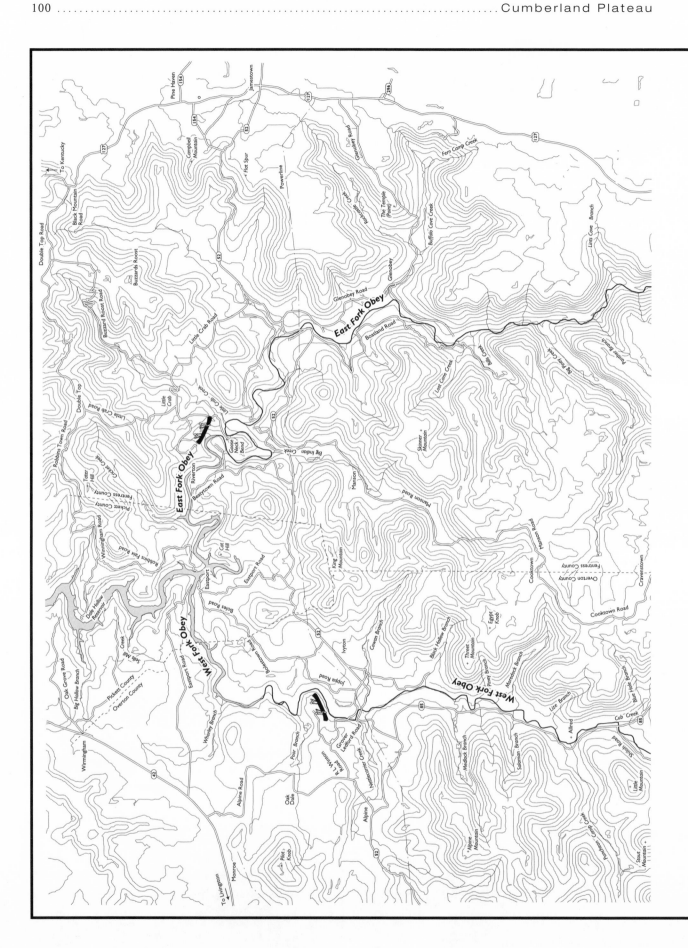

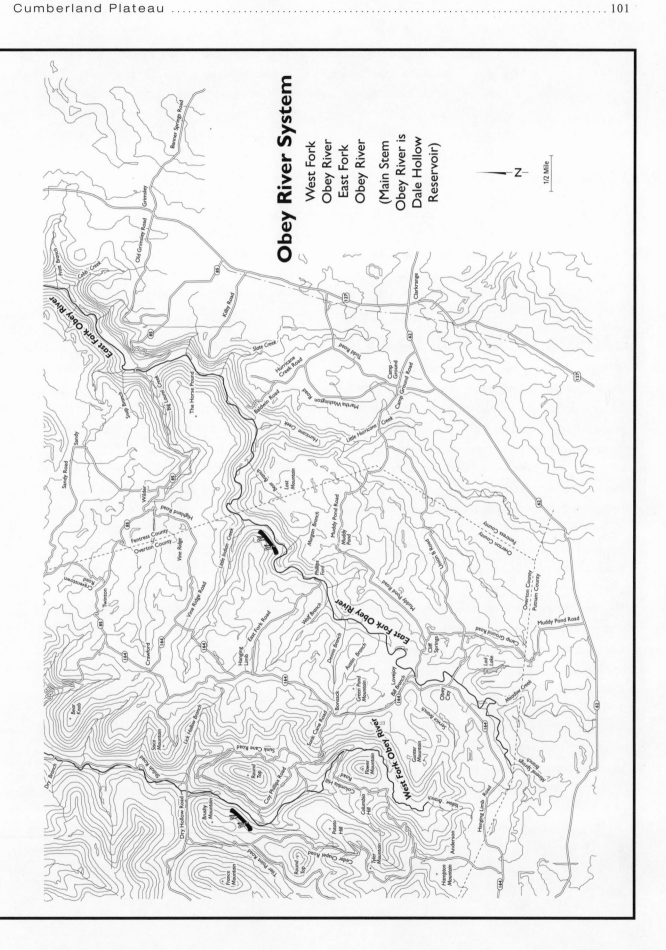

## Obey River System

West Fork
Obey River

East Fork
Obey River

(Main Stem
Obey River is
Dale Hollow
Reservoir)

N

1/2 Mile

downstream from the TN 85 bridge, the West Fork winds below massive, timbered mountains that extend right to the banks of the river. Its level of difficulty is Class II, except where the stream loops away from the paralleling highway a mile and a half below the access at Allred. Here the West Fork enters a short but beautiful canyon with tall, vertical rock walls and borderline Class III rapids and ledges. Emerging from the canyon, Class II rapids occur frequently as the stream nears the TN 52 bridge crossing. Below the TN 52 bridge to the lake, rapids are encountered less often. Scenery remains spectacular, however, with exposed rock and rugged plateau mountains continuing even as the West Fork joins the lake pool. An excellent choice when most other rivers in the Cumberland Plateau are too high to run, the West Obey is lively and exciting with comparatively little in the way of hazards. As on the East Fork, the width of the stream rarely exceeds forty feet; thus, deadfalls and logjams constitute the greatest danger to paddlers. Access is fair to good, especially in the upper section where TN 85 accompanies the river.

# It Takes a "Local" to Save a National River

Dam-building fever was running high in Morgan County in the late 1960s. A handful of local politicians and would-be land speculators were yelling, "We need a dam on the Obed River." They went to the Tennessee Valley Authority with a request that the river be restudied (for about the third time) to try to justify a dam. TVA responded by organizing a local watershed development association (those same politicians and speculators) and launching a series of studies. The watershed development politicos went into high gear in protecting their turf. All opposition was shouted down. The local newspaper published any and everything which extolled the virtues of the dam but wouldn't publish even a letter in opposition. In 1968 The Tennessee Scenic Rivers bill was introduced into the Tennessee State Legislature and included the Obed as one of the rivers to be included. Extreme political pressure from the local state representative resulted in dropping the Obed from the state bill before final passage. The propaganda machine was working full force and the parade was rolling.

But suddenly rain! Rain fell on their parade. But not enough rain to fill their proposed reservoir! TVA's studies could not support a cost/benefit ratio that would justify the dam. One big problem was that the yearly flow of the stream wouldn't fill a gorge-high reservoir. (Think about that for a moment!) TVA backed away from the proposal. When the National Wild and Scenic Rivers Act was passed in late 1968, it included the Obed as a study river for possible later addition to that system. This got the attention of the old watershed development group and they moved immediately to oppose national status for the Obed. The battle lines were drawn again.

But during that time, things were changing in Morgan County. A new radio station was established in Wartburg, and it broke the blackout on news. The editorship of the newspaper changed, and some county officials were replaced. The old watershed group was losing considerable public support. I managed to produce a weekly talk show on outdoors recreation for the local radio station. A considerable amount of time on that show was devoted to promoting national status for the Obed. Bob Lantz (author of this guidebook) had moved to Morgan County, and he and I organized the Obed River Council. With the help of a few loyal members we published an Obed River information brochure and distributed it to every mailing address in the county. We wrote countless letters, countered negative

# The Obed–Emory River System

What do you get when you combine high natural rainfall, sheltered canyons, generally inaccessible terrain, protected wildlife habitat, and free-flowing waters? You get a wild and scenic place. It's possible that if you find enough such contiguous acreage you'd have a nationally significant wild and scenic place. And the Obed–Emory River system in Tennessee has all those attributes and is, indeed, a wild and scenic place. In fact, it is Tennessee's only National Wild and Scenic River—but it is a river that does the national system proud!

With the type of cascading clean, clear water almost nonexistent in the populated eastern United States, this deeply cut, free-flowing river system is a statewide favorite for whitewater canoeing—in season. Through a quirk of political boundaries, only half of the Obed–Emory system is nationally designated, but of that half, a full forty-two of the forty-four protected miles qualify as "wild," the highest wilderness classification. And wilderness canoeing it is!

newspaper ads with letters to the editor (sometimes in the same edition, thanks to warnings from friendly editors), ran our own ads in the paper, bought ads on the radio, and provided speakers at public hearings.

By the time the Bureau of Outdoor Recreation completed its national river studies and issued its report in 1973, public support had shifted dramatically, although the old watershed association was putting up a brave front, so the battle continued. Before the election of 1974, conservation interests had convinced Marilyn Lloyd, the eventual winner of the local congressional seat, on the merits of the Obed River. The BOR studies had recommended ninety-eight miles of the Obed, Daddys Creek, Clear Creek, and Emory River for inclusion in the National System, about equally divided between Morgan and Cumberland Counties. Introduction of a bill by Mrs. Lloyd in 1975 to include the entire ninety-eight miles in the system caused an explosion in Cumberland County, a rural area in a different congressional district. Land speculators, developers, mining interests, and second homeowners on the streams in that county had not been convinced of the merits of national status. Mrs. Lloyd's bill failed to clear the congressional committee. In the meantime Bob and I enlisted the help of a personable local retiree to go about our county, talking to people and obtaining signatures on petitions of support. In a few months he brought in a large folder full of pages of signatures. Copies of this tremendous show of support for the project in Morgan County were presented to Mrs. Lloyd and to Sen. Bill Brock, who agreed to sponsor a revised bill in the state senate. Mrs. Lloyd agreed to revise her bill and reintroduce it later. In the meantime, Morgan County had elected a county executive who even went to Washington to offer testimony of support. The bill establishing the Obed Wild and Scenic River was finally passed in 1976 and included only the Morgan County part of the proposal plus a few river miles in Cumberland County, which is wholly within the state-owned Catoosa Wildlife Management Area. Implementation on the Obed has been extremely slow and it is still faced with many threats from developments upstream in Cumberland County, so the battle to save the Obed goes on and on and on.

—Don Todd
Wartburg, Tennessee

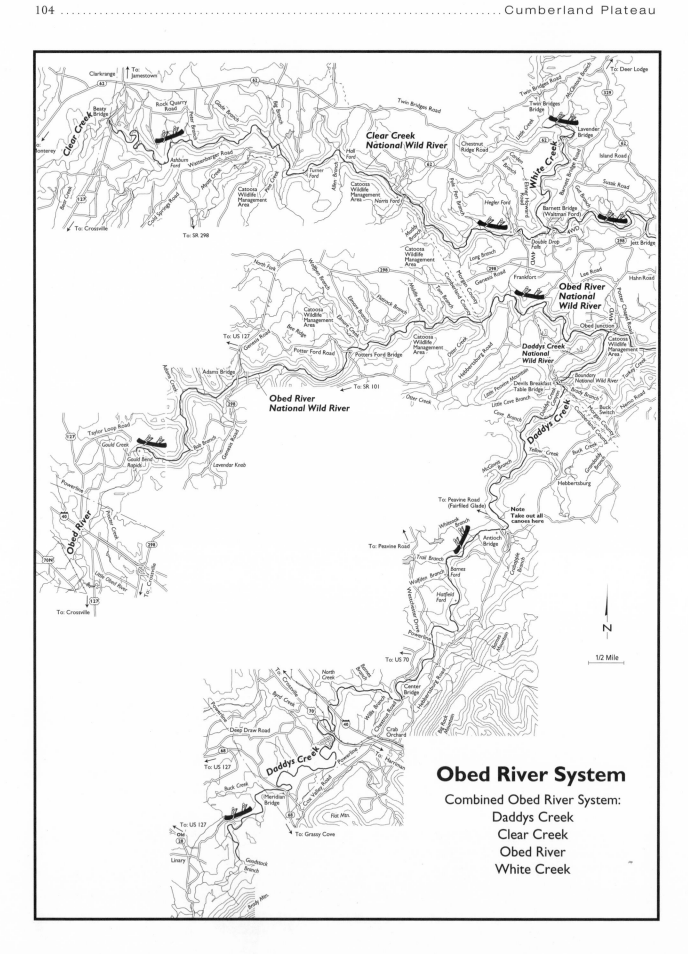

# Obed River System

Combined Obed River System:
Daddys Creek
Clear Creek
Obed River
White Creek

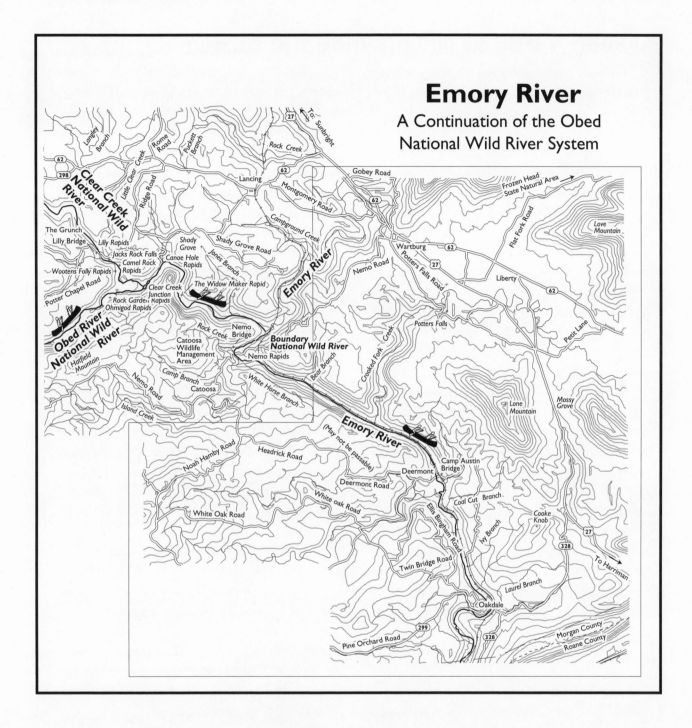

Emory River
A Continuation of the Obed
National Wild River System

Actually, the nationally protected waters of the downstream Obed–Emory river system gather together from three upstream sources: Daddys Creek, the Obed River, and Clear Creek. Although these tributaries mix and match the river and creek designations, all are about equal in size as they come together within a couple of river miles to add equal proportions to the mainstem Obed flow. And then about five miles downstream, another tributary, Emory River, drops in with a flow no greater than any of those upstream tributaries, but steals away with the name. The Obed has met its "Mile 0," and the Emory continues with the National Wild and Scenic River flow.

# Building a Bridge while Silting the Stream

Lavender bridge today is a long concrete span running from ridge to ridge high over White Creek on Tennessee State Route 62 in Morgan County. A long, grassy slope down to the stream from a deadend parking area on an abandoned segment of old SR 62 provides a convenient put-in for canoe runs down to Clear Creek and, eventually, to the Obed Wild and Scenic River. Before 1985, however, Lavender bridge was a low, short span on a narrow, two-lane road that wound down one side of a ravine and back up the other. The new bridge is less scenic for sightseers on the Cumberland Plateau, but local citizens who depend on SR 62 travel under all weather conditions appreciate both the improved safety and the time it saves.

Construction of the new bridge on two tall concrete piers and a long, high, earthen approach ramp did not require any innovative engineering by the Tennessee Department of Transportation (TDOT) or its contractor. The length and height of the earthen ramp which had to be built did create the potential for major erosion problems, however, if the introduced soil was not stabilized throughout the construction process. Unfortunately, it was not. Significant amounts of soil were washed into White Creek, blanketing the streambed with silt at the construction site and for a considerable distance downstream.

Biologists with the Tennessee Department of Health and Environment (TDHE) documented the destruction of aquatic life in the affected reaches of White Creek, but were unable through agency channels to bring about timely corrective and punitive actions. Photographic evidence of the obvious problem gathered and reported by citizen environmentalists also failed to gain TDOT or TDHE official acknowledgement of the problem or formal action by TDHE against TDOT.

The Tennessee Scenic Rivers Association (TSRA) and two of its individual members

(a well-qualified engineer and a member of the state legislature), along with Tennessee Citizens for Wilderness Planning, filed formal complaints under provisions of Tennessee's Water Pollution Control Act, alleging that TDOT and its contractor had polluted the waters of White Creek. When the TDHE commissioner dismissed those complaints as groundless, the two environmental organizations and the two citizen complainants indicated that they would appeal his ruling to the Water Quality Control Board, which has the authority to overrule his decision.

Early in the complaint process, TSRA had initiated its own program of biological stream monitoring to assess White Creek stream water quality at the bridge construction site, as well as upstream and downstream. In preparation for the formal appeal process, they retained the services of a consulting engineer who could testify concerning the inadequacy of TDOT erosion-control measures on the project. And they recruited pro bono attorneys from the TSRA membership to guide and support TSRA officers in formal hearings to come.

For TSRA, two major issues were to be pursued in their conflict with TDOT and TDHE. The first dealt with disputed facts. TSRA charged that TDOT and its contractor had polluted the waters of White Creek when they failed to control soil erosion in replacing the old Lavender bridge. TDOT and its contractor argued that there was no evidence that the waters of White Creek had, in fact, been polluted.

The second issue focused on differing interpretations of Tennessee's Water Pollution Control Act. Senior officials in TDOT and TDHE argued that (a) provisions of the Water Quality Control Act do not apply to state agencies and (b) one agency of the state cannot take actions against or regulate the activities of another agency of the same government. TSRA and the other environmentalists interpreted the law differently, holding that the Water Quality Control Act does regulate state agencies, as well as other agencies and individuals, and that TDHE is obligated to take actions against other state agencies if they contribute to the pollution of waters of the state.

The anticipated public hearing before the Water Quality Control Board never took place. The battle occurred, instead, in the "discovery" process, in which complainants and defendants sought to determine what evidence the other side intended to present in the public hearing. Attorneys for TDOT and the bridge contractor issued subpoenas for all complainants, including the state biologists who had originally documented the pollution problem and their supervisors. TSRA's pro bono attorneys, in turn, subpoenaed not only the state biologists and their supervisors but all TDHE officials up the chain of command to the position where it was believed the decision had been made that TDHE would not attempt to enforce water quality standards against TDOT.

Settlement came in the form of an agreement that TSRA and other complainants would not pursue the issue of guilt in this particular case if TDHE and TDOT would acknowledge that our interpretation of the Water Quality Control Act was correct and that "The TDOT and (xxx) Construction Company, Inc. are 'persons' as defined by T.C.A. Section 69-3-103(1S) and

subject to the Water Quality Control Act." They agreed also that "the TDOT and its contractors are required to comply with all requirements of (the Water Quality Control Act) for its road and bridge construction activities, including the acquisition of a valid permit from the Commissioner of TDHE for each project which will cause or is likely to cause pollution." They agreed further that in the future "the TDOT shall apply for and obtain a valid water quality permit from TDHE for proposed construction projects appurtenant to Tennessee waters, prior to the advertisement for competitive bids for each project."

This all took a few years to accomplish. A lot of water had passed below the new bridge. Erosion had stopped at the Lavender bridge site by the time TDHE and TDOT proposed their settlement. The silt in White Creek was spread over many river miles downstream and could not feasibly be recovered. Any fine imposed on the polluters likely would have been small. But the potential benefits to the environment from a change in the ways TDHE and TDOT would go about bridge and riparian highway construction was huge. TSRA and other complainants felt that the settlement represented a major victory for the environment.

—Ray Norris
Nashville, TN

The Obed–Emory, in Cumberland and Morgan Counties, is a major drainage of the northern half of Tennessee's Cumberland Plateau, a highly wear-resistant sandstone remnant of prehistoric marine geology. Over the eons, the streams in the area have only cut narrow defiles in the hard sandstone caprock. These waterways are now noted for their steep-sided "gorge" topography. As the streams carved their narrow ways, large, bus-sized boulders tumbled off the undercut gorge walls, many landing in the water's flow. And the natural pool-drop and descending-elevation whitewater became even more interesting as blind passages, undercut rocks, and tricky crosscurrents were added.

The Obed–Emory is technical whitewater—not of the pushy variety, where enough cresting waves will finally swamp your canoe, but rather of the water-reading-required variety, where a lack of skillful multidirectional maneuvering will leave your canoe plastered all over the front of some stream-splitting sandstone. But do not despair. On your (long) hike out, while climbing through some hard-found break in the nearly continuous gorge-wall rimrock, if you pause and look back at the view, you'll note the incredible beauty of this undisturbed natural wilderness. You'll see a verdant forest with excellent second-growth and possibly some virgin forest. Huge hemlocks and white pines vie with the ever-present streamside rhododendron and mountain laurel to command your attention.

The same riverway boulders that alter the canoeist's downstream run also support lush lichen, mosses, and ferns. And with such abundant and fertile flora comes a similar abundance of fauna. In fact, a large part of the Obed–Emory system lies within a large state game preserve, the Catoosa Wildlife Management Area. Deer, turkeys, hawks, bobcats, rattlesnakes, and copperheads all noticeably inhabit the area. Undoubtedly you'll see one of the above on your sojourn in the area. Just remember: this river system is free flowing! A rainfall pushes the flow rates up within hours, but within days of a sudden storm, the water has passed completely on by. So learn to check the water's flow at put-in. And take note of incipient weather. Don't expect much canoeing opportunity in the long, dry months late in the season, but if you hit it right, you've got it all going for you: exciting whitewater, beautiful scenery, and a taste of the primeval wilderness.

## White Creek

When the rivers are running high enough to scare the experts off lower Clear Creek, you can have a great run on the upstream tributary, White Creek. A put-in at Twin Bridges in western Morgan County allows an interesting three-mile warm-up toward Lavender bridge, the big concrete structure at TN 62. Between Twin Bridges and Lavender, the scenery is pastoral with a hint of bluff, while the omnipresent rhododendron screens most of the bankside views.

White Creek has swift water and straightforward rapids, but remember that high water levels are needed to float this high on the watershed. Blowdown strainers are possible anywhere on White Creek due to the narrow, intimate nature of the streamway. Below Lavender, the rapids become more technical and the necessary skill level increases. But the visual interest increases, too, as you drop the twenty feet per mile into Clear Creek canyonlands. You'll be amazed at the water flushing by on Clear Creek as the confluence comes to view. You'll also experience a twinge of regret as you paddle out of the close and intimate little sidestream that you've experienced for the past seven miles. Drop below White Creek's delta island at the confluence and ferry over to the righthand shore of Clear Creek. Above you is the new one-lane Barnett bridge (also known as the Waltman Ford bridge). Look around in the pool below that bridge and you can still see the rusty steel spans that washed out in 1973. Look up again at the level of the bridge and imagine the water level above that. A lot of water rushed through these streams on that day in May of 1973. You might keep that in mind if it is raining.

## Clear Creek (US 127 to Obed River)

Its name is its description. Clear Creek is a small, intimate, clean-water stream. But its name hides the fact that Clear Creek provides one-third of the nationally significant waters of the Obed National Wild and Scenic River System. Paddlers who visit the system soon find out that actually Clear Creek is the most favored whitewater in the entire Obed system. It forms the boundary between Cumberland and Fentress Counties before entering Morgan County and finding its confluence with the Obed River. The creek starts narrow and intimate for floaters who put in at the US 127 bridge. Blowdown obstructions and other pastoral hazards are common on this little-run part of this high-on-the-watershed float.

Sharp-eyed canoeists will note that the farther they float, the deeper the stream cuts into the terrain. Creekside banks become bluffs. The meandering stream gains a stronger, swifter character, and outside intrusions on the streamway cease. It's twenty miles to the next bridge, with numerous Class II drops along the way. And twenty miles is too far for a single-day whitewater trip, so the canoeist is challenged while directing a camping-gear-laden canoe through the shoals and rapids.

Two Class III rapids are found in this upper section, but they are easy to portage. By the time you reach the earlier site of Burkhardt's concrete cabin (downstream left at river mile 15), you'll be within the boundaries of the national system. Along the big pool at the cabin site, an old logging road can be found within the left bank floodplain. This road connects (just downstream) to the ancient Norris Ford Road, which is now a four-wheel-drive-plus, washed-out creekway that offers the first (emergency) vehicular access since the US 127 bridge at mile 29.

Down at about mile 9 you come to a major access, Barnett bridge (also called Waltman Ford bridge). But before you get there you have to get past Double Drop Falls. It is common to portage this Class III rapid when loaded with camping gear. At the Barnett Bridge access area, White Creek enters the stream from river left and almost doubles the flow. Shed your camping gear and enjoy the brisk five-mile run to Jett bridge. This particular segment of Clear

Bluff on Clear Creek. A river runs under it. Upper Clear Creek passes completely under this overhanging bluff. Photograph by Walt Mayer.

Examining Clear Creek. The first NPS superintendent in charge of the newly designated Obed National Wild River takes his first on-site view of upper Clear Creek (with this guidebook's author and a renowned river photographer). Photograph by Jim Robertson.

Creek has the longest paddling season; it can still be run when the rest is too low. It's also the best introduction to the Obed–Emory system in the entire watershed. It's got beautiful scenery, solid Class II rapids, and reasonable access to the bridges.

If you've piloted your craft without mishap to Jett, then you're ready for the short, snappy, and renowned Jett-to-Lilly run. Probably more canoes float this short, two-and-a-

Clear Creek below Jett. Leaving Jett Bridge on Clear Creek, a group of paddlers space themselves out to run the narrow chutes and rapids single file.

half-mile run than any other section in the system. It will make for a delightful hour in your life. The clean, clear waters of Clear Creek (the best water quality in the entire river system) playfully jump, funnel, and splash while your canoe bounces, rocks, and rolls on down the twenty-foot-per-mile gradient. An obvious discontinuity in the river gives notice that you're approaching The Grunch, named after the sound the aft end of your

Lilly Rapids above Lilly Bridge on Clear Creek. This marks the exciting end to the most enjoyable two miles of floating (Jett bridge to Lilly bridge) in the entire Obed National Wild River system.

canoe makes after the rest of your craft clears that pushy, three-foot waterfall. Around the bend is the Washing Machine, always operating on its spin dry cycle. And those are just preludes for Lilly Rapids just upstream of the take-out at Lilly bridge.

Lilly is the longest rapid on this section and allows the canoeist plenty of opportunity to show off for the spectators on the bridge. There is no more access below Lilly bridge, but there are still one and a half miles of Clear Creek before its confluence with the Obed. But those one and a half miles drop at 67.3 feet per mile. That is dangerous by anyone's ratings. Jacks Rock Falls, Camel Rock, and Wootens Folly are three mean Class IV's in rapid succession. Good, high-quality, whitewater canoes have been torn to shreds by this trio. And yet there's more. In fact, you can see the waters of the Obed and still be eaten

Mouth of Clear Creek. The mouth of Clear Creek as it enters the Obed River is marked by this unusual overhanging rock. This marker can be seen from either river, but few can see it unless they are out paddling in the Obed National Wild River system. Photograph by Jim Robertson.

alive by the last big offset double drop in an unnamed rapid just above the confluence. Canoeing below Lilly is for well-experienced paddlers following normal safety procedures and paddling in groups with a minimum of three craft.

The next convenient take-out (and next bridge crossing) below Lilly is at Nemo bridge on the Emory River (just past the Obed-Emory confluence), 7.1 miles downstream from Lilly. So do not set off lightly to view the Clear Creek confluence or you just might end your float with a hike. (At the Obed/Clear Creek confluence, a trail scales the end of the point of land that separates the two rivers—while on Clear Creek look to river's right just before the confluence. Start climbing the talus slope on the end of the point and you'll intersect the trail at the base of the bluff caprock. It's a tough chug as you steeply ascend 450 feet; but the trail does wind up through the caprock and onto a ridgeway dirt road heading toward the eventual rural settlements. Take care of your own problems if possible; the people out there are hard-pressed enough with their own survival.)

## Daddys Creek

Daddys Creek is a long stream. It flows for miles and miles. But it's built upside down. Most conventional streams tumble out of their watershed mountains then slow down to a pastoral finish. This stream meanders atop the plateau uplands, gathering a little water here, a little there, and a little more from elsewhere. Finally, after most of its miles have been spent wandering, the creek begins a major cut into the sandstone caprock of the Plateau. And it quickly drops into the Obed gathering grounds. This "major cut" has a name (and a well-deserved reputation among plateau "creek boaters"): Daddys Creek Canyon.

Two "Legends" on Clear Creek. One legend is Dick Wooten. The other is that Blue Hole Canoe of his (with no added flotation). The National Wild Clear Creek is at high water, but none of it is in Dick's boat . . . yet. Photograph by Julie Keller.

Daddys Creek Canyon. Don't run this section in an open canoe. OK, you can run it if the water is right, the weather is right, your equipment is right, your skills are right, and you are with the right companions. There are lethal boat-eating undercuts down in this inaccessible National Wild and Fierce River. Photograph by Julie Keller.

Daddys Creek. Low flow in the fall as the water leaves Daddys Creek Canyon. It is now time to hike and rock-hop through that gorge to enjoy its beauty (and scout the keepers if you really don't have any better sense than to paddle through such awesome terrain).

Not only is this stream backwards, but it also has no middle ground. Starting in northeastern Cumberland County and flowing into Morgan County, you'll find pastoral, easy floating in the upper reaches and terrifying, dangerous whitewater below. If there is plenty of water in the system, you might have enough flow for the pastoral, meandering float from Big Lick to Linary. Portage the dam at Linary (just above TN 28) and continue your placid way to Meridian, US 70, and Center bridges. You'll see evidences of mining and farming all along the way. At times the landforms close in and you penetrate some shallow canyons.

Below Center bridge the gradient picks up and your canoeing becomes more serious. Take out at the Antioch bridge. Don't boat below this bridge until you've hiked the three miles of Daddys Creek Canyon below the Yellow Creek confluence to scout the action. Here you'll see the distorted piles of massive boulders that torture the streamway (not to mention the boater); Class IV and V rapids set in a drop of one hundred feet per mile amid the pounding and crashing water. Not only are there dangerous undercut rocks in this section, but in one place there's an undercut bluff that's probably the single most dangerous spot in the entire Obed–Emory system. Portage in many cases is difficult to impossible. (It's hard to front a house-sized boulder with a boat on your back.) This is the most difficult and hazardous section of the entire system. The scenery is outstanding.

About a mile below this canyon is the Devils Breakfast Table bridge and the boundary for the national system. This bridge is a put-in for the lower Obed run with the last two and a half miles of Daddys Creek being extremely scenic and the water a solid Class II. You then come to Obed Junction and will probably continue to more taxing paddling on the Obed, or you can carry out on the four-wheel-drive access road on the Obed River's left, across from the confluence.

## Obed River

The "wild" and "scenic" Obed doesn't really start out that way. In fact the early flow is tied up by the city of Crossville in Cumberland County in some tributary lakes and a necessary water plant. After cycling through the uses of Crossville, the waters for the upper, upper

Upper Obed River. The upper Obed River above Adams bridge. Here an excellent tandem team negotiates a precision fourteen-foot turn in a sixteen-foot canoe.

Obed below Obed Junction. Springtime on the Obed River. Wetsuits help the coldwater paddlers keep their minds on their progress through the rapids. And with no extra floatation, they better keep focused on their paddling effectiveness.

Obed River run finally push past US 127 and I-40 and head off cross-country toward the Catoosa Wildlife Management Area. US 127 is a tough, steep put-in, but maybe that's good, because this upper, upper stretch of the Obed River features tough, steep rapids. It's a narrow stream up here, and high water readings are required before the run is feasible.

This section of the Obed is called the Goulds Bend run, and it starts easily and ends placidly, but in the middle the bottom drops out at 80 feet per mile! Knucklebuster and Hellhole are Class IV rapids, but the Esses should be portaged. You can tell the Esses because the stream makes two, sharp, 90-degree turns in opposite directions, and to all the world it looks as if a 16-foot canoe couldn't swing that far in those tight spaces. Many canoeists walk out from this spot in the river. Landowners have posted much of the access at Adams bridge, so be particularly careful during take-out or in parking shuttle cars here.

A mile below the bridge, the river enters the Catoosa Wildlife Management Area and simultaneously crosses the boundary for national designation. Automobiles cannot reach Potters Ford bridge during turkey or deer hunts (or when the Catoosa is closed for winter road care), so it is best to check with the Catoosa managers before planning a trip below Adams bridge. Many solid Class II rapids, with a couple of surprising III's thrown in, characterize this extremely scenic and wild float between Adams bridge and Obed Junction. At

Obed National Wild River. Overlooking the Obed National Wild River at about River Mile 4. (The Widow-maker rapid shows up to the left far downstream.) This view site is atop a bluff much like the one seen on the other side. From this vantage point, an equally awe-inspiring view can be had looking upstream to the right as the river rounds the bend heading down from "Canoe Hole." Photograph by Jim Robertson.

sixteen miles, this trip is too long for a day trip; consequently, this is probably the least-run section in the system. Obed Junction is actually the confluence of Daddys Creek and the Obed River and was named at the turn of the century when an old narrow-gauge logging railroad used to come down Daddys Creek and turn down the Obed. The old bridge pilings are still visible at the confluence. There's a four-wheel-drive access road out on the Obed River's left here. Actually, there's a trail out on the river's right just down from the confluence, but it will lead only to a road in the middle of Catoosa that may not be of

Water-level View of Obed. A canoeist's view of the Obed National Wild River. Views like this provide great reasons to go paddling! Photograph by Jim Robertson.

much help. (Your best bet when forced to leave the Obed past this point is to try to scale the bluffs on river's left.)

Below Obed Junction you enter the wild and woolly Obed that most floaters talk about. This run usually starts either from the four-wheel-drive Obed Junction road, or from two miles up Daddys Creek (above the junction) at Devils Breakfast Table bridge. The run ends ten miles below the junction at Nemo bridge on the Emory. The water from Daddys Creek doubles the flow of the Obed, and the river gets pushy as the gorge gets deeper. A rapid called 90-Right/90-Left kind of lets you know what to expect. The next one, Ohmigod!, is actually very similar but is entered via a blind approach. Sturdy whitewater canoes have been ripped to pieces under the rocks during high-water attempts at this rapid. And shortly thereafter, the Class IV Rockgarden has spilled many an expert and taken a life. Many excellent canoeists portage Rockgarden.

There follow more narrow drops, more chances for pinned canoes, more opportunity to walk out (remember, to the left). And then you reach Clear Creek junction. A long cascading delta rapid propels you into Canoe Hole, where an old logging road provides four-wheel-drive-plus access to the river (most people park at the top and portage the quarter mile up or down the bluff).

Beyond here the canoeing settles down to three great Class II or more rapids in a row with the added excitement of The Widowmaker making a fourth. The river slows down, letting the canoeist marvel at the scenery. A slow pool or two allows time for some reminiscing before a large side-wall cut ahead signals the railroad tunnel and tracks running along the Emory. The overgrown pool found here is actually the confluence of the Obed with the Emory. The name changes because the river turns 90 degrees; but 90 percent of the water comes down the Obed. Look off to the left in the bend of the river and you'll see a small tributary sneaking in under the ever-present bankside foliage. That's the Emory River, and you are now on that river.

A frolicking mile of a wider river and some interesting shoals bring you to the old iron bridge at Nemo. In May of 1973, when Barnett and Lilly bridges washed out on Clear Creek and Antioch and Devils Breakfast Table bridges washed out on Daddys Creek, the water lapped over the deck on Nemo bridge. It's interesting to think about as you wind up your long, eventful whitewater run.

## Crab Orchard Creek

Can there be too much water in the Obed system? Rarely. But it has happened. Should you see water lapping at the deck of Nemo bridge, such as Don Todd found during the flood of 1973, it's time to backtrack out of that narrow river gorge and get up onto the plateau. However, a nice early spring flood of 8,000 to 12,000 cfs on the Emory at Oakdale gauge is common enough. Well, those levels bring out the feeder stream waters. And such waters bring out the "creek boaters." Creek boaters are a subset of whitewater paddlers, which in themselves are a subset of the river runners, which, of course, are a subset of all self-powered canoeists. And it takes a group of well-supported creek boaters to enjoy dropping down a tight, twisting, boulder-bordered cascade. But under the right conditions, Crab Orchard Creek is all that, and it's there to enjoy. As Monte Smith notes in his 1995 edition of *Southeastern Whitewater* when referring to Crab Orchard Creek: "With the right flow level this can be the most fun trip in the Obed/Emory watershed, if not in the entire Southeast." Monte noted in his 1990 edition of *A Paddler's Guide to the Obed/Emory Watershed* that Crab Orchard Creek offered "Continuous whitewater! No long pools. Not even short pools. Just rapid after rapid after rapid." The reason for quoting Monte so much here is that long before he ever put his trip notes to paper, Monte discovered this particular run and enthusiastically popularized it. He wrote and published articles in whitewater journals. He described the trip in paddlers' newsletters. He took pictures and gave talks about this run. But only the "concept" was conveyed for many years, because he could rarely get a trip organized at the same time as the necessary water flow remained at the 10,000 cfs level. And that's one of the problems with "creek boating."

Crab Orchard Creek is a 13.5-mile run in continuous Class III water. Gradients up to 80 feet per mile are included in the run. Such a trip requires all whitewater safety precautions, including at least the minimum number of participants, whitewater-worthy equipment, whitewater-worthy paddler skills, knowledge of the current flow rates, rescue gear, support from those who have already paddled the stream, and an ability to abandon gear and walk out, if necessary, midway through the trip. (It has been necessary before.) Make your first run on this stream in the company of others who have already been down the incline. Use one of Monte's guidebook write-ups for particulars. But a good Class III paddler can get a great introduction to "creek boating" on this stream.

## Emory River

The Emory actually deserves no better than to share the same fate as the other Plateau streams. At first, the river flows placidly for miles and miles, then it careens a couple of miles down a series of rockslides until dropping into a pool on the Obed. And that should be it— the tributary feeding a mainstem. But by a quirk of geology, the Emory River retains its name after joining the much bigger Obed, which we now find is actually an overgrown "tributary" to that little Emory stream. The Obed has terminated at its Mile 0, and the new, improved Emory continues toward the Clinch and the big Tennessee Rivers.

Upstream in its headwaters in northeastern Morgan County, the little Emory drains a lovely covelike valley amid the towering peaks of the Cumberland Mountains. (This happens on the backside of Frozen Head State Natural Area.) Scenic farmlands on the valley floor are offset by the hardwood flanks of the adjacent mountains. The stream is slow and pastoral near Gobey. You will also see many traces of past and present strip mining all along the Emory as this stream penetrates deep into a coal-bearing region of this part of the Appalachians. The Emory is second only to its neighbor, the New River (of Tennessee), in the extent of strip mining in its watershed. You will notice the murky water quality as you float the Emory. (You will also see the active strip mines and the ineffective silt traps on the more poorly situated ones just before you reach the Obed.)

The upper part of the Emory is a pleasant, easy float from under the new US 27 bridge and on to Montgomery bridge (where John Muir stayed overnight on his "thousand-mile walk to the sea"). Below Montgomery bridge the stream continues its Class I flow for three more miles to where the solid rock riverbed finally begins to break up. At this point the Emory River falls off the Cumberland Plateau.

For two miles, the canoeist drops at sixty-two feet per mile, crashing between boulders as the narrow stream is bounced back and forth by the steep-sided terrain. It is best to run this section at marginal water flows. Too much water can push even expert canoeists beyond their reach. Portages are not difficult and are feasible alternatives to some of the dead-end drops, especially at the higher water levels. Interesting abandoned railroad tunnels are visible on both sides of the river toward the end of this canyon. Finally, the railroad bridge over the Emory signals the upcoming confluence with the Obed—an entirely different river. It's big and wide and has much more water, and the water quality improves. After a mile of cascading joyrides,

Emory River—extending the National Scenic River. The lower river settles into a pleasant Class I and II run. But you have to get through the entrance rapid to get there. Photograph by Julie Keller.

the iron bridge of Nemo comes into view. It is only this short section of the Emory between the Obed confluence and the Nemo bridge that is included in the national system.

Just below the bridge and out of sight around a bend, a Class III rapid awaits. Nemo Rapid is a bouncy double-dip into a plunge-pool recovery basin. This signals the beginning of a nine-mile run to Oakdale. It's Class I and II. You're floating on the combined waters of the entire Obed–Emory system, so the season lasts longer. The river is wider, but it channels up as the flow decreases. This section is ideal for the beginning canoeist to try out the Obed–Emory experience. The Catoosa Wildlife Management Area is still on the river's right, but a railroad track runs on the river's left (it can be a trail out for emergency use). The scenery and water remain attractive. Midway, you pass under the Camp Austin bridge. Several long pools make you complacent, but the Class II or more rapids below Camp Austin and Oakdale bridges should wake you up again. Take out at the Oakdale bridge. The park-like area around the bend belongs to one of Oakdale's law enforcement officers, and permission to use the area is difficult to obtain. This run is a pleasant drifting mountain scenery run and almost a relief from the crashing whitewater of the upper Obed stretches. There are about five more free-flowing miles left, then the Emory feeds the clean mountain waters to the tailwaters of Watts Bar Lake on the Clinch and Tennessee rivers.

## Piney Creek of Rhea County

"Creek boating" opened up a few runs that were relatively unknown until their boats of choice got shorter than fourteen feet in length. If you could not swivel a sixteen-foot canoe down the narrow, tight streamway, then it used to be that open canoes didn't make the trip.

But the creeks were still there, and the paddlers were still looking for them. Finally, as skill and equipment made some advances, a few canoeists began floating those narrow, tight creeks. And rumors about "Piney Creek in Rhea County" began to be heard. Located on the Cumberland Plateau's Walden Ridge escarpment overlooking the great Tennessee River Valley in east Tennessee, this little stream is in rugged, wild, remote terrain—land not suited for human habitation. It's not even fair to request any rescue aid in land like this, and a paddler trying to walk out is just as apt to fall off a twenty-foot bluff as to get woefully trapped in the omnipresent rhododendron and laurel thickets. The put-in is on the dead-end graveled Wash–Pelfrey Road creek crossing and the take-out is ten miles downstream at Shut-in Gap Road. And there is nothing between these two backwoods roads anywhere near this stream except boulders, bluffs, ledges, hemlock, white pine, rhododendron, laurel, and clean, clear water.

Wash–Pelfrey Road is the right fork after Mountain Road out of Evensville, Tennessee, climbs the Walden Ridge escarpment and splits to head off, on the left side, toward Liberty Hill. Shut-in Gap Road is a road climbing that same escarpment directly out of Spring City, Tennessee, (not TN 68). Piney Creek runs through a narrow, deep gorge on the ridge above the escarpment. It is a narrow stream with scenic side branches tumbling in as waterfalls all along the way. The float down this creek is rated Class IV and V and mostly suitable for closed craft. There are numerous strainers, keepers, and undercut rocks. The portages are difficult and numerous. The run is too long to dally during any of the many scoutings and portages required. Nightfall can easily overtake a large, slow-moving group. High water levels are needed. The only gauge nearby is over on the Tellico River (not in the same watershed, or even in the same mountains), where it has been found that a Tellico reading of 800 to 1,200 cfs generally provides the level needed to float the Piney.

# Little Sequatchie River

The Little Sequatchie River is a spectacularly beautiful, wet-weather, Class II whitewater run. Like its big brother, the Sequatchie, the Little Sequatchie cuts a steep, wooded gorge in the southern end of the Cumberland Plateau. Plunging out of the mountains in northern Marion County, the Little Sequatchie carves its way through the Plateau as it flows southward to its mouth at the Sequatchie north of Ebenezer. Runnable only in late winter, spring, and during periods of heavy rain, the Little Sequatchie is an absolute delight. Steep, timbered mountainsides converge at the edge of the intimate and diminutive thirty-five-foot-wide stream. Though close to Chattanooga, the setting is pristine and rugged, with lush vegetation along the banks in most sections.

Most of the upper Little Sequatchie is inaccessible. However, by paralleling the stream on a dirt farm road, persistent paddlers can work their way upstream to put in. Short but certainly eventful, the run is a good Class II float with one Class III area that should be scouted. Hazards in the top section, other than the rapids, are deadfalls and a number of islands that make for a few very tight passages. Swift water in conjunction with brush jams, particularly in congested spots around the islands, provide ample opportunity for the unwary to become entrapped.

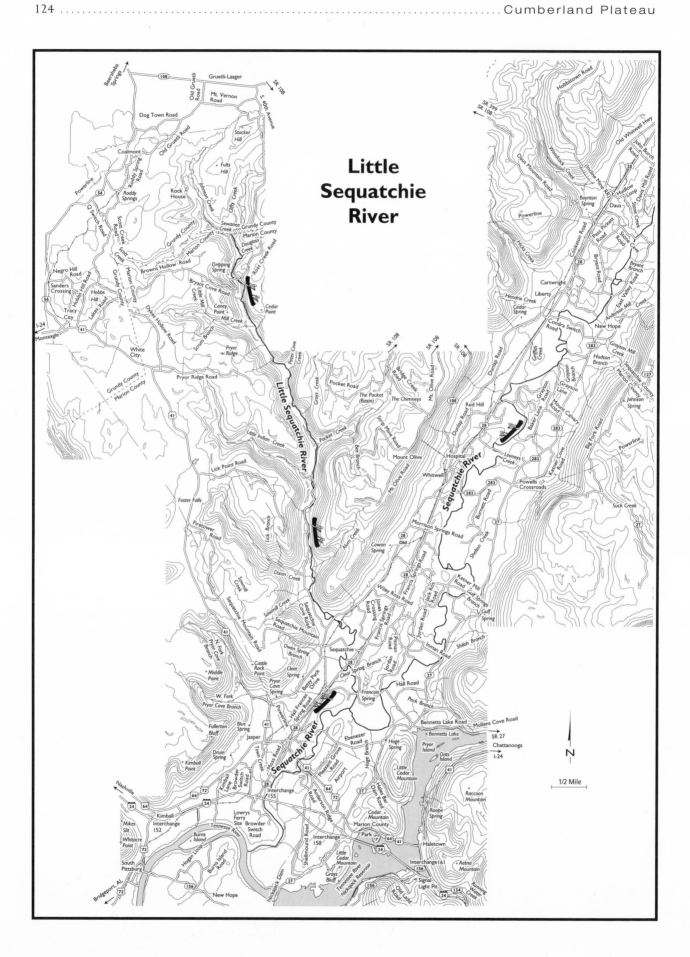

Little
Sequatchie
River

Below SR 27 the Little Sequatchie flattens out a bit, with most of the whitewater turning into benign riffles and shoals. Mountains recede, and cultivated land encroaches on the river. Banks and bottom are primarily of mud with fewer rocks than were in evidence upstream. Steep and approaching six to eight feet in height, the banks are generally shaded with hardwoods. Islands, particularly small brush islands, persist almost all the way to the river's mouth near Ebenezer. As with the upper section, frequent strainers represent the greatest hazard. By the time the Little Sequatchie reaches the Sequatchie, it is running through almost flat-bottom farmland. Runs on the Little Sequatchie are too short for canoe camping, although trips can be lengthened by following the Sequatchie downstream. Access along the lower Little Sequatchie is fair to good.

# Big Fiery Gizzard Creek

Deep within the southern Cumberlands, the Fiery Gizzard flows through the heart of an intimate, historical, beautiful natural area. The South Cumberland Recreation Area is one of the premier outdoor sites to visit in Tennessee. But the creeks there support better hiking than floating. After moving only a mile or two into the Fiery Gizzard terrain, you begin to feel the inherent remoteness of the area. Bluffs, falls, forest, and game trails combine to bring out your explorer instincts. But others have explored there earlier. Davy Crockett, Herman Baggenstoss, and Doug Cameron all left their marks before you. Crockett probably named the place by spitting out a too-hot turkey innard at his campfire along the creek. Baggenstoss spent a long and productive lifetime in the headwaters of the Fiery Gizzard and succeeded in establishing political protection for this pretty prize (and, along with his brothers, made the best salt-rising bread in the oldest bakery in Tennessee). Cameron decided to paddle the Fiery Gizzard and thereby got that stream into this guidebook. By living nearby and watching the daily rainfall, he was able to actually find a rain-soaked day when that stream could float a boat. He talked some Sewanee cronies into bringing their canoes and they actually made their descent on the Fiery Gizzard. So it can be done. And what a beautiful place to be. After consultation with Doug and a study of the documenting photos of his Blue Hole canoe at Blue Hole falls, the official advice from this guidebook is Take a hike!

# Sequatchie River

The heavily timbered and rugged Cumberland Plateau, a classic rift valley, gentle year-round, Class I river flow—these are the elements that make the Sequatchie River a true "sleeper" among the canoeing resources of Tennessee. There are over seventy canoeable miles on this relatively rural stream. And all of it drains down the center of a five-mile-wide valley embedded in the southern part of Tennessee's Cumberland Plateau.

The Sequatchie Valley is a rift valley, said to be one of only two in the world. The waters for this river rise in Grassy Cove in southern Cumberland County, only to be blocked from passage to the valley by Bear Den Mountain, one of the walls of the totally enclosed

# Grundy's Fiery Gizzard

The gorge along Big Fiery Gizzard Creek and Gizzard Creek near Tracy City goes by the prosaic name of Grundy Forest State Natural Area according to the officials at South Cumberland State Park. It is better known by residents and the hundreds of thousands of annual visitors as Fiery Gizzard. The Fiery Gizzard is an important remnant forest, left over from the last Ice Age. The plant community found in the Gizzard is typical of Wisconsin, not Tennessee. Allan Strand, a visiting professor at the nearby University of the South, stated that such a forest community cannot be found short of the Smokies. It is the cool shade and the moisture of the Gizzard that have enabled this special place of light and beauty to remain.

The Fiery Gizzard is also an important recreational resource. Hundreds of thousands of visitors come every year. Most hike, backpack the trail to Foster Falls, and enjoy the cool respite of swimming holes and waterfalls on hot summer days. Boating would seem unlikely, since the stream goes underground when it reaches down to the limestone layer underlying the sandstone cap of the plateau, but it has been run several times during heavy rains. The first known descent was made by Steve Puckette, Van Nall, and Doug Cameron in January 1980.

The headwaters of the Fiery Gizzard rise near Tracy City, which runs its own water district. The droughts of the mid-1980s led the State of Tennessee to require Tracy City (through a consent order) to provide an adequate water supply for the people it serves out to a forty-year horizon. For almost twenty years, Tracy City has been at odds with the state about its water supply. The town gets its water from an abandoned deep mine. The water in this mine, according to one state water quality official,

has had a pH level of 2, the acidity of gastric juice. The situation has lasted for years and has caused most of the water system's pipes to be weakened or destroyed (no telling what it's doing to people!).

To remedy this situation, Tracy City is proposing to dam Big Fiery Gizzard Creek just north of Highway 56/41, creating a ninety-five-acre lake, costing all taxpayers (not just the local water users) 4.5 million dollars. This lake would take up to one million gallons of water a day from the little stream. Such a depletion of flow of the stream would irreparably change the Gizzard. Currently the runoff levels vary from annual spring floods to bare trickles in dry Octobers. To change to a constant flow below the dam, as proposed by the engineering report, would alter the ecosystem that has become dependent on the natural ebb and flow. This is the same issue being debated nationally concerning the Grand Canyon. Local politics and jealousies keep the city from forming alliances with adjacent water districts, which have more than adequate capacities. Even a nearby suitable, existing lake with a willing seller has been ignored as a solution.

This is a good illustration of the way water is managed in Tennessee, and we can expect to see more and more small dams appear as we address our water problems piecemeal. There is no regional or watershed planning for water, and expansions like those in Tracy City do not even have to increase wastewater treatment capacity. Tracy City, in fact, has no wastewater treatment. The primary form of pollution in the clear, cold waters of Fiery Gizzard is the human intestinal bacterium, E. coli!

—Doug Cameron
Sewanee, TN

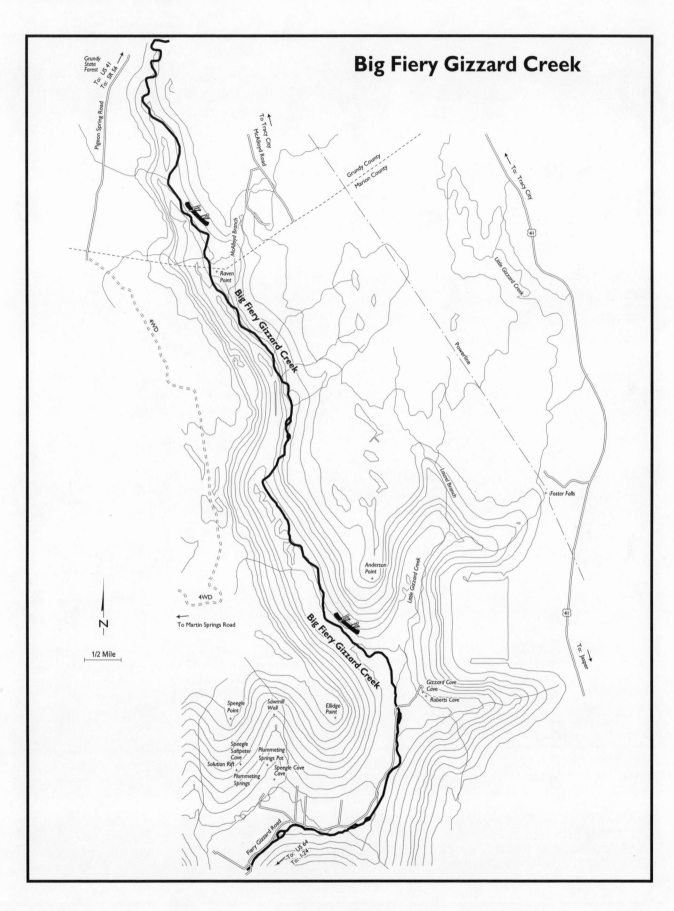

# Big Fiery Gizzard Creek

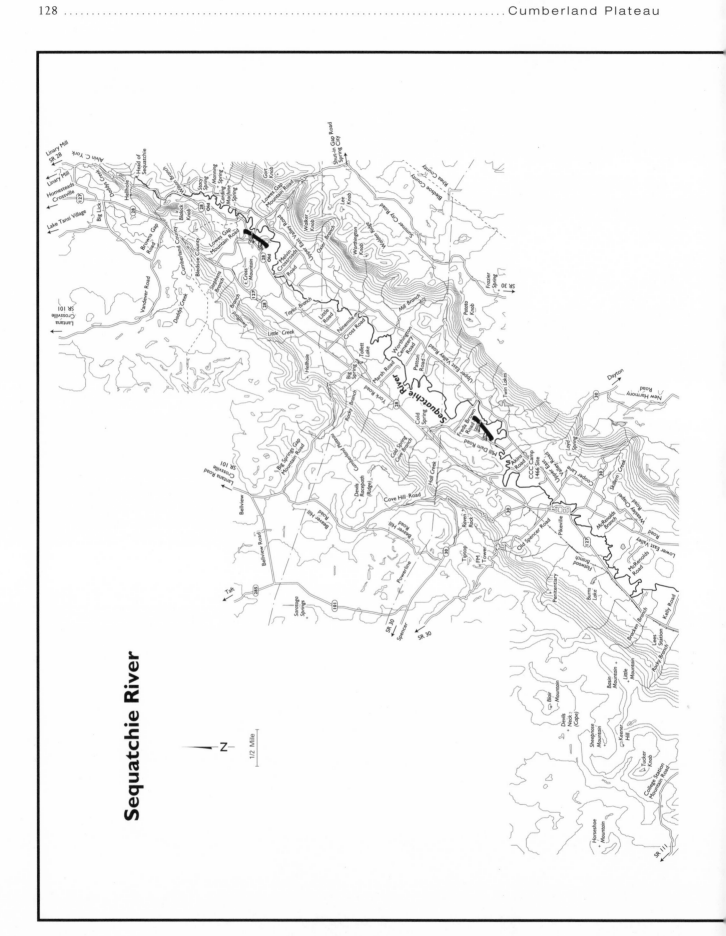

# Sequatchie River

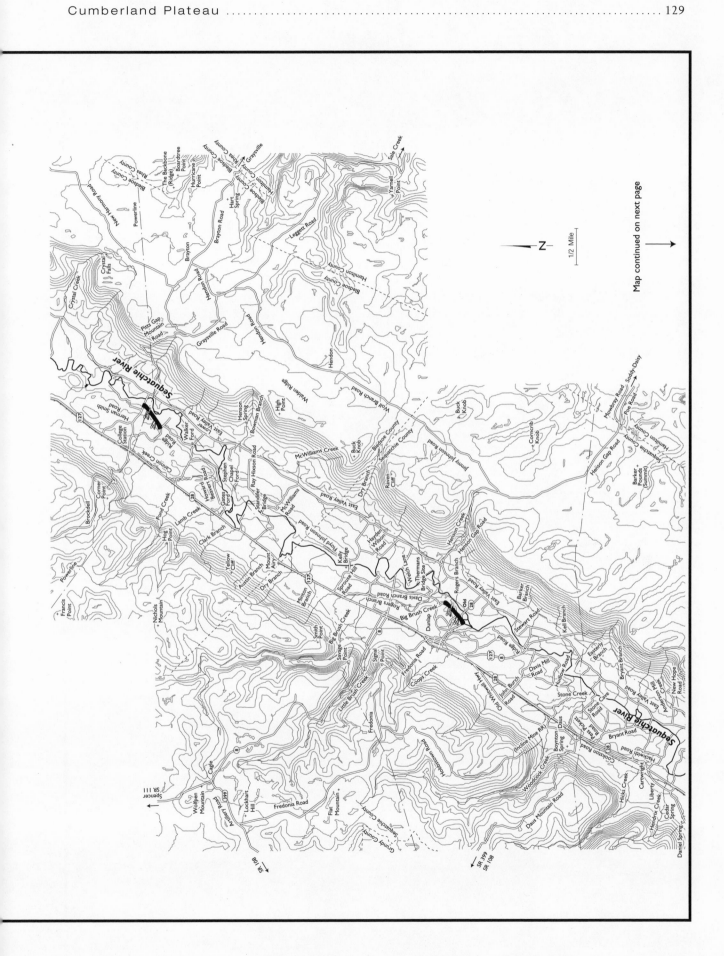

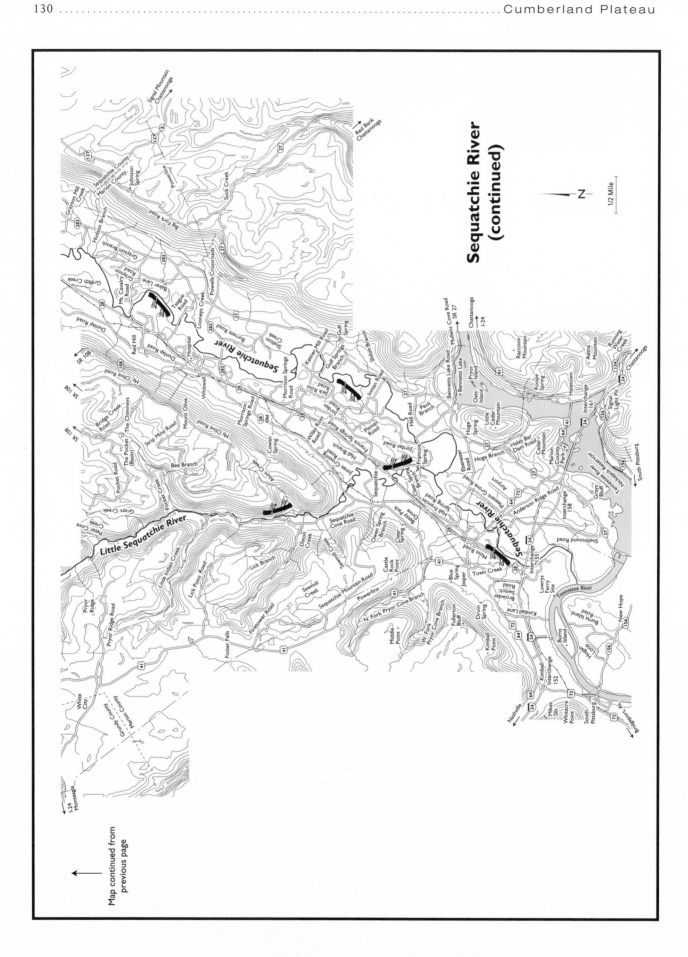

**Sequatchie River (continued)**

N

1/2 Mile

Map continued from previous page

cove. Nature answers gravity's call by running the stream waters four miles underground before it re-emerges at the head of the Sequatchie Valley as a good-sized stream. The stream follows the deepening cut of this rift in the plateau and parallels the general direction of the Tennessee River (twenty miles to its east) until that larger river makes its dramatic turn west at Chattanooga. The Sequatchie River never deviates from its southern (with a western tilt) direction through Bledsoe, Sequatchie, and Marion Counties; it is, therefore, intercepted by the Tennessee River forty more twisting Tennessee River miles downstream from that city of Civil War, river-bluff fame. The same type of river bluffs can be found along both sides of the Sequatchie Valley, and many times both sides are visible from the river.

The main part of the highland Cumberland Plateau on the river's right and the plateau remnant, Walden Ridge, on the river's left are each about 1,300 feet higher than the gently flowing Sequatchie. The river valley is generally narrow (about five miles in width), and both escarpments to the plateau elevations are steep-sided sandstone bluffs. The scenery from river level is the most spectacular you'll find on a Class I float stream in Tennessee. The river is accessible at many points as US 127 uses the upper part of the valley as a path south toward Chattanooga. The valley is basically agrarian, with a linear array of small towns linked by the river and the paralleling highway. The heavily wooded escarpments are noted for their spring and fall beauty. Steam-powered railroad excursions leave the famed Chattanooga depot every year during both those seasons just to travel the length of the valley during those colorful times. Canoeists, of course, are treated to the same vistas, with the added opportunity of glimpsing indigenous river and woodland wildlife.

Sequatchie River. The Sequatchie River, a quiet water wonder in the heart of the Cumberland Plateau.

Old Indian fish traps and later remains of river mills and their low mill dams can be found along the way. Ketner Mill (at about river mile 17), built in 1824, grinds corn to this day. (Portage the new ten-foot dam.) Vaguely remembered and certainly underutilized, the Sequatchie River is an ideal place for family floats. The river is now served by a local livery in Dunlap. The Pilkingtons at this Sequatchie River canoe base know local flow conditions and more. They have always been very helpful to Sequatchie canoeists whether the paddlers use the livery service or not. The Sequatchie is worth looking into; it is unique pastoral floating in the heart of the rugged Cumberlands.

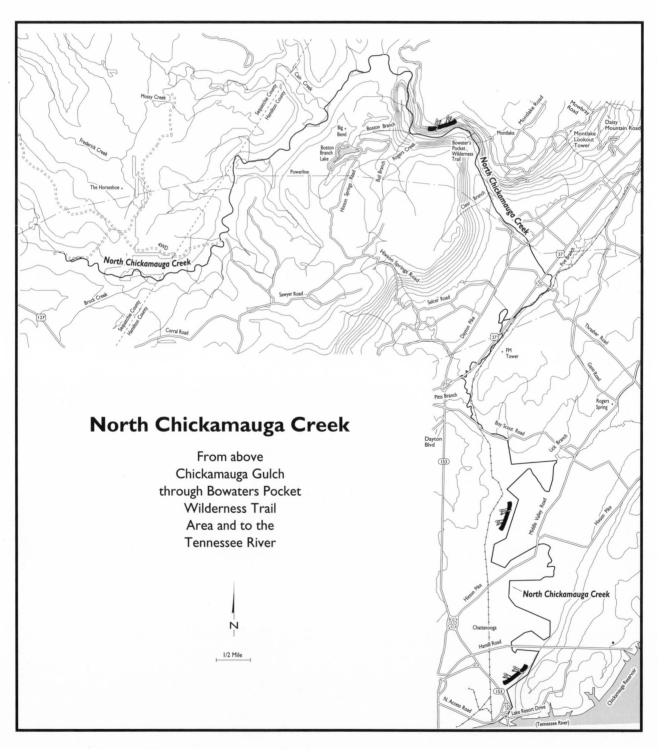

# North Chickamauga Creek

From above
Chickamauga Gulch
through Bowaters Pocket
Wilderness Trail
Area and to the
Tennessee River

N

1/2 Mile

# North Chickamauga Creek

No relation to South Chickamauga Creek in the same area, this northern drainage into the Tennessee River (just below Chickamauga Dam) comes flying out of Sequatchie County's North Chickamauga Gulf indentation into the eastern Walden Ridge escarpment of the Cumberland Plateau and drops—with a thud—onto the abbreviated Tennessee Valley floor offering more than sixteen miles of pastoral canoeing amid the northern Chattanooga suburbs in Hamilton County. Looking west from US 27 at the stream crossing, you can see the rockbound gulf, the origin of this spring-fed stream—a no man's land from which issue the cold, clear canoeing waters for the valley-floor paddlers. A Bowaters Pocket Wilderness trail follows an old railway alongside the streamway as it crashes out of the plateau. Hiking up into that gulf is a worthy exercise if you like falling water and boulders.

As you turn away from the gulf and paddle along into the valley, you will note how the road construction, shopping center, and other human activities degrade the water quality mile by mile. However, the residents along here are particularly sensitive to the scenic value and water quality of this creek and have done an inspired job of protecting it. Their work continues to improve the stream in this increasingly metropolitan area. This effort makes it doubly important that you do not litter North Chickamauga Creek. If you can't carry out more than you brought with you, stay off the creek and out of their backyard.

The entire run of the creek below US 27 is pastoral and pleasant with riffles and pools. Put-ins are on private land, so common sense should prevail for parking, permission, and so forth. The take-out in the immediate area of Chickamauga Dam is on a public-access Tennessee Valley Authority Reservation. Here the creek is lined with riprap (laid rock reinforcement of the riverbank). Note that, at times, on the last mile or two, the current of the creek may actually run upstream due to heavy discharge at the dam on the Tennessee River just above the mouth of North Chickamauga Creek.

# Cumberland Valley

## Dale Hollow Lake Canoe Trail

Although this book is oriented toward flowing water, several opportunities for good paddling do exist on some of Tennessee's many lakes. The following description of the Dale Hollow Lake Canoe Trail was written by Tennessee Scenic Rivers Association members Ohio Knox and Bill Mitchum for the Nashville District of the U.S. Army Corps of Engineers' canoe guide to the Cumberland River Basin.

The trip starts at Eastport Dock where the east and west forks of the Obey River come together in Pickett County, Tennessee. The trail winds its way down the Obey River arm of the lake through densely forested areas with steep slopes and an irregular shoreline. Approximately ten miles downstream the trail passes Sunset Dock, Byrdstown Bridge (TN Route 42), and Obey River Recreation Area, the largest recreation area on the lake. From this point on, the lake gradually opens up with heavily wooded drainage basins on both sites of the lake, contributing to the clearness of the lake water and the lack of siltation throughout the entire lake. Wildlife is usually abundant on the lake, with ducks, deer, muskrat, and an occasional eagle being seen. Traveling on down the lake, the trail passes points of interest, such as Trooper Island, operated for underprivileged boys, by the Kentucky State Police, and several recreation areas such as Lillydale, Willow Grove, and First Island. The trip can be ended at Dale Hollow Dock or continued to the dam and finished at Pleasant Grove Island Recreation Area, located directly across from the dam. The entire trip is approximately fifty-five miles long with ideal camping spots all along the way.

Upon completion of the trip, you may want to visit the Resources Manager's Office, the National Fish Hatchery and the Power Plant directly below the dam.

If you desire additional information or would like a map of the lake, contact the Resource Manager, Dale Hollow Lake, Celina, Tennessee 38551. Fishery—Excellent. Dale Hollow is noted worldwide for its record-producing smallmouth bass. In addition, fishing is excellent for walleye, largemouth bass, Kentucky bass, white bass and crappie.

## Obey River

Although most of the Obey River below the confluence of its east and west forks is situated out of sight and out of mind below the placid waters of Dale Hollow Lake, the river continues to exist in abbreviated form for seven miles below Dale Hollow Dam to its mouth at the Cumberland River. Runnable all year with easy access, the lower Obey winds alternately below limestone palisades and along cultivated bottom land. Difficulty is Class I. Hazards to navigation consist primarily of powerboats.

# Roaring River System

## Flat Creek

Flat Creek isn't flat; In fact, it isn't even runnable most of the time. When other rivers in the watershed (Roaring River, Spring Creek, Blackburn Fork) are flooded, try Overton County's Flat Creek. It is a short, two-mile, deep-set, narrow creek with some interesting Class II water and a pretty waterfall midway down the float. But be careful: this scenic twenty-foot falls might be the last bit of scenery you'll see. The falls slip up on you, and the smooth, rock-slab riverbottom is hard for braking purchase should you need a fast halt to your downstream progress. Eddy out to the right against the bluff and carry down beside the old gristmill ruins. The rest of the way to Roaring River is quick and easy. Paddle a half mile more to the Ramsey Farm take-out (described in the Roaring River section). This take-out can be arduous and be sure to get permission before using it. Put-in is at the TN 136 bridge. Get permission here, too.

## Spring Creek

Spring Creek, which originates in Putnam County and flows through Overton and Jackson Counties on its way to join the Roaring River, is a local whitewater adventure with a very short running season—a season measured in days, and, unfortunately, these days are not continuous. In the early spring, when the ground is saturated and then a big rainfall occurs, area canoeists emerge like demented, water-soaked mushrooms and direct their winter-pallid, PFD-adorned bodies down this steep, wild, beautiful gorge full of springs, creeks, waterfalls, heavy vegetation, and broken boats. The ten-mile, Class I upper run is characterized by clean, clear, sparkling water flowing gently over small riffles and through shallow pools. It's a narrow stream and heavily wooded on the banks. Numerous intricately carved bluffs are passed as one meanders along with the stream. Blowdowns (deadfalls) and log-jams are the major obstacles for the floater. (Make sure the box culvert under TN 136 is clear before approaching that passage.)

The five-plus miles below the low-water access bridge near Waterloo Falls is the spectacular and difficult Spring Creek "gorge," a Class III to IV run. At this put-in, the water flowing over the five-foot ledge that you see is called Go/No-Go Rapid (because it's the gorge run's gauge). If there's enough water and you can easily run this rapid without dragging, put on your hardhat and go. The water will be muddy because very high-water flow is the only time you can get down this creek. Just around the bend is the thirty-five-foot Waterloo Falls. The mandatory portage is on the right, through the Girl Scout Camp and down the steel stairs. Get prior permission from the Girl Scout Council in Nashville to use this land (615-383-0490). Portaging on the left is dangerous.

Below Waterloo, you meet another five-foot ledge, a warm-up for the Meat Grinder, a 12-foot ledge system around the next bend. It's important to scout the Meat Grinder, for

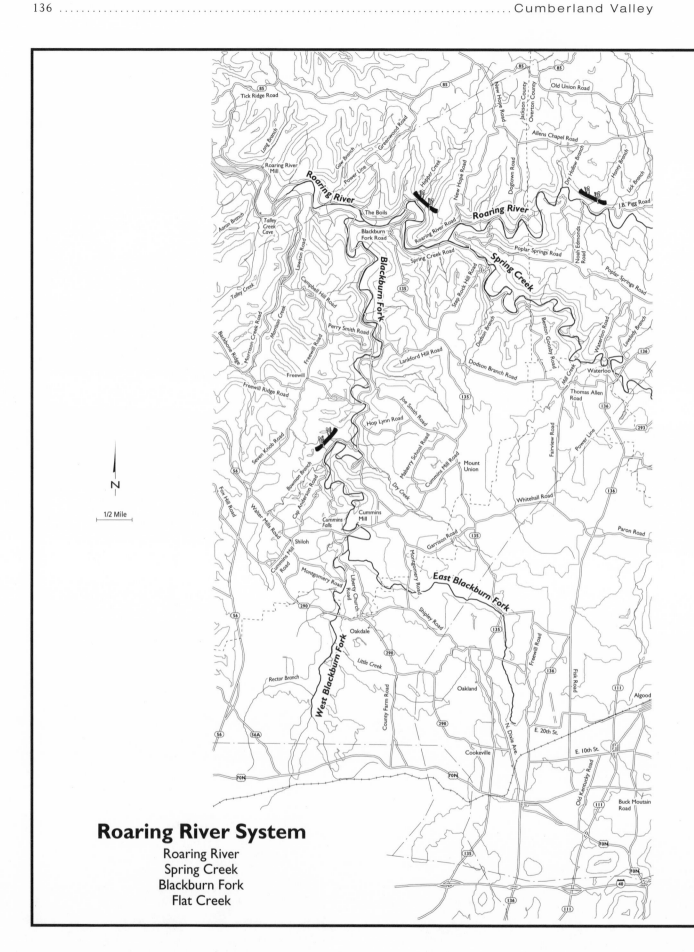

# Roaring River System

Roaring River
Spring Creek
Blackburn Fork
Flat Creek

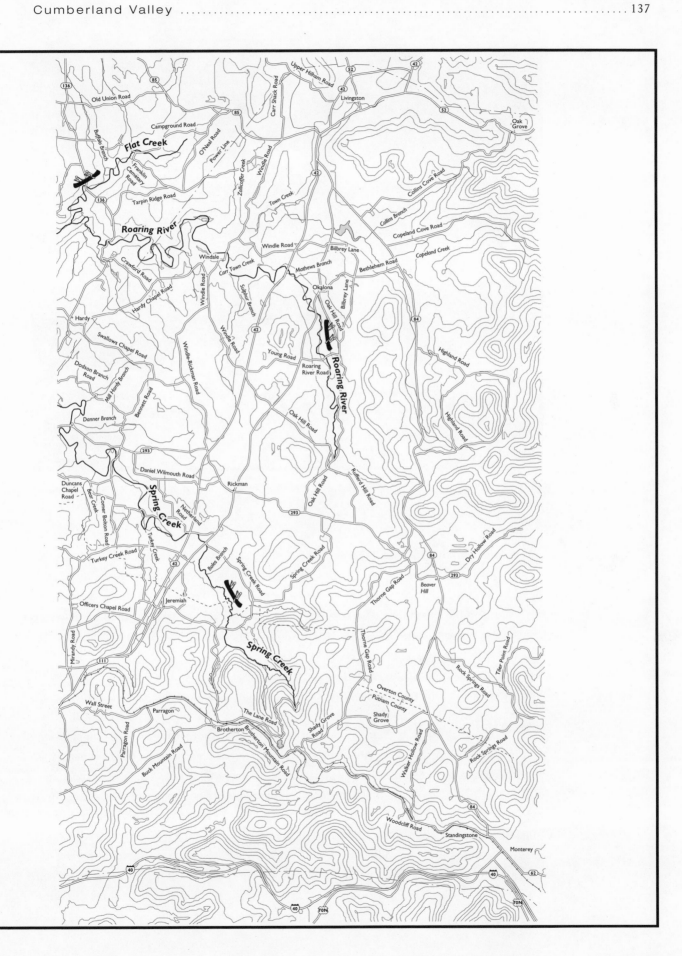

Spring Creek. Water has to be running high, to run Spring Creek. And this is what high running Spring Creek looks like.

it is common to find logs jammed in the rock crevices or rolling in the souse holes during these high-water conditions. Then you go through some rock gardens and around the next bend to Big Daddy, a fast wall-to-wall chute with a big wave at the end. You'll continue through more drops, chutes, and rock-garden dodging until you find a mile of flatwater announcing the take-out. You've traversed an average gradient of forty feet per mile with the first two miles measuring at over eighty-five feet per mile.

The scenery in this intimate little gorge is spectacular and almost totally undisturbed by civilization. About a mile below Waterloo Falls, which itself was a site for an old horizontal-turbine gunpowder mill, the high-volume Mill Creek enters on the left with a beautiful fifty-foot cascading fall striking Spring Creek near midchannel. Another pretty waterfall is visible on the left farther downstream. An emergency access trail can be found on the righthand side about three quarters of a mile below Waterloo Falls (before Mill Creek). This is simply a rough trail to the top of the gorge wall. When the gorge widens, a road appears on the left (near the Jackson County line). A take-out at the nearby Three Gables Ford can be arranged by obtaining permission from the landowner at the white, three-gabled house on that road.

Those wishing to paddle farther may do so by taking out along the road paralleling lower Spring Creek or at the confluence with Roaring River. This adds about three and a half miles of Class I water through pastoral country to your trip. You can also continue ten more miles to Fish Barrier Dam public access on Roaring River.

## Blackburn Fork

Imagine rounding the first bend after put-in on an exploratory float trip and, with no audible advance warning, seeing only treetops ahead. That's what happened to the first group of paddlers on Blackburn Fork. They returned to report that eighty-five-foot Cummings Falls (tallest in the Roaring River system) is not found on the topo maps nor, through a quirk of gorge-shielding acoustics, is it very audible (upstream). But, of course, the treetops on the horizon gave the paddlers a much-needed visual clue that something strange was ahead.

Obtain permission from the landowner to use the dirt road put-in. But do not put-in on Blackburn Fork without realizing the hazard of Cummings Falls a quarter mile below and just beyond the first bend. Keep to the right bank and look for visual clues of your approach to the eighty-five-foot falls. Boats must be lowered by ropes over the sheer rock face on the righthand side of the falls. Paddlers, too, must use the aid of ropes to scale down this same treacherous cliff. So be sure to bring enough throwlines to set up these aids. Allow two hours for this rockface portage for a group of five or six boats.

The scenery in the kettle-shaped canyon around the falls is worth the extra strenuous trip. The drops just below the falls are tight and exciting, approaching Class III. Then the river gradually comes out of the gorge into farmlands. The take-out for this six-mile run is fairly easy at a paralleling road on the right bank where Dry Creek enters. You can add another seven-plus miles by continuing down to the steel bridge on the paralleling gravel road (just before the creek crosses under TN 135 and joins Roaring River). This section of the fork is still narrow and intimate. The water flow is steady, but the scenery is not dramatic. Extended trips can continue down Roaring River past The Boils to Fish Barrier Dam.

## Roaring River

Just the name of this river attracts the interest of most map-scanning canoeists. And if the water level is right, the adventuresome paddler won't be disappointed. Roaring River is a small, two-county (Overton and Jackson) drainage off the edge of the Cumberland Plateau across the narrow eastern Highland Rim that ends under the backwater of the Cumberland River's Cordell Hull impoundment. But before the roar of that falling water is drowned out, a competent canoeist can paddle down gradients reaching seventy feet per mile tight within a scenic gorge.

This river, along with its tributaries, Spring Creek and Blackburn Fork, is a part of Tennessee's State Scenic River System. The brisk drop of the gathered waters was used in earlier times to power wool-carding and grain-grinding mills, and some of the old ruins and foundations are still visible along the flow. Landownership along this river goes back many generations and a feeling of fierce proprietorship still exists among those who live today on the bluffs above the riverbed. Be advised that it is extremely important to obtain proper landowner permission before attempting any property-crossing access to or egress from the river. Such permission is generally readily attainable; but oversight of the proper pre-float civilities can (and probably will) result in an unnecessary confrontation with the local landowner and the legal establishment, who all regard unfamiliar out-of-area canoeists much the same way you would regard a rabid dog heading across the yard toward your front door. DO NOT TRESPASS!

The first six and a half miles of Roaring River, from Windle to old TN 136, is a pleasant, narrow, Class I float. No gauge exists, but there should be enough water flow to cover the ten-foot Johnsons Falls from wall to wall. This falls and the ruins of Johnsons Mill are just below TN 136. (Portage Johnsons Falls; the backwash below is treacherous.) Be sure to obtain landowner permission before using the put-in at the top of this run in Windle. And then, while scouting the water level at Johnsons Falls, be sure to scout the take-out features above that drop as well. You need to be able to recognize the area from the river. It is after the Johnsons Falls portage that the "roar" begins. You will encounter two and a half miles of continuous Class III water as you descend the 70-foot-per-mile gradient through a narrow, 200-foot-deep gorge. There are some spectacular waves and tight maneuvering. Water flow should cover the ledges below the TN 136 bridge, but not cover the old mill race. A good surfing wave is found at the old gauging station, and there are some strong holes just below it. Beyond that, you will find a mass of crosscurrents and dead-ends at the high bluff (on the right), followed by some interesting rock gardens.

The river begins to flatten out (below Flat Creek) in time to allow the paddler to watch for the landmark barn on the right that signals the Ramsey Farm take-out. If the road is too muddy for vehicular approach to the river, you will be treated to a Class V carry to the plateau top. Obtain permission before using this take-out. The landowner is wary (and weary) of people crossing his land. Below this point, the river settles back to a scenic four-and-a-half-mile, Class II run with impressive bluffs and some interesting rapids. The gorge ends at the Arbor Chapel access. Below here, the river runs through a narrow farming valley, and Spring Creek and Blackburn Fork add their flows. Just below the mouth of the latter, at The Boils, a significant amount of additional river flow emerges from subterranean caverns. There are limestone bluffs to see and generally an easy, Class I float to the public take-out at Fish Barrier Dam.

# Calfkiller River

The Calfkiller River is an extremely serpentine stream that originates in southeastern Putnam County and wiggles its way south through White County en route to its mouth at the Caney Fork. Winding through rolling hills with occasional small rock bluffs, the corridor surrounding the basin is heavily populated and developed. Banks are shaded with sycamore and oak and vary in steepness. From the access near the Putnam County line to Sparta, the Calfkiller can be run from mid-December to late April and during periods of heavy rain. The river is narrow in this section—rarely exceeding 35 to 40 feet in width and averaging approximately 30 feet. The level of difficulty for this upper section is primarily Class I, with some borderline Class II stretches. Hazards in the upper section include deadfalls and a partially washed out dam midway to Sparta. Access along the upper section is good.

The Calfkiller runs through the west side of Sparta and widens to 50 to 60 feet before tumbling over a lethal dam above Sparta that must be portaged. Exiting Sparta on the south side, the stream returns to the rural surroundings of farm and woodland terrain. Midway between Sparta and the Caney Fork, the course of the Calfkiller becomes tortuously convoluted with one loop of the river following another. In the middle of this section the stream

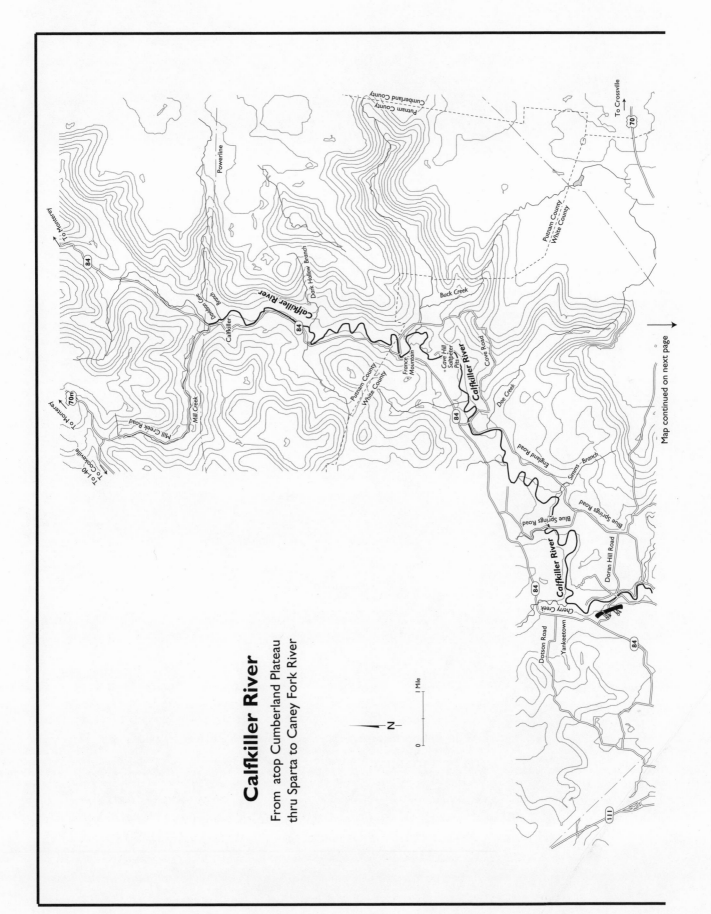

## Calfkiller River

From atop Cumberland Plateau
thru Sparta to Caney Fork River

Map continued on next page

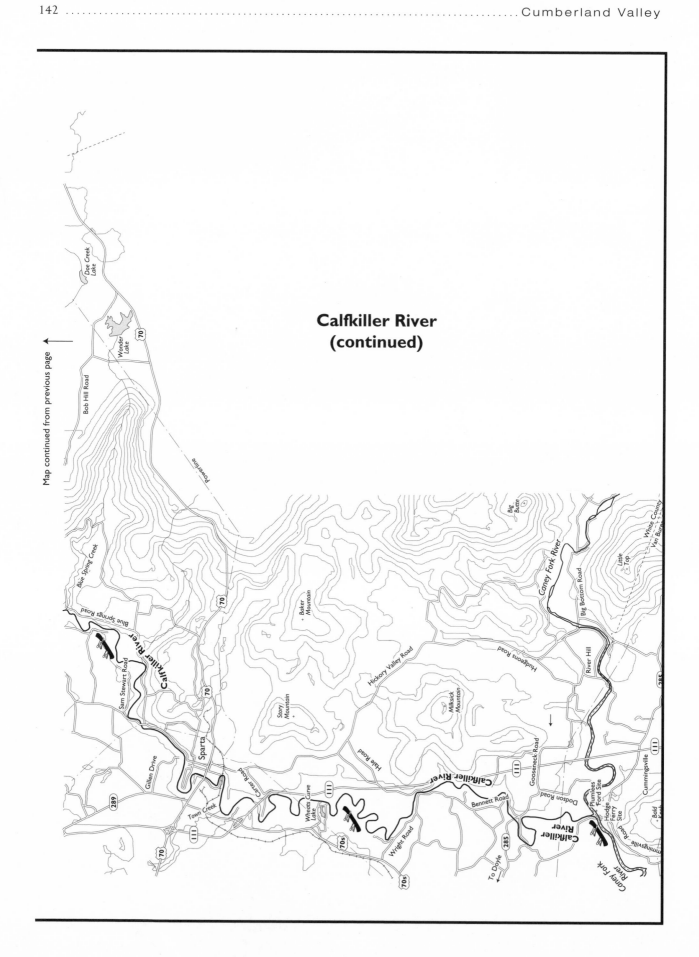

# Calfkiller River
# (continued)

is punctuated by a series of mild, borderline Class II rapids and ledges occurring at 150- to 200-yard intervals. Then the stream widens and straightens out somewhat as the terrain becomes more rugged and wooded. Below here the level of difficulty is Class I. From Sparta to the mouth at the Caney Fork access is limited and hazards to navigation are limited primarily to deadfalls and logjams at bridges. The Calfkiller below Sparta is runnable from late fall to the middle of June.

# Collins River

The Collins River is an inspirational stream. In fact it inspired the establishment of the State Scenic River system.

The upper Collins River is a beautiful, wooded, clear-water family float in Grundy and Warren Counties, with a surprisingly good flow level most of the year. But then again, most who know the sources of the Collins expect this river to provide excellent canoeing conditions. Probably the most primitive, pristine, and premier natural area in the state of Tennessee, the Savage Gulf complex forms the headwaters for the Collins River.

## Mucking About in Rivers

There are different types of river cleanups. The premier one is the neighborhood or regional kind. This entails extensive planning, logistics, and the involvement of the people who live in the area and local governments. It's an ambitious task.

While it's hard work for the organizers and participants, it serves many useful needs. It fosters a sense of community pride and group accomplishment. It brings together community organizations: scouts, neighborhood groups, local government, clubs—you name it—and instills in them a feeling of pride and responsibility for the condition of the stream and area.

Quite often this is also the only way to get the equipment needed to remove things in the streams that are large enough to eddy in.

Another type is the semi-official cleanup done by a group of boaters who are concerned about a place that is special to them. Often this takes the form of a trip planned around picking up what trash they can handle and have fun doing it. This brings together boaters who know and enjoy the same stream but don't necessarily know many of the people who share their waterway.

The kind of cleanup participated in the most often is totally unofficial. I make it a habit to pick things up as I paddle. It's a great way to practice ferrying, eddying, and leaning out on a paddle brace. If everyone who paddled participated, it would heighten the enjoyment for those who follow. If the group in front of you is practicing this time-tested technique, you will have an easier cleanup and more time to enjoy the scenery.

We have few enough free-flowing streams left in Tennessee. We need to do all we can to maintain the qualities we are there to enjoy. Please do your part, no matter whether it is to help organize a full-blown project or to pick up thoughtless people's residue.

—Bob Todd
Whites Creek, TN

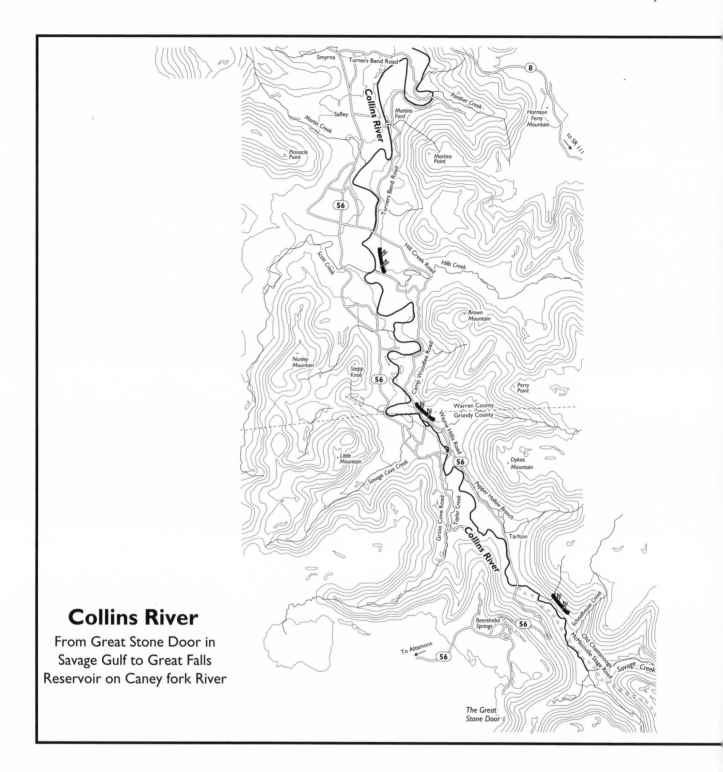

## Collins River

From Great Stone Door in
Savage Gulf to Great Falls
Reservoir on Caney fork River

     Three small creeks work their respective ways out of this heavily wooded, rim-sided, three-fingered complex: Savage Gulf, Collins Gulf, and Big Creek Gulf. From high atop the Great Stone Door on the western escarpment of the Cumberland Plateau, you can see these deep-cut feeder streams descending onto the lower Highland Rim from their respective highland Plateau gulfs. At the foot of the plateau, these streams combine their cascading waters to form the pastoral (and canoeable) stream, the Collins River. Much of the drainage flows from the heavily wooded gulfs, some of which still contain remnants of virgin forest.

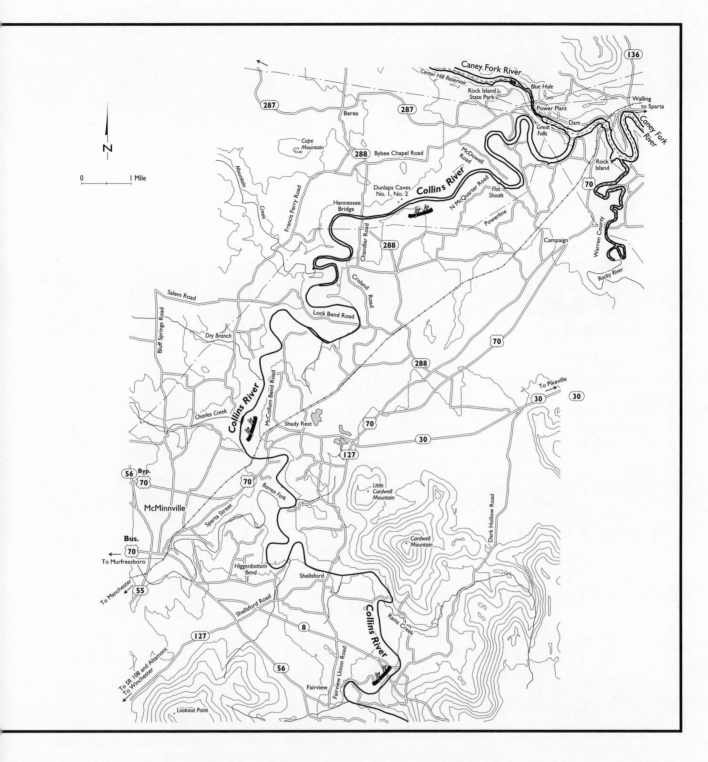

Yet another significant part of this flow comes from the Blue Hole of the Collins, where Big Spring emerges also at the plateau's foot. So clean, clear, flowing water await the paddler at the put-in of this newly combined stream.

The first 9 miles, from Mt. Olive to Irving College, are a real pastoral treat. During the next 14 miles, the residential character (and trash) increases, yet the general topography and scenery are still enjoyable. Finally the press of the suburbs of McMinnville overwhelm the rural waterway for the next 7 miles, until the backwaters of Great Falls Dam (on the Caney Fork

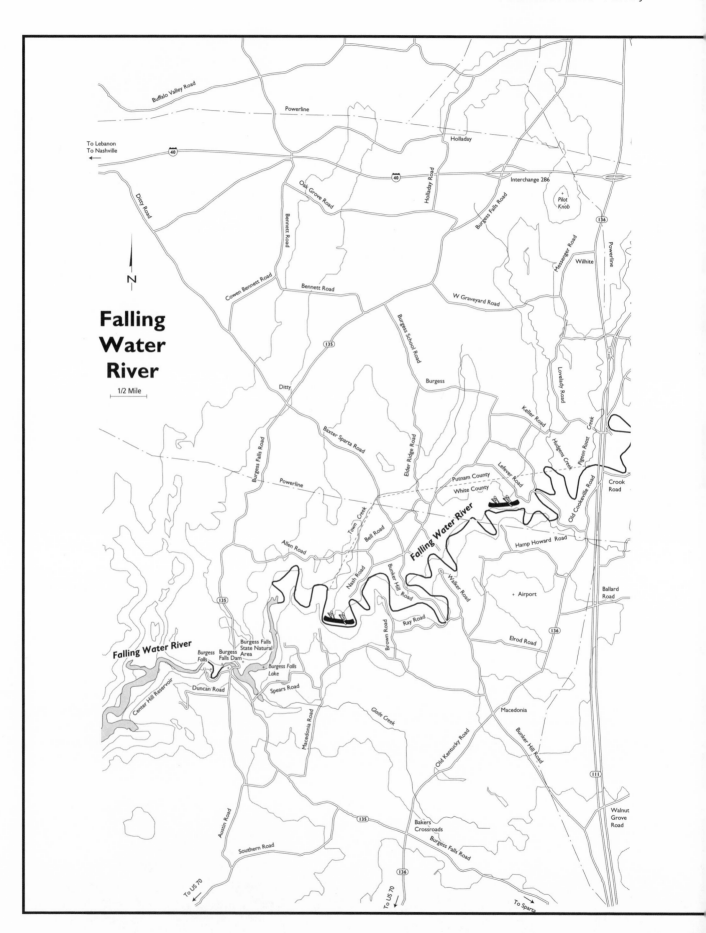

N

**Falling
Water
River**

1/2 Mile

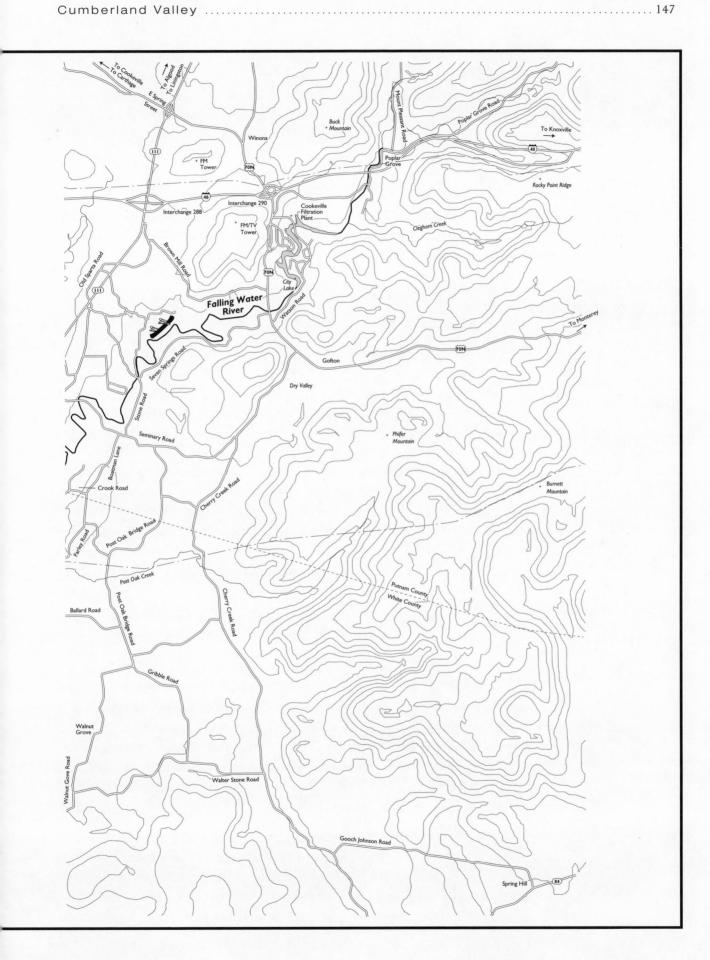

River). You may still canoe 20 more miles on riverine slackwater to just above the dam where the Collins joins the Caney Fork. Interestingly, the Collins parallels the Caney Fork, with a ridge separating the two channels. However, this parallel section of the Caney Fork is downstream of the Great Falls Dam, while the Collins is backed up by that same dam. That ridge separates two streambeds, each heading in opposite directions, and this whole mess is interrupted by the dam. The dam impounds and artificially raises the level of the Collins on the one side of the ridge, but only water released by the dam and flowing down the Caney Fork is in the unimpounded (lower) bed on the other side of the ridge. The interesting facet to all this is that the ridge leaks. So some of the Collins water bypasses the dam and cascades out of the downstream ridge face and tumbles down as a scenic waterfall into the Caney Fork riverbed below the dam, which therefore turns into kind of a naturally evolved unnatural waterfall.

# Falling Water River

Most of Falling Water River is flat; the rest is vertical. This river skirts metropolitan Cookeville and ends by dropping over 100-foot Burgess Falls into the tailwaters of Center Hill Lake. There are three longer than 7-mile, Class I segments of the Falling Water River that make nice pastoral, afternoon paddles for Cookeville canoeists. From the Old (US) Highway 70 crossing to TN 42 is an 8-mile run. (Watch for barbed wire across the river.) Continuing to Old Baxter–Sparta highway (Ditty Road) adds 7.4 miles; and on to Burgess Falls Dam (above the falls by the same name) adds yet another 7.1 miles. That's it for canoeing on the Falling Water River.

Below the dam is a short run of Class III water until you get to a 30-foot drop over a shoulder of rock (with a vertical fall on river's right). Downstream 150 yards is the sheer, 100-foot Burgess Falls. Below the dam is very dangerous and only navigable to experts who know and understand fully the consequences of any miscalculation or accident in those turbulent waters. There is really no reason to canoe below the dam.

# Smith Fork Creek

The paddler Ohio Knox once burst into a quiet, thoughtful canoe-oriented discussion between friends to announce excitedly that he had located "the largest creek in the world!" Who are we to doubt his well-traveled word? A little map work ascertained that, indeed, Smith Fork Creek traverses three counties and offers almost thirty miles of floating opportunities, but Ohio and his party are the only known boaters who have documented their visit. And shortly thereafter, Ohio moved to New Mexico. So with a caution that this is an unverified account, we bring you Ohio's description:

> Sometimes considered the largest creek in the world, Smith Fork Creek is a very pretty stream featuring scenery typical of the Middle Tennessee area. The creek flows gently over a bed of limestone with frequent, easy riffles and some deep pools. The water quality is good and is generally quite clear except after heavy rainfall when runoff from adjacent farms increases turbidity considerably.

Be cautious of the small mill dam on the stream, as well as occasional blow-downs. Upon reaching Liberty, the first high limestone bluffs are seen. Below Liberty, Smith Fork passes through a beautiful valley of farms and woodlands with pretty bluffs on the outside of major bends. Camping throughout the Smith Fork Creek is by permission of landowners only.

The trip can be extended by continuing past the TN 141 access two more miles to the Caney Fork River (near one of the I-40 crossings) and continuing three more miles down the Class I Caney Fork River to the community of Stonewall on country road 6299. The Caney Fork flow is dam controlled.

# Lower Caney Fork River

The lower sections of the Caney Fork River seem the exact opposite of their mountain brother of the upper stretches. Pastoral and generally well behaved, the Caney Fork flows leisurely below Dodson, in south-central White County, to the backwaters of the Great Falls Lake. Spending the last of its awesome energy in a few slightly higher than Class I riffles just below Dodson, the Caney Fork widens to 80 to 95 feet and flows placidly below well-vegetated, tall banks as it approaches the mouth of the Calfkiller River. The surrounding terrain is rolling farmland and woods. On the western end of Great Falls Lake at the mouth of the Collins River is the Great Falls powerhouse and dam. Below the dam begins the shortest run described in this book and possibly the shortest run described anywhere. Consisting of approximately 300 yards of river and two Class II (III) rapids with an easy shuttle back up to the top, the run is both entertaining and excellent for dry-weather practice. Runnable whenever the power plant is generating, the first rapid consists of big waves, while the second is nothing more than the river's last drop into the lake pool of Center Hill Lake.

In northern DeKalb County, below Center Hill Dam, the Caney Fork is once again released and sent on its way. From here to its mouth at the Cumberland River near Carthage in Smith County, the Lower Caney Fork winds beneath majestic limestone palisades and meanders through fertile farmland and shady woods. Water levels will vary considerably according to how much (if any) water is being discharged at the dam. While running fast and deep when the power plant is going full tilt, the Caney Fork is littered with gravel bars when the generators are shut down. Camping along the Caney Fork below the vegetation line or on gravel bars is not recommended, since water levels can fluctuate widely and without warning, subject to the dam releases.

# Bledsoe Creek

Can determined boaters "create" an entirely new waterway? A while back, a few gas-conscious canoeists in Gallatin, in Sumner County, grew tired of traveling the state in search of free-flowing waters. They pooled their resources and bought a topo map to see what might flow near their own back doors. And that was the start of another American mini success story.

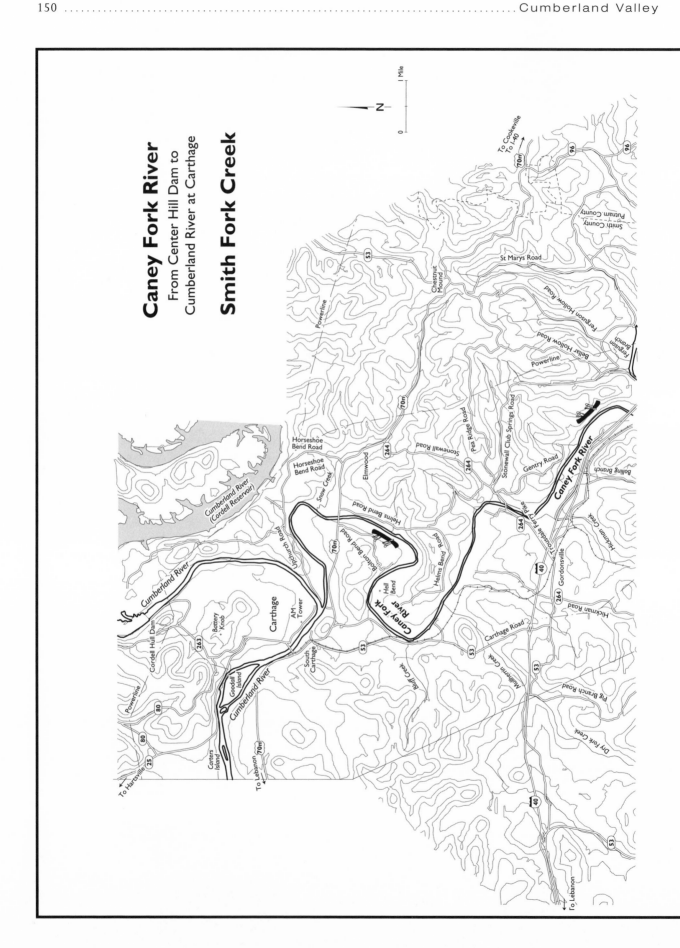

**Caney Fork River**
From Center Hill Dam to
Cumberland River at Carthage

**Smith Fork Creek**

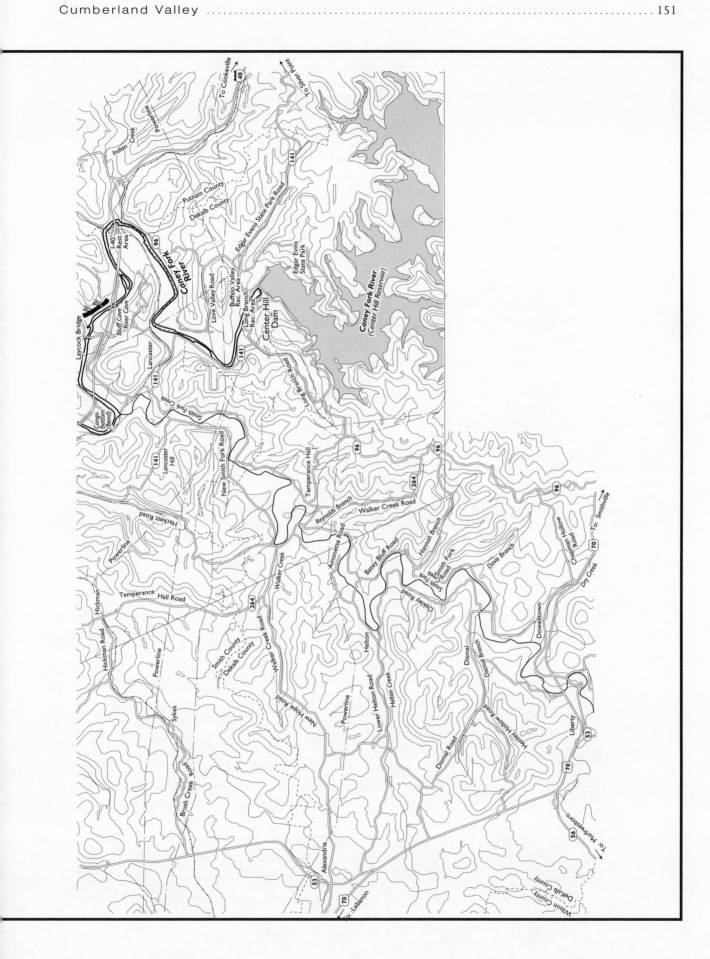

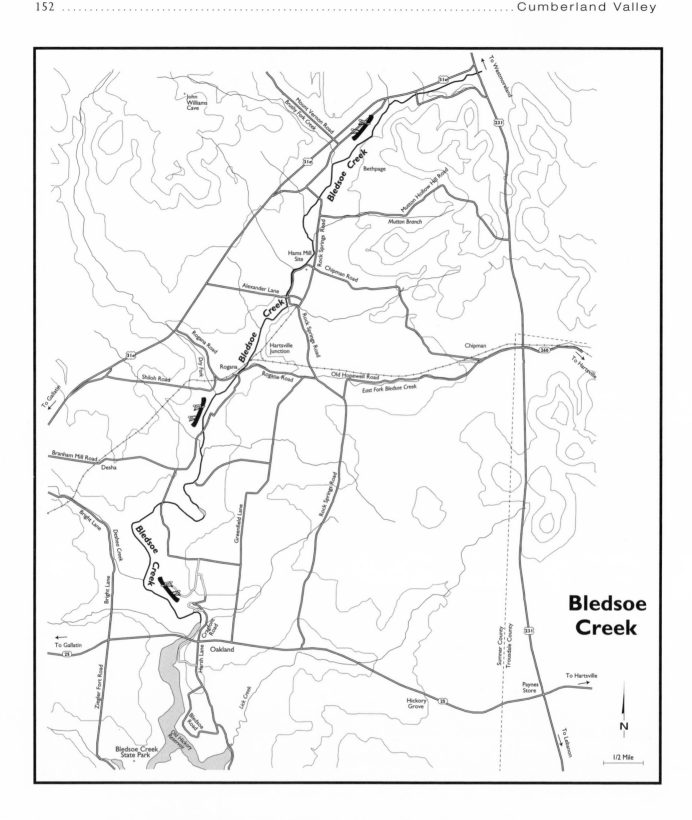

**Bledsoe Creek**

Through clever reckoning and daring exploration, they established the 5.3-mile Bledsoe Creek canoe trip and immediately issued a call to all the canoeists of the state to join them on this Class I adventure. Since their announcement happened to coincide with the dead of the winter and nothing else was happening anyway, their call actually attracted a contingent of Nashville floaters who had opted to sleep late on those cold winter mornings and, hence, could not get any farther away from town anyway due to the seasonal shortness of daylight. And the traditional midwinter Bledsoe Creek trip was born.

This is a pleasant 5.3-mile, three-hour float over riffles and shoals with relatively clean water (as clean as you could expect through the heart of active farmland), a rockbed, and mudbanks. Small limestone bluffs will be found at times, cattle crossings at others. (Cows can be unpredictable; canoes have been stepped on in Bledsoe.) The stream moves quickly, and, midway down, the winterized paddlers will find a five-foot, double-ledge drop, a Class II rapid.

As the backwaters of Old Hickory Lake still the flow, the creekbed rounds a scenic, low, bluff-lined bend and an obvious swimming hole is entered. Up to the left and across a field is the back door of a big stone house: Cragfont, built by Gen. James Winchester around 1800. This home is open for tours and visits by back door canoeists are acceptable. From here to the fishing ramp at TN 25 you will be paddling Old Hickory slackwater (and breaking ice if your timing is right). Bledsoe is best run when water levels are generally high.

# The Stones River System

The Stones River offers canoeists of the highly populated (Nashville) Central Basin a pleasant rural float near their back doorsteps. Almost in the epicenter of the state, in Wilson, Cannon, Rutherford, and Davidson Counties, this river system drains the surrounding Highland Rim and flows through the basin's premier bluegrass region until the flowing waters finally meet Nashville's Cumberland River just east of the capitol city. There may be no other tributary river in the state more steeped in Tennessee history than the Stones. At the river's confluence, John Donelson and Andrew Jackson set up their baronial homesteads a few short years after establishing the rest of their flatboat companions in and around Fort Nashboro. Later, Civil War battles seesawed across the river. Now Opryland, USA, shares those same rivermouth bluffs, and country music echoes upriver off the modern suburban countryside.

Upriver on the Stones, and upstream of the major U.S. Army Corps of Engineers' J. Percy Priest impoundment, you will find eleven small mill dams (on the three main branches of the river), attesting to the density of the early settlements along the waterway—a high enough dam density to allow the pioneer grain grower better bartering terms when he decided it was time to grind his grist. The main river forks have canoeable flows most of the year, but after spring rains upstream tributaries offer exciting runs. Bradley Creek, Cripple Creek, and Overall Creek are floatable in season. (Overall Creek has the best rapid in the central basin, about a hundred yards south of Old Nashville Highway. This is a double ledge with an eight-foot drop. There's just enough room, twenty feet, to recover between the ledges.)

## Stones River, East Fork

This whole stretch is usually very clear, clean-looking water. From Woodbury to Readyville, you will find a ten-mile, pastoral float with a few ripples and some fast bends to the river. The backwater means you are approaching the dam for Readyville Mill (watch out for some single-strand fence wire across the river in a couple of places). The historic Readyville Mill

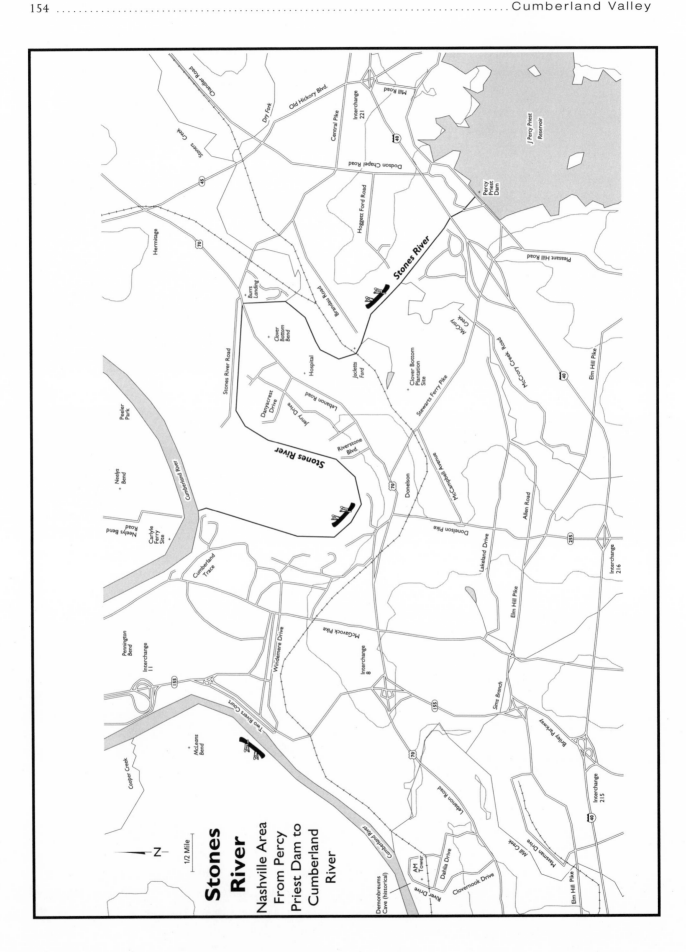

**Stones River**

Nashville Area From Percy Priest Dam to Cumberland River

should be visited before you start on downriver toward Halls Hill Pike. One can purchase waterground flour and many other items at the mill and store.

At about two miles down, there's a concrete slab, low-water bridge that usually needs to be portaged. Below Halls Hill Pike, the stream meanders past more farmland and interesting bends until you come to the old log-mill dam about 3.8 miles below the pike. This dam is breached in the center, leaving a 12-foot chute. Portage or scout before running to make sure the chute is clear and the water level safe. (The old mill burned out about 1975.) Below this mill the riverside scenery picks up with high banks and bluffs.

About 3 miles below the burnt mill, Cripple Creek enters on the left, adding significant flow. The 6.5 miles from Browns Mill Road to Lascassas Pike is one of the most scenic stretches of the river, a winding stream with high rock bluffs.

About 1.5 miles down, pooling will be noticed as you approach Browns Mill Dam. The old mill is still operable and a most impressive structure at over 80 feet high. You will come on the mill and dam rather suddenly. Portage the dam on the left side. A handy abutment extends back at an angle from the dam face. The dam is closed and posted. There has been vandalism. The owner has been happy to allow responsible canoeists to enjoy the stream and admire the mill, but do not trespass.

Then start back to the flow and the beautiful rock bluffs, swift turns, wildlife, and wildflowers. There is a fun rapid to play at the next bridge. The take-out there is easier than the one 3.6 miles on down at Betty Ford Road. At the latter, one must traverse a very high 75-degree angled concrete ramp for about 20 feet to reach the road. It's difficult, but not impossible. Pooling begins about two miles after Betty Ford Road from the back-up of the old Walter Hill Dam. The Murfreesboro water intake is about two miles above the dam (on the left). The large, estate-like VA hospital grounds are on the left just beyond this. Take-out is about a hundred yards above the dam at a boat ramp on the left. Portage the dam. There is a nice parkside put-in below the dam. You now have two to three miles of free-flowing river left before the J. Percy Priest impoundment. Take out at the Corps of Engineers' Mona Ramp off Jefferson Pike on the right.

## Stones River, Middle Fork

With spring flow, you can put-in at the Elam Road, concrete-slab, low-water bridge just below a small dam for a nice scenic five-mile float to Shelbyville Highway (US 231). This float can be stretched another mile to Salem Pike (TN 99) if you don't mind portaging three dams during this mile run. Most choose to cartop that stretch. Just above the TN 99 bridge, the higher-flow West Fork joins the Middle Fork to make a year-round floatable stream.

## Stones River, West Fork

During high springtime flows the upper West Fork (above the Middle Fork junction) can be run. This is a popular float because it has some good Class II water (right in the center of the Central Basin). Put in at Walnut Grove Road and take out four miles downstream at Crescent Road. The next 2.5-mile run is inadvisable because a private owner has built a dam upstream of the next bridge (Barfield Road) and will not allow trespass on his property for portaging of his dam. Below Barfield Road you will find a fast, exciting run, but care must be taken at two low-water bridges that should be portaged. This is a short, three-mile run

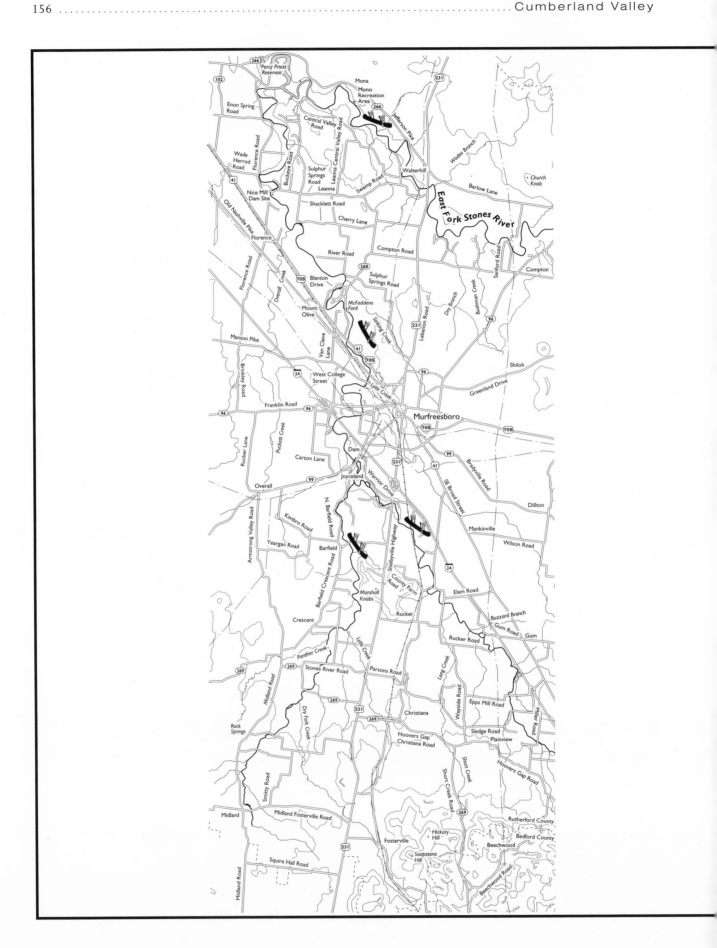

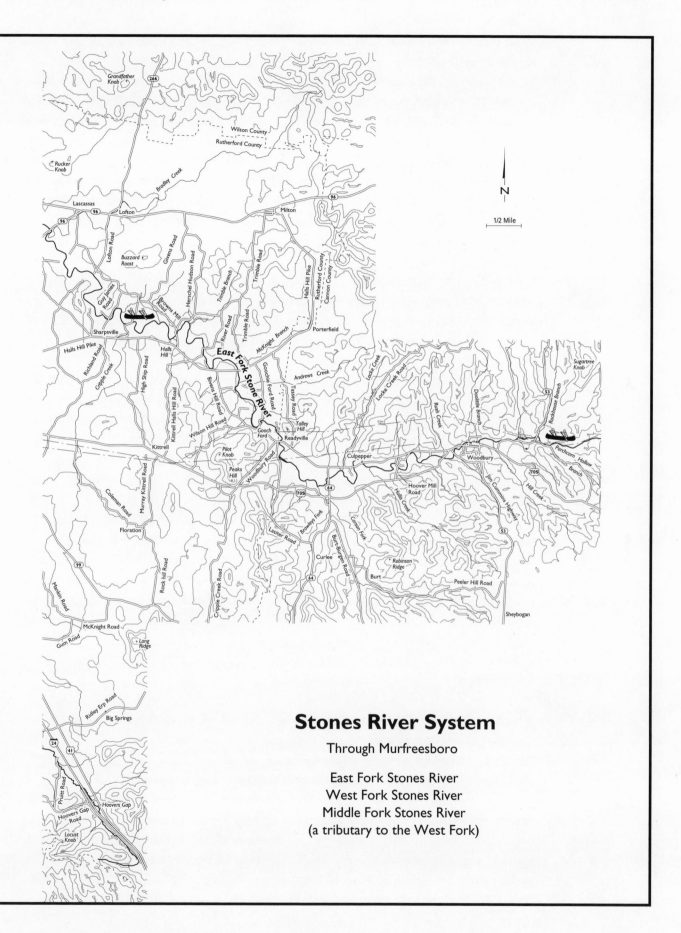

**Stones River System**

Through Murfreesboro

East Fork Stones River
West Fork Stones River
Middle Fork Stones River
(a tributary to the West Fork)

to the pool above the dam under Salem Pike (TN 99) where the Middle Fork joins the West Fork. Portage the dam on the right side and continue for a short interesting float under I-24 and under the old Franklin Road bridge. Better access is found at the new Franklin Road bridge (TN 96) near the freeway. Below here, on the right, is the old Fort Park, now a Murfreesboro City Park. However, only a short section of the stream is free flowing, as it quickly enters the pool area behind the Sportsman Club Dam at Manson Pike. Take out at the right at the Sportsman Club. The dam has a current around the left side that forms a sharp drop over rocks that diverts a canoe to a parallel course with the dam face if one tries to run it. It is a tricky maneuver to pull away from the lethal curl at the dam face caused from the overflow. This run has been fatal. It is strongly advised to portage and put in well away from the back flow.

Below this dam is one of the most exciting runs on the West Fork. However, the river runs through Murfreesboro and the pollution and trash through the upper section are unsightly and discouraging. There are several drops with a nice falls, Chris's Crunch, beside the Stones River Country Club golf course. From this point on, beautiful homes and back yards belie the upstream pollution. After the above rapid, access can be found at Thompson Lane.

The final ten miles of this stream to Nices Mill Recreational Area on Percy Priest impoundment make for a continuation of pleasant pastoral midstate floating. The wildflowers are beautiful. There is enough drop to make the float interesting. Immediately to the left after the bridge, a stone wall marks the spot where 18,000 soldiers fell in the Battle of Stones River in the Civil War. This national monument on the banks of the stream is a popular picnic area. About two and a half miles downriver you cross under a new high bridge and come to a low, two-and-a-half-foot dam with a easy run. The dam is a momentary catch for the effluent from the nearby modern sewage treatment plant. It is a good plant, but you must still realize that you are sharing the river with the people of Murfreesboro, and you will have every reason to hit that chute square in the center. There is more pastoral floating below the drop, then you come to the pool behind the old Nices Mill Dam. Here is the useful Corps of Engineers take-out ramp. At times, there is a mile more below the dam that is free flowing before the impoundment slackwater, but take-out from J. Percy Priest Reservoir is difficult.

# Sycamore Creek

A bubbling and lively Class I stream, Sycamore Creek is born in southern Robertson County and flows southwestward across Cheatham County before running into the Cumberland River. Treelined and studded with gravel bars and brushy islands, Sycamore Creek runs over a rocky mud bottom between three- to six-foot mudbanks. The scenery is superb. It consists of rugged rolling hills, exposed rock bluffs, and cultivated bottomland, alternating with stands of hardwood forest. Paddling is both brisk and enjoyable, with rippling shoals and numerous navigational challenges as the stream snakes around small islands. The level of difficulty is Class I or higher throughout, with strainers and a mill dam being the primary hazards to navigation. The stream's width averages from 30 to 40 feet. Access is fair to good. Sycamore Creek is floatable below US 41A during the spring and following periods of heavy rain.

## The First (Actually, the Second) State Scenic Rivers Act.

Passage of the Tennessee Scenic Rivers Act was not easy. In fact Tennessee was one of the first states in the nation to move in this direction. (Although actions by both states predated national legislation, actually Ohio beat Tennessee by six months in getting its state scenic river system signed into law.) In the early 1960s, legislators throughout the country recognized the beauty and the value of maintaining our rivers. There were many expressions of interest and support for free-flowing rivers in Tennessee with particular attention placed on the whitewater gorges of the Obed and the pastoral, fishing-renowned Buffalo. On the other hand, at the time, and regularly thereafter, misinformation and miscommunication have triggered negative reactions from some landowners on various designated rivers who felt that their ability to farm and utilize their lands as they see fit would be permanently impaired. The need for broad-based education and focused communications seems to be an enduring lesson we have learned since the enactment of our state's system. Time and again rivers have been removed from the system due to local political actions. The intent of the legislation was laudable but it remains to be seen if we can learn to balance the interests of all involved to protect the rights of the landowners, the rights of the public and the natural right of the rivers to remain free flowing, clean, and clear.

—Victor Ashe
Knoxville, Tennessee

## Big Turnbull Creek

Big Turnbull Creek—or simply Turnbull Creek as it's sometimes known—runs north through southeastern Dickson County and the southwestern corner of Cheatham County before reaching its terminus at the Harpeth River at Kingston Springs. A narrow, meandering stream, Turnbull Creek flows through cultivated bottomland bordered by wooded, rolling hills. From time to time, high, timbered bluffs extend to the river's edge. The stream's level of difficulty is Class I, with numerous gravel bars and small, channel-constricting brush islands to keep the paddling lively. Hazards to navigation consist of deadfalls and logjams. The stream's width averages from 30 to 40 feet. Turnbull Creek is runnable in spring and during periods of heavy rain downstream of the TN 96 bridge. Access is available but difficult.

## Harpeth River

In the heart of Middle Tennessee, the Harpeth offers a change of pace for the thousands of metropolitan residents who know enough to walk out their back doors and cart their gear to the nearest neighborhood put-in. The Harpeth is a State Scenic River within Nashville's Davidson County. It is also a stream with over one hundred rural miles of Class I floating, from upstream of Franklin (in Williamson County, near Harpeth River mile 90) to the Cheatham pool on the Cumberland River (in Cheatham County at Cumberland River mile 152.9).

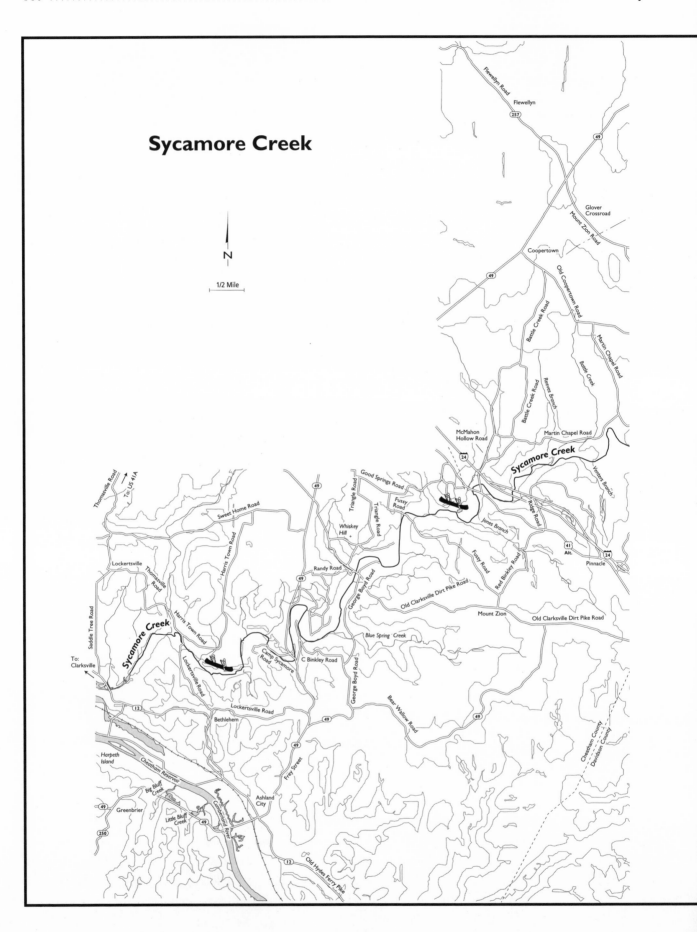

**Sycamore Creek**

N

1/2 Mile

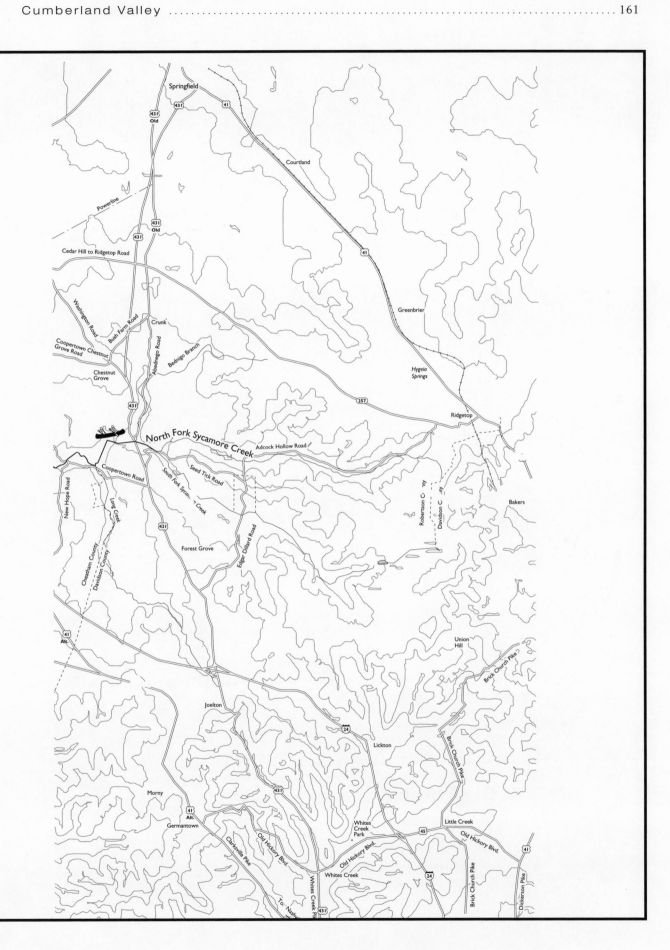

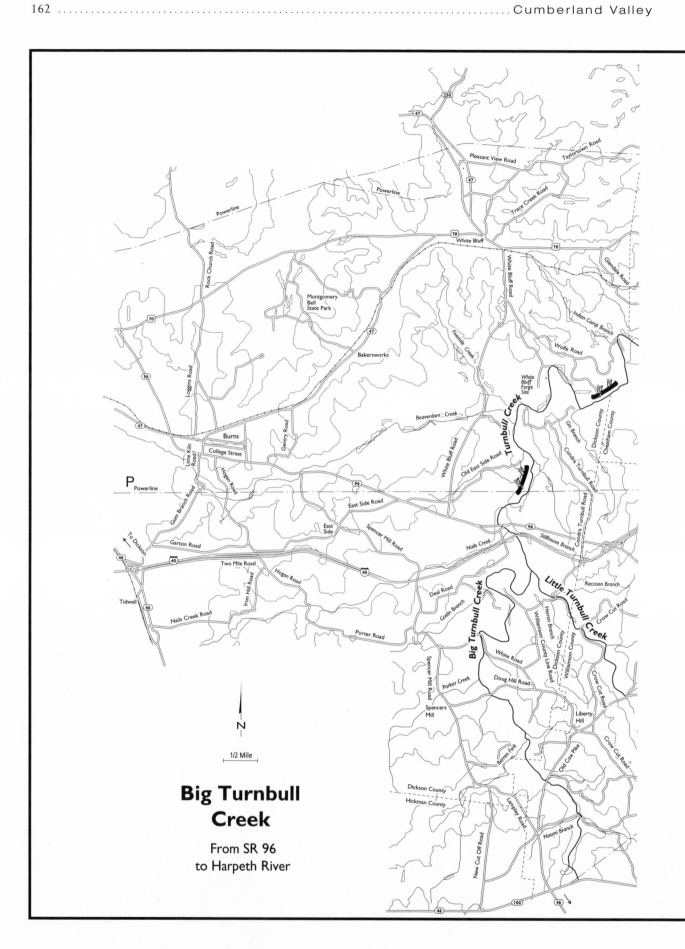

# Big Turnbull Creek

From SR 96
to Harpeth River

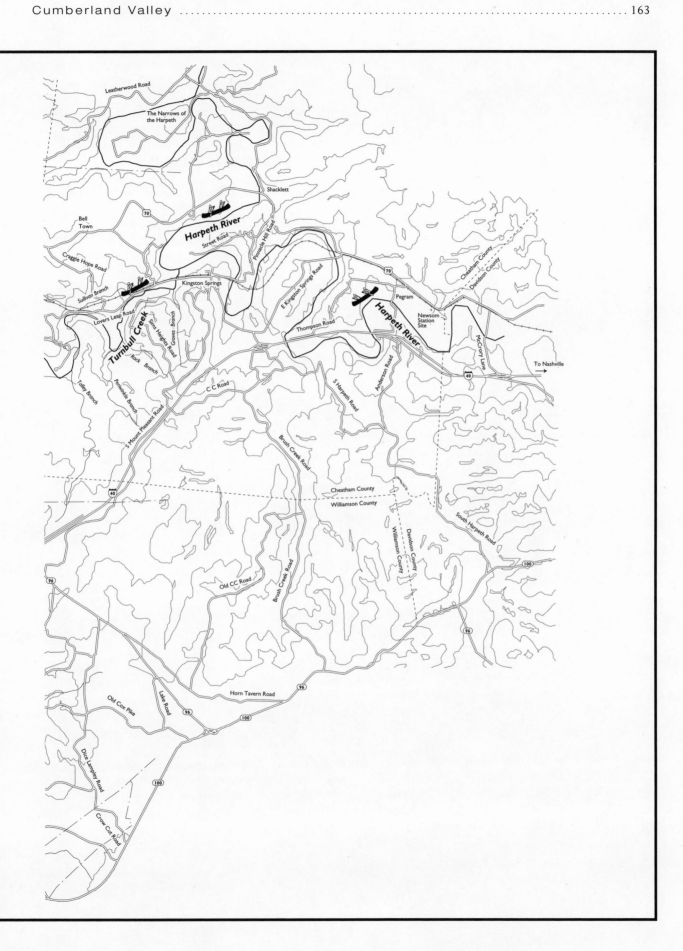

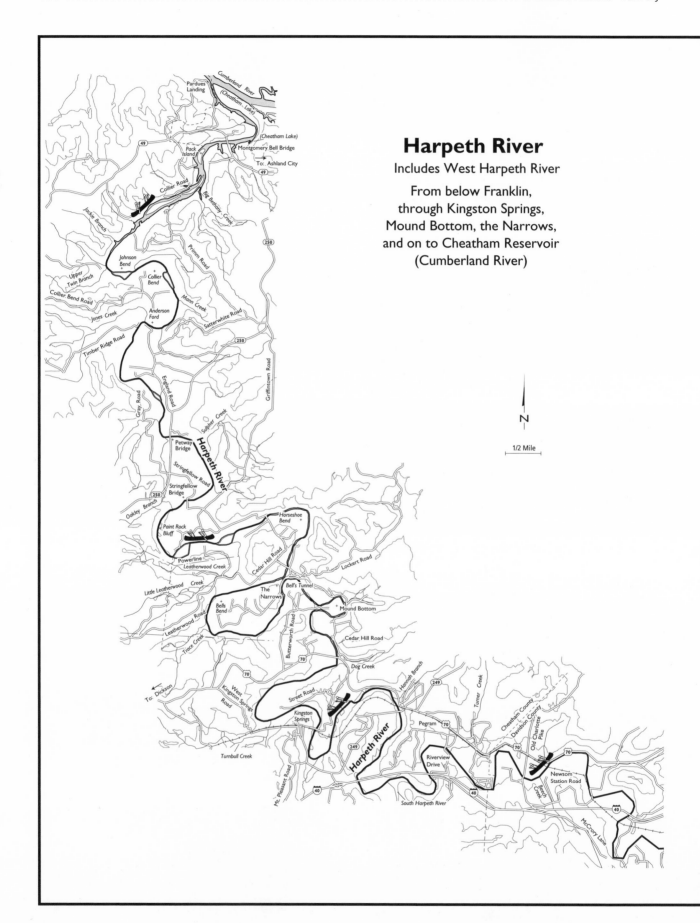

# Harpeth River

Includes West Harpeth River

From below Franklin,
through Kingston Springs,
Mound Bottom, the Narrows,
and on to Cheatham Reservoir
(Cumberland River)

N

1/2 Mile

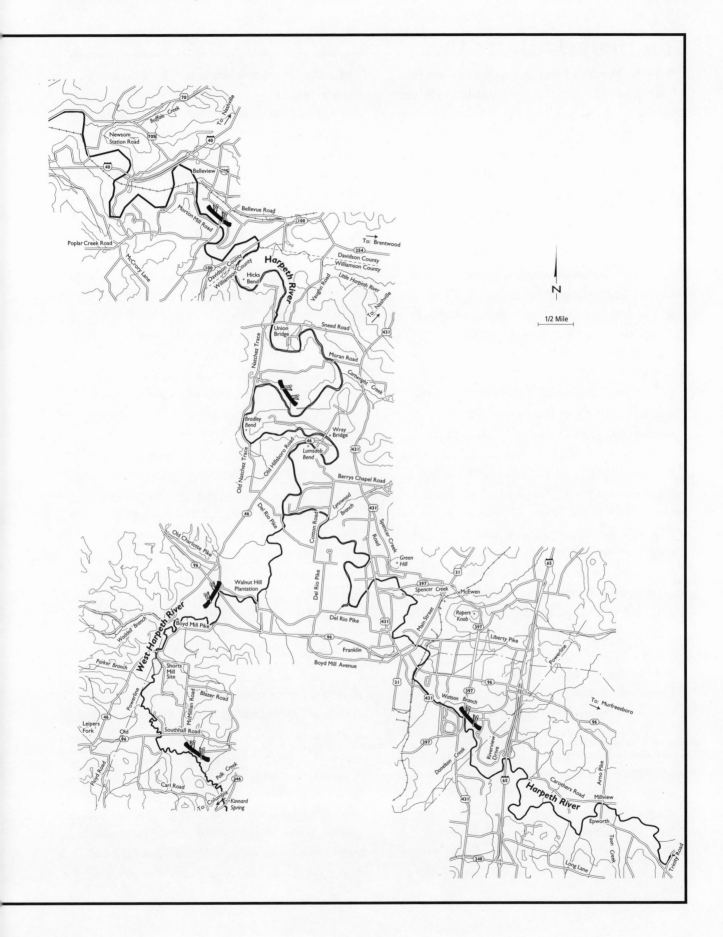

# The Historic Harpeth

The Harpeth River and its tributaries—the Little Harpeth, South Harpeth, and West Harpeth—form one of the true river treasures of Middle Tennessee. Beginning in Rutherford County, the river flows 117 miles through five counties before emptying into the Cumberland below Ashland City.

The valleys of the Harpeth are rich in history. Five major archaeological sites are located along the river, and there are at least two ancient rock paintings and one petroglyph on bluffs along and overlooking the river. Mound Bottom, situated in a bend of the Harpeth in Cheatham County, is one of the largest prehistoric human habitation sites in the southeastern United States.

At the Narrows of the Harpeth, a state-owned historic site, the river makes a six-mile bend and returns to within 180 feet of itself. Sometime around 1804, Montgomery Bell, one of the area's earliest settlers, realized that the fifteen-foot drop in elevation on the downstream side of the Narrows presented a commercial opportunity. Utilizing slave labor, Bell constructed a tunnel through the rock ridge separating the two sections of river. He then established the Pattison Iron Works at the outfall, using gravity flow to power the mill wheel. It is believed that many of the cannonballs used in the War of 1812 were made at this site. Bell lived at the top of the hill overlooking the Narrows. He died there in 1855 and is buried across the river in a small grove of trees.

The Natchez Trace crossed the Harpeth and the Little Harpeth in Williamson County, and Andrew Jackson, Aaron Burr, Meriwether Lewis, and other early pioneers, bandits, boatmen, and soldiers passed that way. The Harpeth flows past antebellum homes and mills and through the fields where the Battle of Franklin was fought in 1864. Over 6,000 Confederates

and 2,300 Union soldiers lost their lives along the Harpeth.

Although the Harpeth could certainly be considered "stressed" and "threatened," it has escaped outright ecological disaster. There are no dams along the entire length of the river. Water quality is a visible problem most of the year because of agricultural runoff. The exception is the winter season when the sediments settle, and the clear, sparkling water makes the Harpeth a delight to paddle.

Most of the Harpeth and its tributaries drain rural farmland. However, it has suffered also from urban pollution and runoff. Several years ago a large number of battery casings were found in the Harpeth where it passes through Franklin, and fish kills from city sewage used to be a common occurrence. Williamson County has been Tennessee's fastest-growing county over the past decade, and that development and its resultant runoff have posed new threats for the river. Similarly, a considerable amount of new development has occurred in southwestern Davidson County that could also become a problem. The river now borders the area's newest, and one of its largest, shopping mall complexes.

The Harpeth was designated as one of the state's first scenic rivers when the Scenic Rivers Act was passed in the late 1960s. However, because of opposition by private landowners, all of the river except the eleven-mile portion in Davidson County was removed from the act the following year.

In recent years a group of citizens in Williamson County have formed the Harpeth River Coalition to gather information about the river, monitor what is happening to it, and educate local citizens about the wonderful resource that is literally in their backyard. Thus far, however, large landholders along the Harpeth and its tributaries have resisted efforts to bring the Williamson County section of the Harpeth under state protection again.

An effort has been underway in Davidson County to build a greenway along a segment of the Harpeth that runs through a residential area. Such a greenway would increase recreational opportunities and enhance the property values of adjacent landowners, so one would expect that such a proposal would be favorably received. Instead, there has been nearly irrational opposition. There are, clearly, apprehensions about opening up private property for public use, and residents cite the fear of increased crime as one of the major reasons for resisting the greenway concept. They apparently believe that a greenway would provide a new venue for attack by muggers and rapists and a new avenue of escape for burglars!

Anyone who has been around rivers very much knows the basis for the resistance to public access. Rivers—especially at isolated bridge crossings—have often been where rowdies congregate to shoot guns, party, get drunk, and dump trash. The fact that river conservationists are not the ones who do these kinds of things

cuts little ice, and the recent renewed resistance to any regulatory or governmental "taking" of private property has further decreased the prospects for expanded public use of rivers.

Except for an annual spring flood or two, the Harpeth and its tributaries are the gentlest of streams. They are pastoral, wooded, mostly shallow, and quite scenic. They provide abundant and perfect opportunities for family recreation such as canoeing, wading, fishing, and learning about river ecology. Greenways would add walking, jogging, photography, and perhaps bicycling to that list.

As more and more development and growth occur along the Harpeth, there will be also an increased demand for public recreation. The pressure will increase, and sooner or later landowners will come to realize that a protected river and regulated use of it and its corridor are in their best interests as well as those of the public. And in the populated Middle Tennessee area, this gem of a riverway winds through the rural and urban countryside awaiting its deserved protection.

—Ed Young
Nashville, TN

The Harpeth means history! The farther downstream you travel, the further back in time you reach. This major historical conduit will float you through the disastrous Franklin battlefield of the Civil War; then it will take you further back to an outlaw time along the Natchez Trace; finally. you are in the heart of a pre-Indian culture circa A.D. 1200. A sampling of places to look for includes:

River mile 73: The old Natchez Trace stone bridge over an incoming tributary.

River mile 61: Bellevue Methodist Church (1912); Riverside (1860); Bellevue I (1787).

River mile 54: Newsom Mill (1862), a state restoration project.

River Mile 33: Mound Bottom, a bend in the river now owned by the state, with ceremonial and burial mounds dating to prehistoric times. A petroglyph scepter appears on a bluff on the other side of the river overlooking the ceremonial sites.

River mile 30: The entrance to Montgomery Bell's 1819 diversion tunnel. This is an 8-foot-high-by-16-foot-wide tunnel driven through solid rock under a piece of the land called The Narrows. The river flows over five miles around a big bend coming back to within 200 feet of itself on the other side of this narrow ridge. During the river's low stage, Bell's diversion tunnel is capable of delivering 40 cfs over the 15-foot drop in the river between the two points. He used this head to power an iron forge.

River mile 26: Montgomery Bell's grave, across the river from his tunnel's outfall.

River mile 21: Impressive, 200-foot bluffs. Another prehistoric petroglyph painted on the bluff, which apparently represents the sun and moon.

The Harpeth system is generally pastoral with a few solid Class II rapids thrown in to wake the paddler up. In Williamson County, the stream is generally in a limestone bed with mudbanks. In Davidson County, it is mud with mud. In Cheatham County, where the river cuts into the Western Highland Rim, the bottom remains mud, but the banks begin to firm up and limestone bluffs begin to appear. The last five miles will be on the Harpeth's backwaters of the Cumberland River's downstream Cheatham Dam. Many of the upper river miles are held by private landowners. Do not trespass or camp.

# West Harpeth River

If there is enough water to float on the Harpeth main stem near Franklin, then there will be enough water to float on the West Harpeth below Leipers Fork. And, in fact, the trip might be more enjoyable on the west side of the river system. The West Harpeth is not a wilderness stream, but its setting is rural and access is good. This is the Harpeth system's own "Franklin bypass." Although floatable water levels are sparse that far upstream in the watershed, the river keeps its character, and the fishing is considered good by locals all the way upstream from Leipers Fork to the US 31 bridge. There has been a lot of history played out, back and forth across the low banks of the shallow, riffled West Harpeth. Its a good off-season float when the water table is charged and the rest of the world is watching the bowl games.

# The Red River System

The Red River originates in Sumner County, Tennessee, and flows north into Kentucky, draining northern Sumner and Robertson Counties in Tennessee and Simpson and Logan Counties in Kentucky before dropping back into Tennessee through Robertson and Montgomery Counties en route to its mouth at the Cumberland River near Clarksville. In both Kentucky and Tennessee, the Red is a pleasant pastoral stream running over a rock, sand, and clay bottom within thickly shaded and heavily vegetated, tall banks. Surrounding terrain consists of fertile, gently rolling farmland.

The North Fork of the Red River is runnable downstream from Prices Mill in Kentucky from late November through early June. West of Adairville, Kentucky, near the small town of Dot, the South Fork of the Red joins the North Fork. From here to its mouth

**Red River System**
Red River
Sulphur Fork Red River

N

1/2 Mile

Continued on next page

the Red is runnable all year in years of average rainfall. The South Fork is runnable only from Adairville to its confluence with the North Fork from December through mid-April. Like the North Fork, the South Fork is winding, shaded, and cozy. Deadfalls caused by bankside erosion are a problem on both forks, while a series of old mill dams from Prices Mill to just below the KY 591 bridge necessitate several portages on the North Fork.

The level of difficulty for both of the forks is Class I or higher, with enough ripples, sandbars, and shallows to ensure an active trip. The average width of the North Fork is approximately 55 feet, while the more diminutive South Fork averages 45 feet (broadening

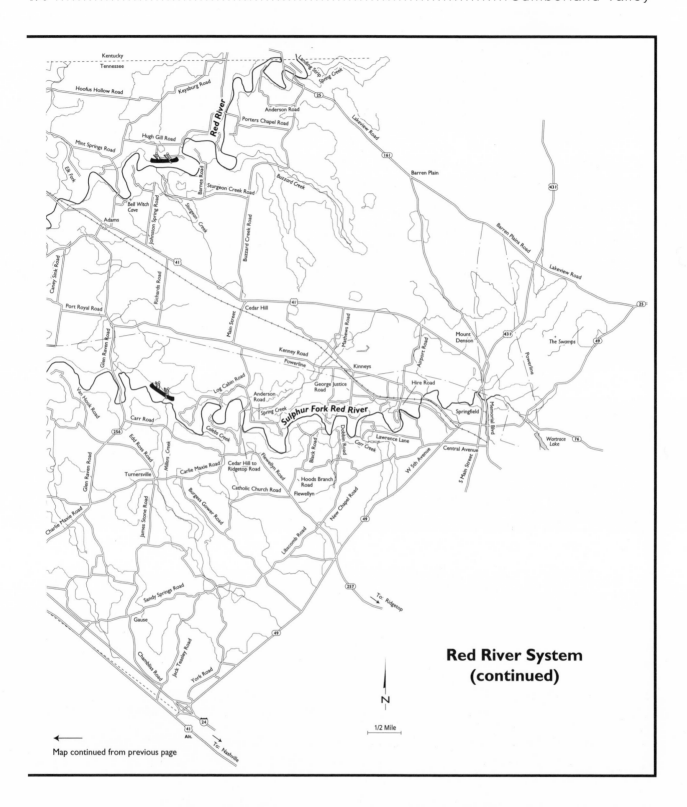

**Red River System
(continued)**

N

1/2 Mile

Map continued from previous page

to around 65 feet at its mouth). Below the confluence of the forks, ripples and small shoals occur less frequently and the river widens noticeably. Streamside terrain and flora remain much the same in this lower section, and the river continues to meander in serpentine fashion. The level of difficulty is still Class I, as long sluggish pools replace the swiftly moving current characteristic of the two forks.

## Sulphur Fork Creek

At historically rich Port Royal, the Red River is joined by Sulphur Fork Creek, which flows west from Robertson County near Springfield, one of Tennessee's earliest settlements. A small, intimate stream from thirty-five to fifty-five feet in width, hardwood canopied, and following a convoluted course, Sulphur Fork Creek is primarily a wet-weather stream running through woodland and rolling farm terrain. Sulphur Fork Creek is Class I water with plentiful small riffles. It can be run downstream from the TN 76 bridge.

Navigational hazards on Sulphur Fork Creek include deadfalls and Hills Mill Dam just upstream of the TN 76 bridge near Walnut Grove. From the mouth of Sulphur Fork Creek there is little change downstream until the Red River enters the more densely populated environs of Clarksville. Entering Clarksville, the scenery remains pleasant as it winds beneath the beautiful homes of an exclusive residential neighborhood. From shortly upstream of the L&N bridge to the confluence, however, the Red runs through an industrial area with debris in the stream and several ugly mining excavations visible. The Red River and its main tributaries are well suited to day cruising since they have many points of access. In that almost all land along the river and its forks is privately owned, however, canoe camping is not recommended.

# Tennessee Valley—West

## Elk River

The Elk is one of Tennessee's friendly, pastoral rivers. Originating in Grundy County, the Elk curves through Franklin, Moore, Lincoln, and Giles Counties before tipping south of the border into Alabama en route to its mouth at the Tennessee River southwest of Athens, Alabama. One of the state's longer drainages, the Elk runs approximately 220 miles from headwaters to mouth; 180 of these miles are in Tennessee.

Flowing along a convoluted course characterized by continuous broad loops, the Elk drops off the Cumberland Plateau onto the Eastern Highland Rim and then along the southern perimeter of the Nashville Central Basin. Above Woods Lake the Elk is difficult to catch at a runnable level. Terrain in the headwaters is rolling to rugged, with steep, wooded hills

## Bluebell Island—A Sparkling Gem of Nature

Bluebell Island is located in the Elk River about a half mile downstream from Patterson Ford Bridge on Tennessee Highway 50 (one mile west of I-24). Each Spring, toward the end of March, the island is covered with wildflowers, notably the Virginia Bluebell (Mertensia virginica).

Dr. Harry Yeatman of the University of the South has found and photographed the endangered dwarf Trillium, Trillium puscillum, on the island. The trees on all but two acres of the island have never been cut and include a fine example of swamp hardwoods (water oak, willow oak, swamp chestnut oak, black willow), mixed mesophytic (basswood, buckeye, and black cherry), riverine species (river birch, sycamore, and ironwood), and limestone indicators (red cedar and redbud). Because it is an island, Bluebell has rarely seen any disturbance. You literally cannot walk on the island in the springtime without stepping on flowers!

Bluebell Island has been a target for the Tennessee Nature Conservancy for many years, and the island has been high on the Tennessee Protection Planning List. Bluebell Island has also been a target for wildflower sellers, who have been sneaking in to steal the island's wealth; and an adjacent landowner recently tried to divert the river through the middle of the island in order to acquire more land for himself.

The South Cumberland Regional Land Trust (Box 615, Monteagle, TN 37356) has obtained an option on the island and is raising the money for purchase at publication time.

—Doug Cameron
Sewanee, TN

# Elk River

### (Includes Tims Ford Reservoir and Woods Reservoir)

N

1/2 Mile

Map continued on next page →

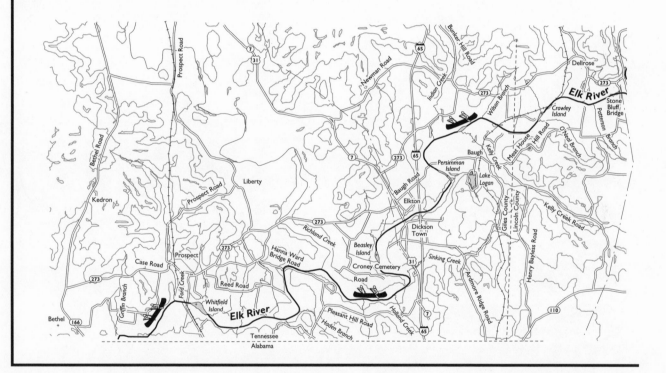

alternating with cultivated bottomland. At Woods Lake in northeastern Franklin County, the Elk is impounded for fifteen miles of its course before being released below Elk River Dam. From here the river is allowed to flow for only five or so miles before it joins the lake pool of much larger Tims Ford Lake. Free once again at the bottom of Tims Ford Dam, moving toward Fayetteville, the Elk winds through high, rugged, steep, wooded, and rocky knobs that slope down to tilled bottomland at streamside. Lined with sycamore, willow, and various oaks, the banks range from 9 to 14 feet in height and vary in steepness. The river's width averages from 45 to 60 feet in this section, with smooth paddling augmented by a moderate current and interrupted only occasionally by shoals (Class I or higher). The level of difficulty

# Elk River
# (continued)

Map continued from previous page

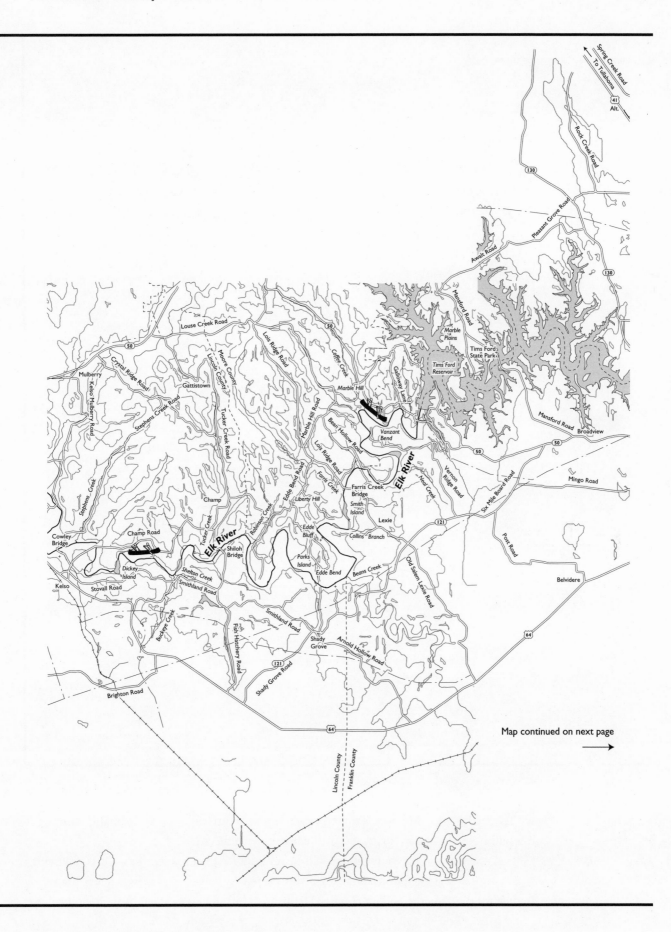

Map continued on next page →

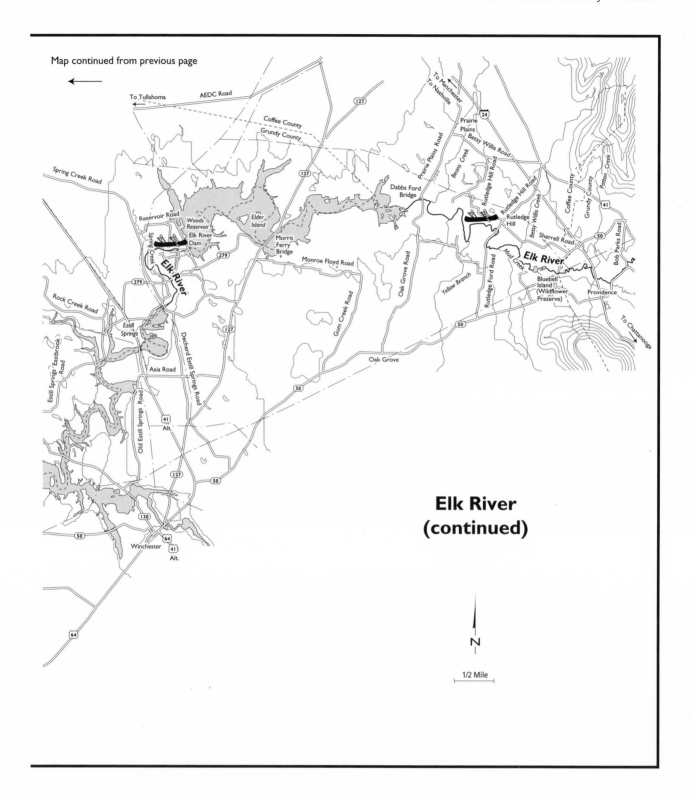

Map continued from previous page

Elk River (continued)

N

1/2 Mile

is Class I with very little in the way of hazards to navigation. Signs of habitation are obvious and frequent but are generally complementary to the view.

Downstream of Fayetteville the Elk passes under some exposed rock bluffs, following which timbered, precipitous knobs are supplanted by tall, but somewhat less dramatic, undulating hills. As the Elk approaches Elkton in eastern Giles County, more gently rolling farmland becomes the order of the day. Throughout, the stream continues to be well shaded and the level of difficulty remains Class I. River width increases from 60 to 75 feet, and the current continues to be helpful. Several hazards to navigation, however, are encountered between Fayetteville and Elkton. Just downstream of the US 231 bridge in Fayetteville are the remains of an old bridge that is dangerous in itself and sometimes catches debris. About eight miles below Fayetteville, near the tiny town of Harris, is a fairly large dam. Although there is a spillway the dam should nevertheless be portaged. A somewhat less-intimidating dam is encountered just east of Delrose. The center section of this dam has been washed away, allowing passage at higher water levels.

Below Elkton the river meanders undisturbed through flat to gently rolling farmland with occasional patches of woods. Scenery is pleasant but not as beautiful as along the upper sections. Hardwoods continue to shade the river, which has widened from 75 to 90 feet. Banks are less sharply inclined and the course of the river a little less sinuous as the Elk crosses into Alabama and on to the Tennessee River. The level of difficulty for the lower Elk remains a relaxing Class I with occasional deadfalls posing the only hazard to navigation.

Access all along the Elk is adequate to good, allowing for trips of varying length. While streamside property is, of course, private, there are many sizable wooded islands that make good camping sites.

# Buffalo River

"Buffalo River, running wild and free, the past comes alive when you talk to me. . . ."

(Opening lines of "The Singing Buffalo," author unknown)

Wild, free, past, alive. This short fragment of a longer poetic expression aptly describes the Buffalo River. There are no dams on this fishing paradise. There are more than 110 miles of floating opportunities. The farther you progress down this surprisingly swift, free-flowing river, the more time seems to back up. The Buffalo drains a quiet, bypassed, Western Highland Rim corner of Middle Tennessee. Names like Slink Shoals, Flat Woods, Blue Hole, Texas Bottoms, Big and Little Opossum Creeks, and Topsy appear along the river's course and are highly indicative of the slower-paced time through which you are traveling.

Take it easy. Gear yourself down to the pace of the river. Then enjoy your chance to participate in this remnant of nature's unhurrying domain. Nature does not get in much of a hurry, but the swift-moving shallow shoals along the way may cause you a few problems if you don't react quickly enough.

The Buffalo is noted for its fine float fishing. But it is noted just as widely for its propensity to dunk the unwary canoeist. When the river bends (and this river is composed mostly of these bends), the current picks up and many times flushes through the undercut, toppled trees lying across the outside of the bend. It is common for out-of-control canoeists and their canoes to flush under those water-level sweepers, too. Hang to the inside of blind bends as much as possible. Many riverside bluffs offer scenic backdrops to fertile fishing holes. Springs feed the river, and there's even one place where a noisy miniature whirlpool in a still pool announces a sink that removes a share of the river's flow.

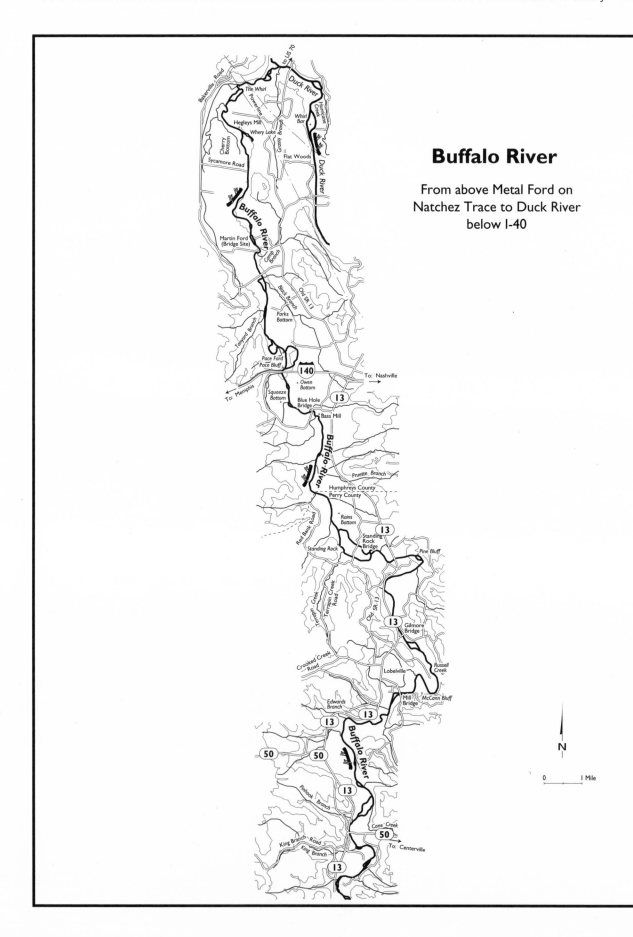

**Buffalo River**

From above Metal Ford on
Natchez Trace to Duck River
below I-40

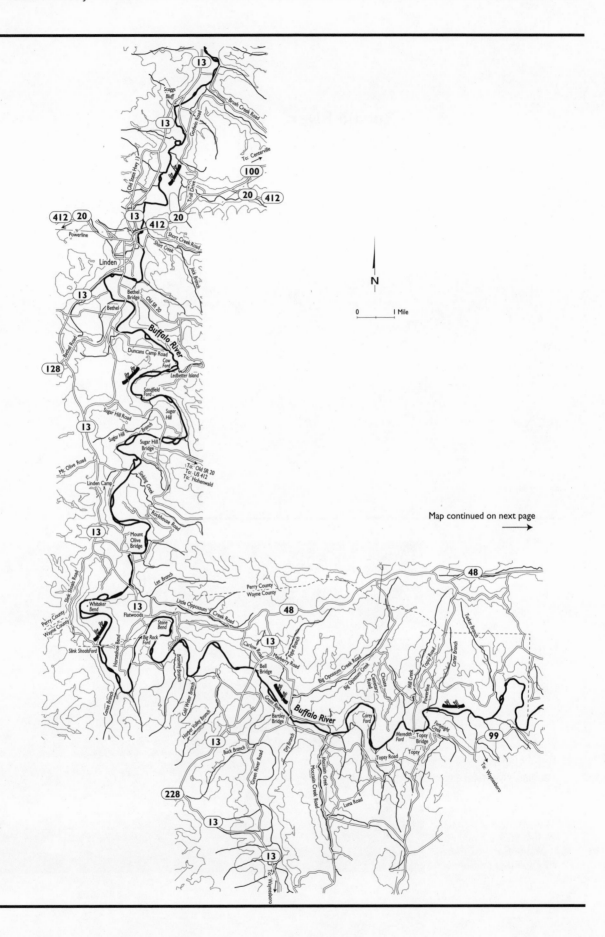

Map continued on next page →

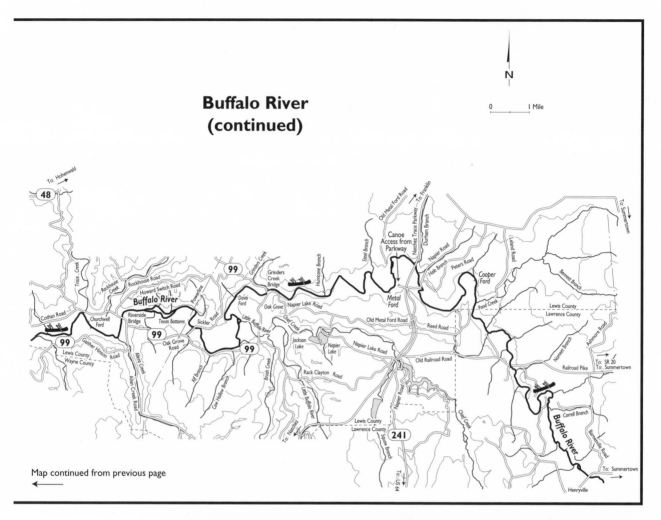

## Buffalo River
## (continued)

N

0          1 Mile

Map continued from previous page
←

Buffalo River Rest Stop.

"Actually, this side-surfing ledge is at the Metal Ford put-in. The beautiful Metal Ford access is a rest stop on the Natchez Trace." Photograph by Ann Spencer.

Generally, the higher-water late winter and springtime runs can be made from Metal Ford near where the Natchez Trace crosses the river at about river mile 102, or even higher up the river at Henryville bridge at mile 117. At low water, late summer and fall trips can usually still be floated starting near Flat Woods at about mile 60. Many liveries are now available around the Flat Woods area at the big bend where the river turns north.

The spectacular 110 miles of free-flowing floating the Buffalo River offers is truly one of the most popular float and fishing resources in Tennessee. And deservedly so.

# Duck River

In 1974, the Duck River provided over 265 miles of free-flowing floating through the heart of Tennessee. Shortly thereafter, TVA closed its non-power-producing Normandy Dam at river mile 248.5 and effectively shortened the free-flowing canoeing opportunity to below the dam site. Unfortunately, Normandy Lake drowned out the major shoals and rapids of this river—a part of the river with much interest for canoeists. Immediately below Columbia, water quality problems resulting from the city and its industry hinder recreational use of this river for many river miles. Finally, below Centerville, this major drainageway of Middle Tennessee again becomes a pleasant float, but the size precludes any major shoals of interest. The stream is quiet and slow.

Under the waters of the Normandy impoundment, the old riverbed winds through one of the richest archaeological regions in Tennessee. The river and its attendant woods in the Eastern Highland Rim were an established Native American hunting area. Many old Indian campsites were found by intense pre-impoundment TVA digs at many of the same spots where canoe floaters used to stop to sift the sands for arrowheads. Now the natural, rich, self-fertilizing, phosphate-laden spring floodwaters in the basin are held back by the Normandy Dam (rather than spread out in the historically useful and carefully managed pattern over the riverside croplands), and the residue from the resulting too-rich "Normandy-Green" algae feeding on the cooped-up nutrients drifts down in the impoundment to settle over those same sands.

After the Normandy Dam construction, TVA worked on a second major obstruction to the river near Columbia. Even after the concrete was poured, the remaining earthworks costs alone proved too expensive to justify the project, and the project was terminated. The river has been diverted around the damsite construction, and it is a strange barren float in the construction area near the damsite. There remains pleasant paddling on the Duck, and, indeed, a float trip through the downstream Hickman County area retains much of the pastoral appeal that used to exist all along the 200-mile floatway.

Beware of low-level dams on the Duck. Many early water supply and mill dams still provide lethal backrollers during periods of significant flow. Wherever a mill appears, a dam is likely to be. Be sure to scout (from the bank!) for flush-through breaks in the dam, or else portage. When a back-roller occurs below a dam, do not attempt to run that dam, no matter how small the drop may appear. Portage and live!

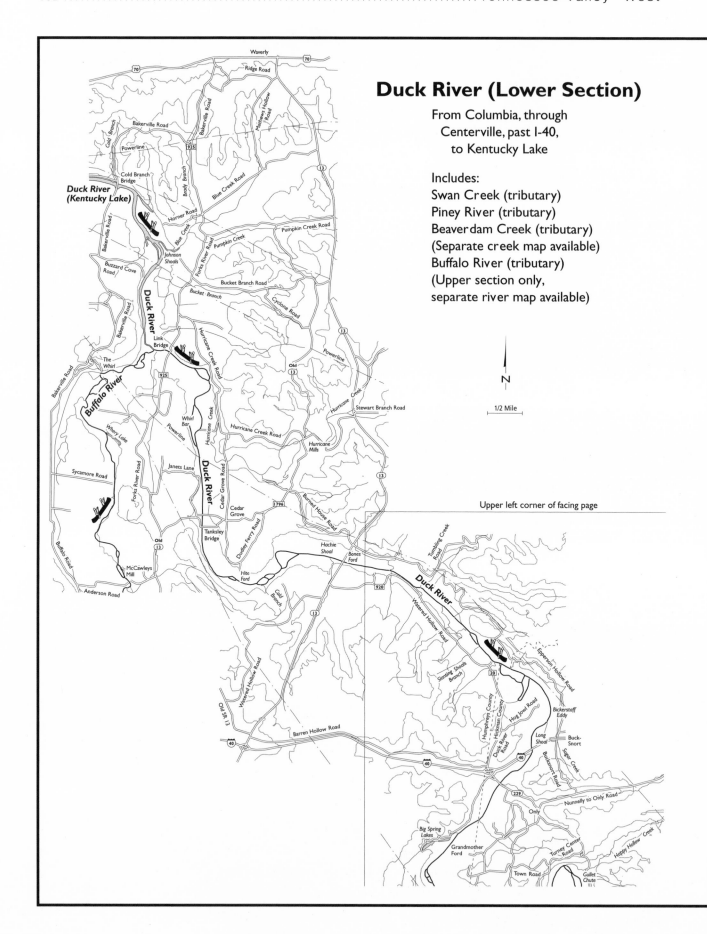

# Duck River (Lower Section)

From Columbia, through
Centerville, past I-40,
to Kentucky Lake

Includes:
Swan Creek (tributary)
Piney River (tributary)
Beaverdam Creek (tributary)
(Separate creek map available)
Buffalo River (tributary)
(Upper section only,
separate river map available)

N

1/2 Mile

Upper left corner of facing page

920

Tumbling Creek Road

Snake Creek

Watered Hollow Road

Grandfathers Building

20

Slanting Shoals Branch

Emerson Hollow Road

Bickerstaff Eddy

Sugar Creek

Humphreys County
Hickman County

Hog Jowl Road

Long Shoal

Buck-Snort

Lower right corner of facing page

N

1/2 Mile

Map continued on next page

To: SR 230
Possum Hollow Road

40

Bucksnort Road

Duck River

229

Nunnelly to Only Road

Smith Road

Taylor Creek Road

Piney Road

Powerline

Dodd Hollow Road

Only

Happy Hollow Creek

Little Piney Creek

Little Piney Road

Old Richmond Road

Taylor Creek

Taylor Creek Road

Piney River

Big Spring Lakes

Grandmother Ford

King Branch

Turney Center Road

Town Road

Little Piney

Powerline

Capshaw Hollow Road

Lowes Bend Road

Scotts Ford

Field Island

FM Tower

Briggs Chapel Road

Hicks Ford

Fields Bend Road

Baker Road

Logshoal Island

Gullet Chute

Perry County

Alexander Ford

Murphree Eddy

Coble to Only Road

Lovets Shoal

Wright Road

Pantner Branch

Easley Bend Road

Duck River

Easley Bend

Eastern Shoal

Backwall Hollow Road

Burchard Town Bend

Burchard Ford

Roman Road

Wright Bend Road

Miller Road

Beaverdam Bridge

Lovett Island

Whitson Bend Road

Whitson Bend Road

Trace Creek

Rocky Branch

Huddleston Bridge

Peroque Ford

Blue Rock Shoals

Beaverdam Creek

Skull Creek

50

Wolf Creek

Wolf Creek Road

Brian Pond Branch

Briar Pond Bottom

Briar Pond Road

Coble to Only Road

Trace Creek Road

Middle Fork

East Fork

Coble

50

Wolf Creek Road

Lowe Branch

Sulphur Creek Road

Sulphur Fork

Bluewater Branch

East Beaverdam Road

50

Glenn Hinson Road

Joe Branch

West Beaverdam Road

East Beaverdam Road

Powerline

# Duck River (Lower Section)
## (continued)

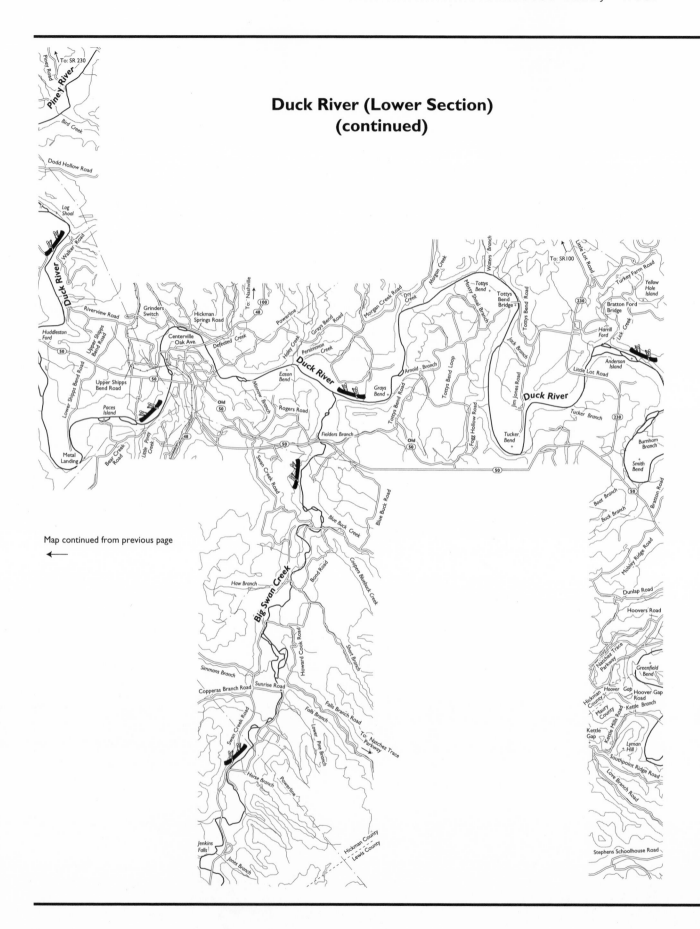

Map continued from previous page
←

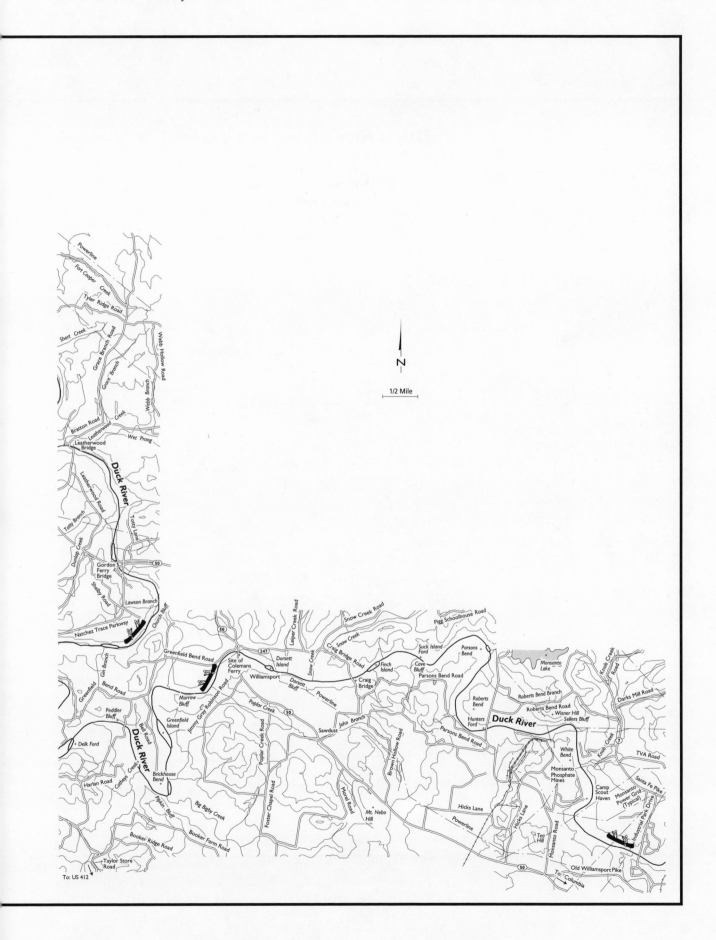

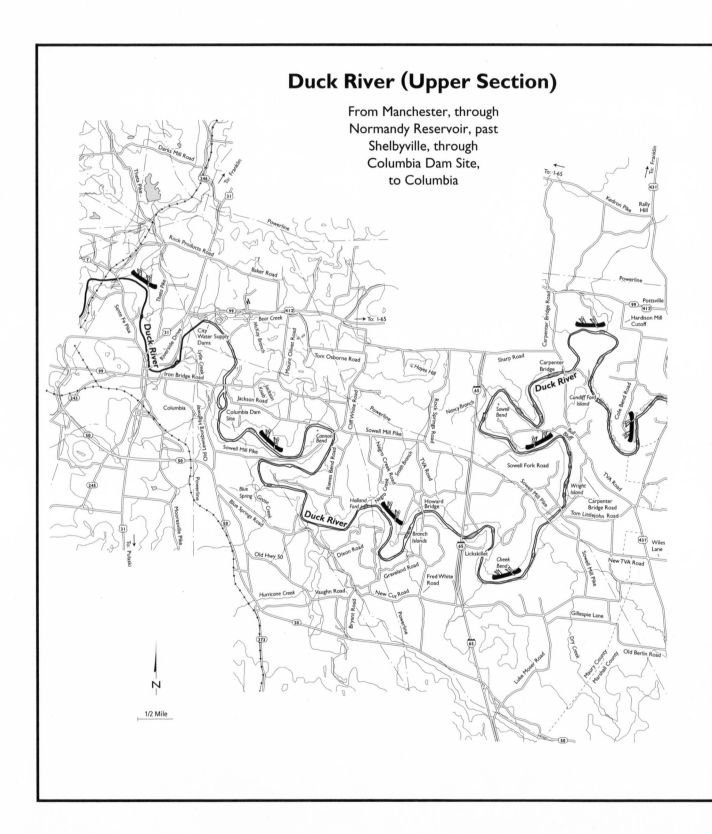

# Duck River (Upper Section)

From Manchester, through
Normandy Reservoir, past
Shelbyville, through
Columbia Dam Site,
to Columbia

Map continued on next page

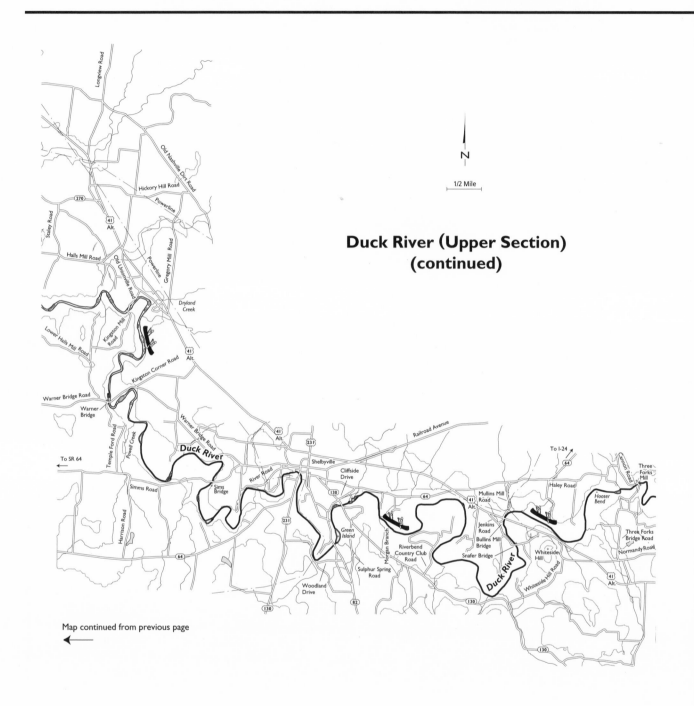

**Duck River (Upper Section) (continued)**

Map continued from previous page

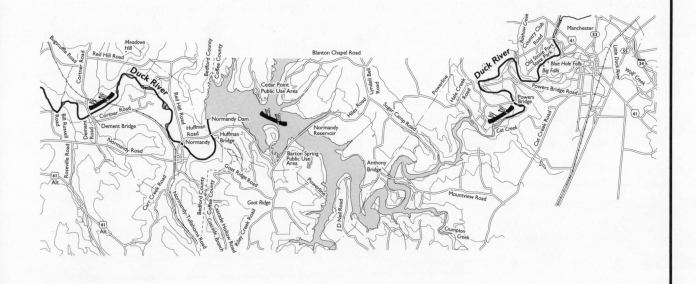

# The Free-Flowing Duck River

## Recreational Value

The Duck River is the longest free-flowing river in Eastern America. Downstream from Normandy Dam the Duck River snakes its way through southern Middle Tennessee for a distance of 272 miles from Manchester, Tennessee, to its confluence with the Tennessee River near Waverly. The beauty of this recreational opportunity is that every inch of the Duck River is within a one-hour drive of Nashville. The Duck River is a lovely pastoral stream in a rural setting perfectly suited for family canoeing, fishing, swimming, tubing, overnight camping, and group outings. The river has a steady and predictable flow and is canoeable year-round. There are numerous access points with friendly and accommodating landowners who have welcomed users of the river for many, many years.

## Wildlife

There is abundant wildlife available for easy viewing from a canoe including deer, wild turkey, rabbits, squirrels, cranes, ducks, beaver, muskrat, and a wide assortment of snakes, turtles, and birds. I have never taken a float trip on the Duck River without seeing an abundance and great variety of wildlife on every stretch of the river.

I particularly remember one of the more interesting canoe trips with my brother, Mark. It was the day after Christmas in 1984, and we were canoeing the Duck River in Eastern Hickman County near Shady Grove, Tennessee, in 40-degree weather when we spotted two large ears sticking up out of the water approximately one hundred yards in front of their canoe. Upon determining that the ears belonged to a very strong swimming doe, we increased paddling efforts to try to close the gap between our canoe and the doe, but made little real progress. After following the doe down the middle of the river for approximately a quarter of a mile, we suddenly heard rustling noises in the brush on the right bank of the river and looked over to find a huge buck stomping and pawing the ground and snorting in the air, trying to attract the attention of the doe. The buck continued to follow the progress of the doe down the river, with the buck refusing to get in the water and the doe refusing to get out. After this standoff transpired for some period of time, the doe finally gave in and swam over to the bank and climbed out of the river, where she rubbed noses with the mighty buck for a few minutes before they both bounded off into the woods beyond the river. This is the type of wildlife experience that you come to expect when canoeing the Duck River.

## The Death of a Dam

In 1972 TVA announced its plan to construct a dam on the Duck River at Columbia under great pressure from Congressman Joe L. Evins, despite the fact that TVA's own feasibility studies in 1933, 1951, and 1966 (and later in 1985) all showed that the project was not economically feasible, returning only forty cents for each dollar invested. Strong opposition from the Tennessee Scenic Rivers Association, Tennessee Citizens for Wilderness Planning, and many other environmental and conservation organizations and individuals, along with a subsequent changing of the guard both in Congress and at TVA, resulted in TVA abandoning the project in 1986.

[Editors note: Murfreesboro canoeist Frank Fly, originally from Sawdust, Tennessee, along the banks of the Duck, has been the lead counsel on the efforts to prevent the construction of the Columbia Dam on the Duck River. He has spent countless pro bono hours helping keep that section of free-flowing river available for all of us to enjoy.]

The Columbia Dam project as originally proposed would have required the taking of 33,000 acres of farmland to impound a reservoir of 12,800 acres of water during the spring and summer months. During the fall and winter months, the reservoir would have been drawn down to only 3,400 acres, thereby exposing more than 9,000 acres of mud flats and shortening the linear length of the lake by a distance of 18 miles. At the original proposed elevation for the reservoir at 630 feet, the impoundment would have stretched all the way to Henry Horton State Park and would have consumed one out of every eighteen acres of farm land in two counties.

Later efforts by a mayor of Columbia and other special interests to revive the project have been met with a steadfast refusal by TVA, which has proposed as an alternative a protected river corridor on the Duck River to increase recreational opportunities for canoeing and other uses.

## Conrad the Clam and Friends

Dr. David Stansbery, retired chairman of the Department of Biology at Ohio State University, has identified the Duck River as having the greatest diversity of aquatic life of any river in the United States, containing some 126 different species. Approximately a dozen of these species have either been listed or are eligible for listing by the U.S. Fish and Wildlife Service as endangered species (including some plants such as the prairie leaf clover). The most famous of these endangered species is the Birdwing Pearly Mussel (scientific name, Condradilla caelata), affectionately known as "Conrad the Clam" by those who have come to appreciate the significance of its presence in this valuable aquatic habitat. It is important to note with regard to endangered aquatic species that all of them previously existed in virtually all rivers throughout Middle Tennessee, but now only live in the Duck River because the water quality in the other streams has deteriorated to the point that they could no longer survive. The richest habitat of the endangered mussels is between Henry Horton State Park and the city of Columbia, particularly the Lillard Mill area, all of which would have been destroyed by the Columbia Dam.

Few people know that the Duck River is the largest single source of the raw materials for cultured pearls in the entire world. The ground-up mussel shells, especially the larger mussel species found in the lower reaches of the river just upstream from the confluence with the Tennessee River, are made into pellets that serve as the raw material for cultured pearls made throughout the world, and especially in the Far East. In addition, few people know that mussels attach themselves to "host fish" by secreting an extremely sticky substance impervious to water. That substance has now been successfully applied to securing dental crowns to capped teeth and has proven to be far superior to the cement that was previously used. Above all, bivalve mollusks are extremely sensitive to even minute variations in water quality, and for this reason alone these species are important in measuring and maintaining the very high water quality that presently exists in the Duck River in comparison with other Middle Tennessee streams.

—Frank Fly
Murfreesboro, TN

## The Perennial Free Family Float

For the past couple of decades, the Tennessee Scenic Rivers Association has sponsored its Family Float Days trip on the Duck River on the first Saturday in June, meeting at 10 A.M. in the restaurant parking lot at Henry Horton State Park. This eight-mile trip, which has been led every year by Frank Fly and Tom Copeland, now represents the longest-standing single trip in TSRA history and covers the free-flowing section of river from the put-in at Lillard Mill to Highway 431, where there is a very nice Class I rapid around the left side of the remains of an ancient Indian fish trap. The largest of these trips was in 1976 with some 56 canoes, including all of the TVA Board of Directors as well as the General Manager and many staff members, along with camera crews from all the television networks in Nashville plus broad radio and newspaper cover-

age. The smallest trip was in 1986 with three canoes including the two trip leaders and one other brave soul. On the latter trip, we endured a pounding rain from the moment of put-in until the lunch stop, at which time the rain stopped and we had a glimmering of sunlight for approximately forty-five minutes until after lunch was completed. As the still-drenched paddlers put back on the river, the torrential rains began again and continued until after the take-out. This trip is expected to continue on the first Saturday in June for so long as TSRA and the Duck River continue to exist, and everyone is welcome with no pre-registration required. Bring lotion on sunny days and rain gear on cloudy ones.

—Frank Fly
Murfreesboro, TN

## Big Swan Creek

Bigger than a creek, smaller than a river, this pretty stream can be paddled during the winter and early spring when the watershed is charged. The nearby Piney River will be passable whenever Big Swan is running. But it might not be true the other way around. This little-traveled treasure is an enjoyable, rural, intimate float. Hazards include blow-downs, sweepers, and the occasional low-water bridge. Also, you should be aware that the rural landowners are not used to finding recreational paddlers intimate with their lands, so treat them and their landholdings with courtesy and respect. Try to make your float enjoyable for all involved.

## Piney River of Middle Tennessee

If size of the stream were the only consideration in granting the label of "river" to a flowing body of water, then the Piney might not be worthy. With all the other Pine(y)s in Tennessee, however, unique beauty, intimacy and clear water which flows at a floatable level most of the year are reasons enough for the Piney to be one of two in Tennessee which are called "river." (The publication "Place Names of Tennessee," Tennessee Division of Geology

Big Swan en route to the Big Duck. The higher waters of early spring make paddling possible higher on the watershed. Big Swan Creek, a tributary to the lengthy Duck River, is a beautiful run. Photo position on Horse Branch Bridge just off Swan Creek Road during a scheduled TSRA club float. Photograph by Ann Spencer.

A favored spot on the Piney River in Middle Tennessee. The Piney River in Hickman County is a tributary of the Duck River. Higher springtime water levels allow this closed-in, pastoral float. (Beware of sweepers.) Photograph by Ann Spencer.

Bulletin 73 lists in addition to both Piney Rivers, twenty-eight streams that have the name Pine(y) Creek or Pine(y) Fork. This does not include the Pine Fork Creeks, which may be a compromise name. Nor does it include the ten or so other names that include Pine(y) as part of the name (select one of the following: Grove, Orchard, Bluff, Island) Creek or Branch or Fork. Cumberland County has three Piney Creeks, each flowing into a different major watershed, a Piney Branch and a Pine Thicket Branch.)

Located only an hour's drive west of Nashville, most people see the Piney River only at its uppermost reach where it passes quietly beneath the high bridges of the east- and westbound lanes of Interstate 40 in extreme southern Dickson County. From this crossing the river meanders generally southward, accepting tributaries and bordering fields and pastures on one side or the other (rarely both) until it feeds into the Duck River about five miles west of Centerville.

## The Fishing Just Isn't the Same Anymore

Beaverdam Creek originates in the hollows and hills north of Hohenwald (High Forest), Tennessee, and flows essentially north until the intersection with SR 48 and SR 100 (known locally as "four corners"), where it gradually turns northwest. There are also some notable springs in the headwaters, particularly Beaverdam Springs. There are other springs throughout the valley watershed.

In past years (thirty to forty years ago) this creek was one of the most productive game fish streams in Middle Tennessee and local people developed the art of making and using gigs to a high degree of skill. Rough fish were also abundant, and local opinion held that the resource was inexhaustible as new fish would migrate from Duck River. During the 1970s, the Tennessee Wildlife Resources Agency stocked Beaverdam Creek with rainbow trout each spring, but the program received a mixed response. Local people resented "outsiders" for fishing "their" creek, but trout lovers highly approved of the program. Nevertheless, due to non-cooperation by local landowners, including destructive gravel mining in the stream, the trout program was eventually discontinued. Today, there are no populations of game fish left in the stream. The reasons for this are numerous and complex.

There have been no beaver on the main stream within memory. However, there are currently several dams and active colonies on tributaries. These beaver were not stocked and are believed to be migrants from Duck River and beyond. Local people view them as a nuisance.

Beaverdam Creek is not a canoeing stream as we generally perceive one to be. During high flow, it might be possible to pole, scrape, and drag most of the way from Milam Branch Road to Duck River, but the trip would resemble a take from a scene in the movie *African Queen* in places. A bigger problem might be in getting permission for passage, as local people view the stream as part of their land. Nevertheless, it is a delightful, clear, cold, clean stream to play in on a hot spring or summer day. There are numerous bridges over the stream downstream of SR 100 and roads (East and West Beaverdam Roads) traverse much of its length.

—Carl Leathers
Nashville, Tennessee

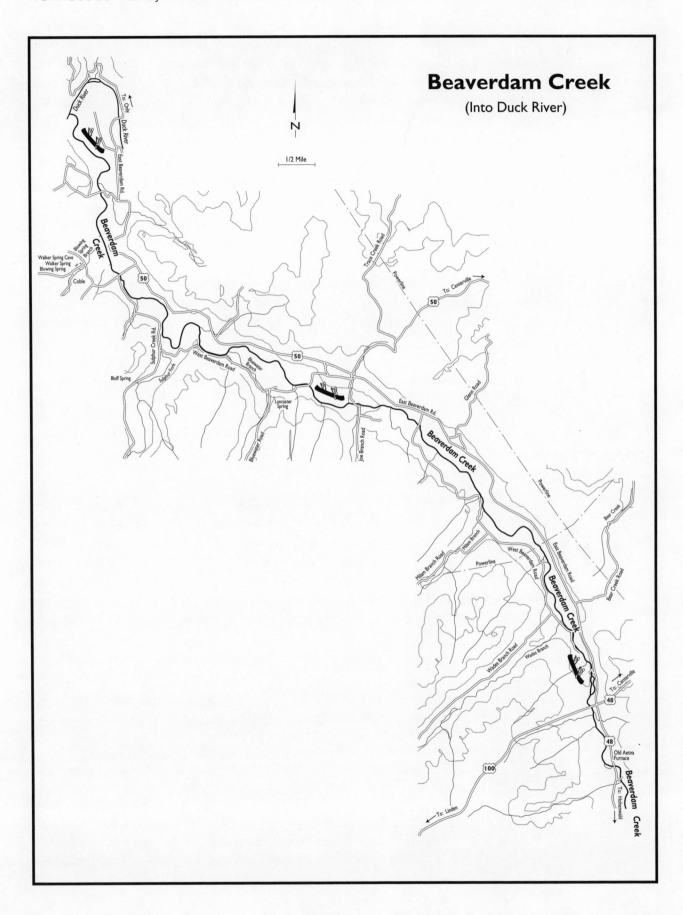

# Beaverdam Creek
## (Into Duck River)

1/2 Mile

N

A float on any section of the Piney reveals a small river with alternating quiet pools and gravel for riffles. Frequently the pools provide excellent fishing for smallmouth bass, bluegill, and, in the upper reaches of the river, an occasional rainbow trout escaped from the tributary Mill Creek where TWRA regularly stocks the fish. Some riffles between pools offer a little excitement with a few standing waves at the bottom. The best way to determine if the section you are interested in floating has enough water is to check out the riffle nearest your proposed put-in. If there is enough water there to float your craft then you can usually count on sufficient water for the rest of the trip. A less-reliable gauge is to determine the Harpeth River reading at Kingston Springs. If the reading is 300 cfs or more then odds are in your favor that the Piney River is runnable from Interstate 40. (Because the two rivers are in adjacent but totally separate watersheds this method lacks precision.)

The main hazards to navigation are deadfalls and strainers. Occasionally canoeists encounter more or less temporary fences (sometimes electrified) intended to keep cattle from wandering up or downstream during the periods of low water. (Local sentiments toward canoeists fluctuate. There have been times when such a fence would have been intended more for the canoeist than the cow. So be sure to practice your normal courtesies of asking permission to park or to cross a field. Swing wide of a favorite fishing hole when it is already in use.)

# Beech River

The Beech River is born, as of late, at the base of Beech Lake Dam north of Lexington and flows southeast across Henderson and Decatur Counties before dropping into the Tennessee River (Kentucky Lake). Similar in all respects to other West Tennessee streams, the Beech runs through channeled banks through woodland swamp and cultivated bottomland. Scarcely 15 feet wide below the dam, the river widens to 30 feet as it passes north of Scotts Hill. Mudbanks are 4 to 8 feet in height and rise almost vertically from the water. Below the small town of Beacon in west-central Decatur County, the Beech resumes flowing through its natural bed. Scenery improves here with increased vegetation and woodlands at streamside and with occasional oxbow lakes. North of Decaturville the river encounters the backwaters of Kentucky Lake. Its level of difficulty is Class I, and deadfalls represent the only hazards to navigation. The Beech is runnable from late November to late May below Rocky Hill with access rated fair to good throughout.

# Big Sandy River

The Big Sandy River originates in Henderson County north of Lexington and flows northeast draining portions of Carroll, Benton, and Henry Counties before emptying into the lake pool of Kentucky Lake (Tennessee River) at Big Sandy. Like most western Tennessee streams, the Big Sandy has been extensively channeled and runs within well-defined, four-foot mud- and

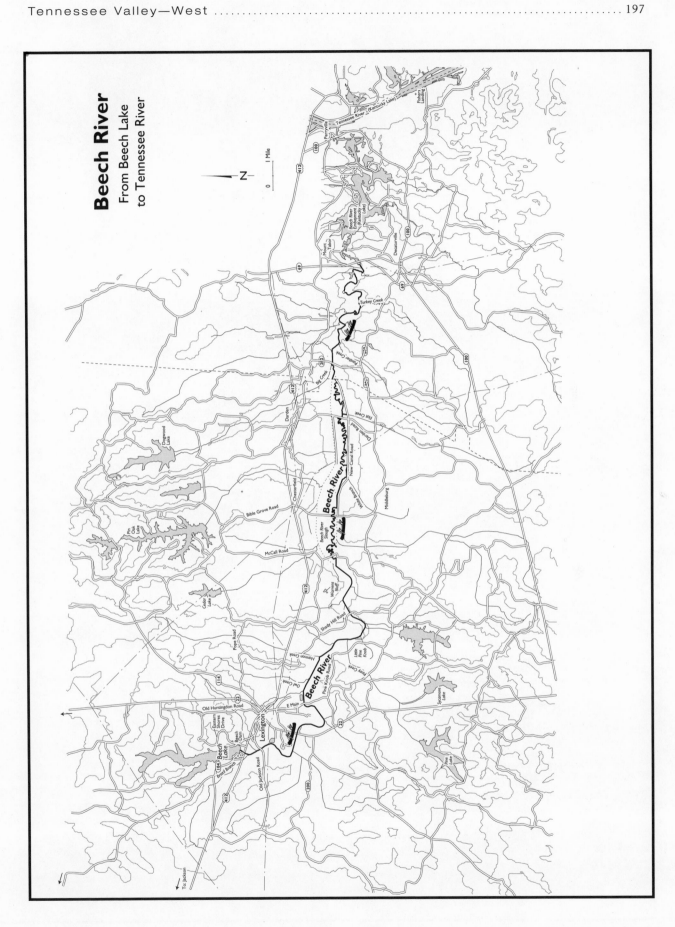

**Beech River**
From Beech Lake
to Tennessee River

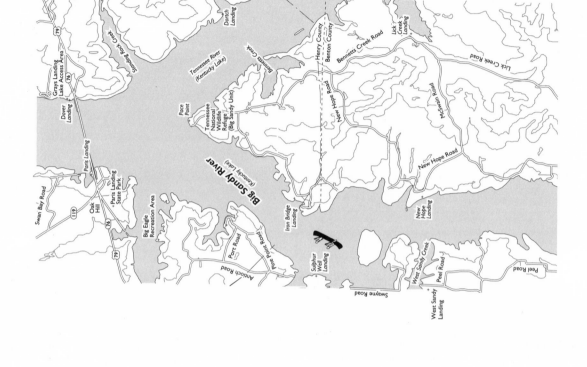

# Big Sandy River

From Natchez Trace
State Forest to
Tennessee River
(Kentucky Lake)

N

1/2 Mile

Map continued on next page

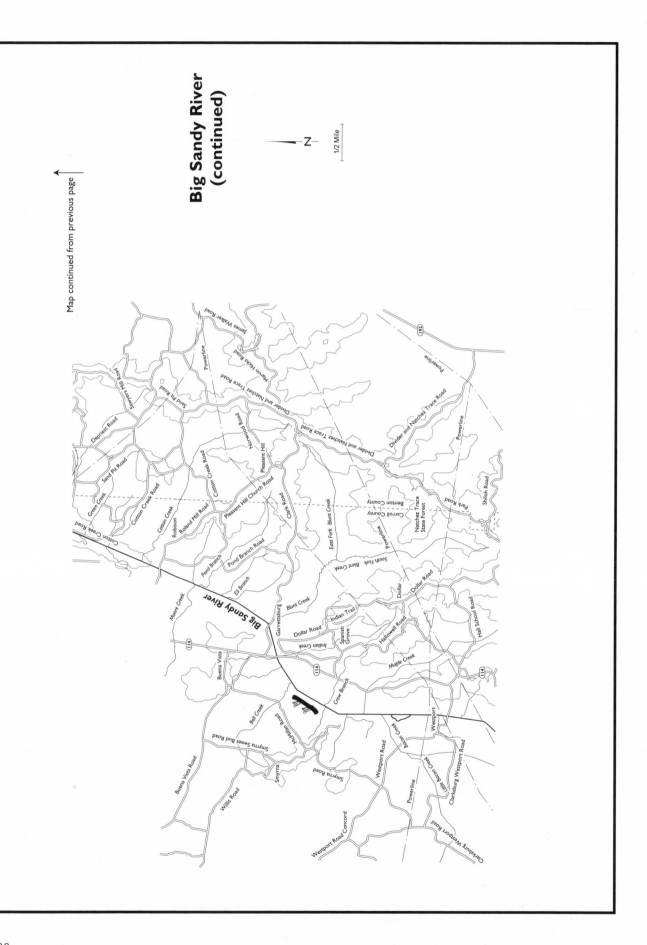

Big Sandy River (continued)

N

1/2 Mile

Map continued from previous page

sandbanks through wooded lowland marshes and farmland. Where the channel bank has revegetated or where prechannelization growth extends to the river, willows and dense scrub predominate. Access is poor except at bridges. Runnable downstream of Yuma in southeastern Carroll County from late November through the end of May, the Big Sandy often overflows its channel during the winter and spring, thus affording access to adjacent marshes and the original riverbed. Like most streams in western Tennessee, there is plenty to be found along the Big Sandy to excite the wildlife enthusiast. Representative mammals include whitetailed deer, beaver, swamp rabbit, striped skunk, and raccoon. Birds, especially waterfowl, are plentiful. Also plentiful in warm weather are mosquitoes and stable flies. Level of difficulty is Class I throughout with deadfalls being the only hazard to navigation.

# Mississippi Plain

## Western Tennessee Overview

The streams of far western Tennessee are an incalculable treasure to the paddler who enjoys wildlife and the enchanted atmosphere of wilderness swamp terrain. To seclude yourself among the proud cypress and lacy willow is to go back in time, to gain a solitude in communion with the heron, the warbler, and the beaver; such seclusion is primeval in its depth and almost completely unknown in today's world. Bordered on the west by the Mississippi River, and on the east by the Mississippi–Tennessee River Divide (a plateau running north to south just west of the Tennessee River) West Tennessee is laced by dozens of streams dropping off the seven-hundred-foot divide down into broad valleys en route to the Mississippi. Most of the streams are typical alluvial rivers following sinuous courses (where not channeled) across the valley. Flooding occurs along each of the rivers to varying degrees almost every year, usually during the winter and spring months, with the duration of each period of flooding being approximately ten days. The valley, or basin, contains several state wildlife management areas and almost fifty private hunting clubs and preserves. Most of the lands in the basin, with the possible exception of those bordering the Hatchie River, are intensively farmed, with the wooded areas consisting of intervening strips and small patches. Because of the agricultural nature of the basin, it is relatively well crossed by county and state roads.

The geology of the West Tennessee area is entirely within the east flank of the Upper Mississippi Embayment region of the Gulf Coastal Plain and includes part of the plateau slope and the Mississippi Alluvial Plain. The land surface forms a broad plateau that slopes southwestward and ends abruptly at the Chickasaw Bluffs. From a height of about 700 feet above sea level along the Tennessee and Mississippi Rivers' drainage divide, the plateau descends toward the Mississippi River to an elevation along the crest of the Chickasaw Bluffs of 400 feet in the northwest and 300 feet in the southwest. The plateau is partially dissected and consists of broad stream valleys and rolling uplands. Other common features of the plateau are hills left by erosion.

The climate of the area may generally be classified as mild with a mean temperature of about 60 degrees Fahrenheit, with freezing temperatures occurring between November and April. Annual rainfall has varied from a minimum of 32 inches to a maximum of 74 inches, with the normal annual precipitation of about 50 inches being fairly well distributed throughout the year.

Woodlands along the streams in West Tennessee are basically riparian, and wetland trees such as tupelo gum, cypress, cottonwood, oaks, river birch, and willows are typical. Common upland trees include oaks and hickories, while low areas, typical of southern swamps, are dominated by bald cypress. In the spring, certain woody plants, such as black cherry, buttonbush, flowering dogwood, trumpet creeper, and wisteria, display showy flowers that enhance the primeval beauty of the streams in the basin. In the fall, blackgum, persimmon, pin oak, red maple, swamp tupelo, and smooth sumac engulf the basin streams in a spectacle of color.

The fauna is characteristic of the southern United States lowlands drained by the Mississippi River. Fish populations are dominated by such forage fish as gizzard shad, golden shiner, bluntface shiner, creek chub, and mosquito fish. Primary game fish include channel catfish, bluegill, sunfish, spotted bass, largemouth bass, black crappie, ant white crappie. Also present are several species of gar, carp, and buffalofish. The amphibian and reptile life along the basin streams is diverse for all forms except lizards. Habitat varies from the delta lowland streams and adjacent river swamps to the dryer upland headwater areas. Three poisonous snakes occur in the West Tennessee lowland—the cottonmouth (water moccasin) is considered common, while canebrake rattlers and copperheads are occasionally seen. The most often encountered snake is the harmless gray rat snake. Among the several exotic amphibians found in the lowlands is the alligator snapping turtle, which has been known to reach lengths of over three feet and weigh one hundred pounds.

The West Tennessee streams are rich in bird life, owing to the variety of habitat provided as the drainages run through marshes and sloughs, dry uplands, open agricultural land, pasture, shrub edges, and forest. Over 250 species of birds are found within the West Tennessee drainages. Some species are transient, some migratory, and others are permanent residents. Birds that breed and nest in the swamp and streamside woodlands include various species of heron, cattle egret, wood duck, turkey vulture, several varieties of hawk and owl, turkey, numerous warblers, and a lengthy list of other songbirds. Common winter transient and migratory residents include the bald eagle, yellow-bellied sapsucker, and fox sparrow. Gamebird waterfowl include a large population of mallards, wood duck, teal, and gadwall, pintail and black ducks. Nonwaterfowl game birds encountered are bobwhite quail, mourning doves, and eastern wild turkey.

Mammals are diverse and plentiful in the varied terrain of the West Tennessee drainages. Common furbearers include mink, beaver, muskrat, opossum, raccoon, gray fox, red fox, striped skunk, and bobcat. White-tailed deer, squirrels, cottontails, and swamp rabbits are considered important game animals. Needless to say, insects abound in the West Tennessee drainages. Stable flies and mosquitoes can be particularly bothersome. Disease carriers present in addition to the various flies and mosquitoes include ticks, mites, and fleas.

As the respective streams of West Tennessee slip toward the Mississippi from the uplands of the Mississippi–Tennessee River Divide in the east, they share much in common in relation to the terrain through which they flow. Most of the major drainages (Wolf and Loosahatchie excepted) originate on the plateau in upland pasture and grassland, or in wooded uplands consisting of open woodlands at higher elevations that are very well drained. Moving downstream toward the Mississippi, the streams flow through croplands into lowland areas where croplands are interrupted intermittently by wooded swamps and sloughs. The latter consist of forested areas where the soil is waterlogged at least within a few inches of the surface during the growing season, and it includes areas around cut-off channels and oxbows. Also encountered are overflow bottomlands that consist of forested, seasonally flooded bottoms where the soil is covered with water or is waterlogged during some periods.

Paddling any of the West Tennessee drainages is a memorable experience. However, what you are most likely to remember depends on the time of year you strike out. During the summer you are most likely to remember dragging your boat and swatting insects. During the winter you may remember ducking buckshot as thousands of hunters converge on the sloughs and oxbows. In high water, you may remember an intimate stream losing itself (and you) irretrievably as it expands into an immense labyrinthine cypress swamp.

Obviously preparation, precaution, and a good measure of common sense are pre-requisite to a pleasant experience in the West Tennessee drainages. Remember to paddle silently and keep conversation to a minimum if you wish to observe the myriad forms of wildlife. If the water is high, take a compass and know how to use it; there is no place on earth easier to get lost than in a West Tennessee high-water swamp. If hunting season is in progress, pick a river or area that is off limits to the hunters. If you do go among the hunters, wear brightly colored clothing, carry a whistle or some other noise-making device to warn them of your presence, and, if possible, mount a florescent bike flag on a high pole on the bow of your boat. Be armed with insect repellent, long trousers, and a long-sleeved shirt when the bugs are on the prowl. Wear a PFD and carry a first-aid kit complete with snakebite kit (and know how to use it).

# Reelfoot Lake

On the first of February in 1812 Reelfoot Lake did not exist. Reelfoot the Chickasaw Indian did, however, and, according to legend, he kidnapped Starlight, a Choctaw princess with whom he was quite smitten. The legend states this was a mutual affection, but mixed mar-riages were taboo. Apparently body snatching was taboo, too, because the legend further states that the wrath of the gods opened the earth, swallowed the entire Chickasaw tribe and covered their lodges with water. Of course, we feel bad about the fate of the young lovers, but ever since February 7, 1812, (when the lake filled), there has been a rich wildlife refuge in northwest Tennessee—a fantastic cypress swamp where mysterious, tranquil canoeing opportunities abound.

Actually, the New Madrid fault line became active in the bitter cold winter of 1811–12 when continuous earthquakes and aftershocks shook the area from December 11 on. Sulphurous vapors often blocked the winter sun and water sloshed back and forth in the Mississippi riverbed. Sand and water spit forth from scattered fissures. The hardest shock occurred on that fateful February 7 and opened Reelfoot basin. Later that day, steamboat cap-tains near Natchez recorded a reverse flow to their commerce way as the Mississippi River backed in and filled Reelfoot Lake.

Reelfoot is just far enough south to escape the normal winter freeze, hence it has become a wintering area for the waterfowl using the Mississippi flyway. In addition, a yearly migration of bald eagles uses the lake and the nearby river as winter hunting grounds for their favorite fresh fish. Much of the area is protected as a national wildlife refuge; the rest is full of hunting blinds. During the late fall and winter, the refuge is closed, and that means that anyone beyond the posted boundaries is trespassing, whether they are simply canoe-camping photographers or bait-spreading poachers. And all are subject to equipment confiscation, fines, and incarceration. It is best to find topo maps of the area and locate these boundaries before paddling off across Reelfoot in the wildlife season. Many access ditches and old bayous cut through the surrounding marshes. The interior of the area is open water, shallow basins. It is best to carry the topo maps to help locate the ditchway desired. Walnut Log ditch is an excellent eastern way into the Upper Blue Basin and the northern cypress-laden wildlife refuges (when open to the public). The state-owned AirPark Inn is a western access to the same area. From the south, the Reelfoot State Park is a good access to the bigger, southern Blue Basin and the interior Lost Pond. Be prepared for open-water wind conditions, and stay close to shore if the weather looks as if it might turn bad. But your trip will be rewarding if you seek great blue heron, ducks, geese, muskrat, beaver, deer—or even the spirits of long-departed Indians.

Reelfoot Wildlife Watching.

Reelfoot Lake in the late fall. Watch the posted signs carefully, for trespass across the wildlife refuge boundaries in hunting season can cause equipment confiscation. (However, young children in the craft can help convince watching authorities that the 'responsible' adults were mostly naïve and ignorant and only wanted to impress the youngsters with the wonders of nature, not flush out the geese for hunters posted just outside the boundaries.) Photograph by Bob Lantz.

# The Forked Deer River System

A large, fan-shaped drainage in the center of Tennessee's Jackson Purchase area is the Forked Deer River system. Running east to west, the Forked Deer and its tributaries drain portions of Carroll, Chester, Henderson, Madison, Haywood, Gibson, Crockett, Lauderdale, and Dyer Counties before reaching its mouth at the Obion River near Hales Point on the Dyer–Lauderdale County line. Made up of three forks imaginatively named the North, Middle, and South Forks, the Forked Deer follows the standard West Tennessee river recipe. Dropping off the Tennessee–Mississippi River Divide, the Forked Deer and its forks run in primarily channeled beds alternately through cultivated bottomland, cypress and willow swamp, and forested lowland. Wildlife is plentiful and diverse throughout the system with the large Tigrett Wildlife Management Area located just downstream of the confluence of the North and Middle Forks. Seasonal flooding is common in the drainage and sometimes allows paddlers to explore beyond the human-made channel into the river's original bed. The level of difficulty is uniformly Class I, with deadfalls and occasional log or brush jams being the primary dangers to navigation.

## Forked Deer River, North Fork

The North Fork of the Forked Deer River flows northwest through Gibson County before heading west into Dyer County to join the Middle Fork east of Dyersburg. Runnable from late fall to June, the North Fork is characterized by its inaccessibility, its diminutive size, and its high, steep banks. The North Fork generally runs through a lowland forest and cypress bog extending an average one-half mile on each side of the river. Just upstream of this runnable area is the Tigrett Wildlife Area. The North Fork is generally shaded by willows, though the trees are situated back a few feet from the bare banks.

## Forked Deer River, Middle Fork

The Middle Fork of the Forked Deer is small, constricted with brush and deadfalls, and not generally suitable for paddling. Paddlers wishing to sample the Middle Fork, which is densely wooded, are best advised to travel upstream from an access point on the North Fork to the confluence.

## Forked Deer River, South Fork

By far the longest of the three forks, the South Fork runs through seven counties before intersecting the Forked Deer southwest of Dyersburg. Runnable downstream of the US 70A bridge northeast of Brownsville from fall to late summer, the South Fork is both beautiful and remote. Flowing through dense woods and marsh lakes that ring the river and extending sometimes as far as one mile on each side of the stream, the South Fork is well shaded by willow and bottom hardwoods along its channeled banks. Access points are rare, and launching is difficult between access points. Downstream, cultivated bottomland intrudes on the wilderness setting and becomes more common at streamside as the South Fork moves into Dyer County. Averaging 20 to 35 feet in width, the South Fork provides some of the better opportunities in the Forked Deer system to observe wildlife. Its banks are of sand and clay and average 4 feet in height with a 45-degree slope.

From the confluence of the North and South Forks, the Forked Deer is extremely remote and inaccessible as it flows in the original bed to its mouth at the Obion. Stream width averages 40 to 50 feet in this section as the Forked Deer passes through swamp woods and farm bottomland. Bottom hardwoods, willow, and scrub vegetation line the river. The banks are of sandy clay and vary in height and steepness.

# The Hatchie River

The Hatchie River, with headwaters in northern Mississippi, is a Tennessee-protected Scenic River and is the only major west Tennessee drainage that is not channeled. Serving as the principal stream basin for Hardeman, Haywood, Tipton, and southern Lauderdale Counties, the Hatchie is extremely rugged and pristine. Slogging through mile upon mile of willow and pine forest, lowland swamp, marsh lakes and oxbows, water prairies, and cypress bogs, the Hatchie is serpentine in its course and primitive and impenetrable in its appearance. Waterfowl and songbirds fill the air with plaintive and animated sounds, while the thick scrub rustles endlessly with the bustling activity of furbearers. Flowing along convoluted passages that overflow into broad marsh lakes during seasonal flooding, the Hatchie is essentially unchanged through hundreds of generations. Willows sink their roots into the gumbo mud of the easily sloping banks that are backed by red oak, cow oak, and sweetgum atop the Hatchie's natural levee. On the far side of the levee, the bottom hardwoods give way to ash, hackberry, overcup oak, and cottonwood as the terrain slants down to the tupelo-cypress brake of the back swamp.

Navigation is tough on the Hatchie and terrain features change substantially with each year's seasonal flooding. Maps help, but they cannot keep pace with the ever-changing topography of the basin. Skill with a compass is indispensable.

The Hatchie is runnable downstream from Pocahontas near the Mississippi state line in southeastern Hardeman County all year. Surrounding terrain is almost uniformly primitive (and sometimes virgin) all along the Hatchie, with infrequent cultivated bottomland and (incredibly) a housing development on the sandy hill terrain near its mouth at the Mississippi being the only spoilers of its wilderness setting. A distinctive feature of the Hatchie basin is its expansive evergreen forests that alternate periodically with the forestation sequence described above.

Access is limited and rescue is difficult on the Hatchie, but the scenery is hypnotically unique and the solitude almost overwhelming. Canoe camping is possible, depending on the water level. Campsites are available for those who are not afraid of the dense scrub on numerous oxbow islands. The level of difficulty is Class I, with brush jams and deadfalls being the primary hazards to navigation.

# Wolf River of Shelby and Fayette Counties

The Wolf River flows east to west, draining south-central Shelby County, and it runs along the northern edge of the city of Memphis before emptying into the Mississippi River. Runnable except in periods of dry weather, the Wolf flows through a channeled bed until it emerges on

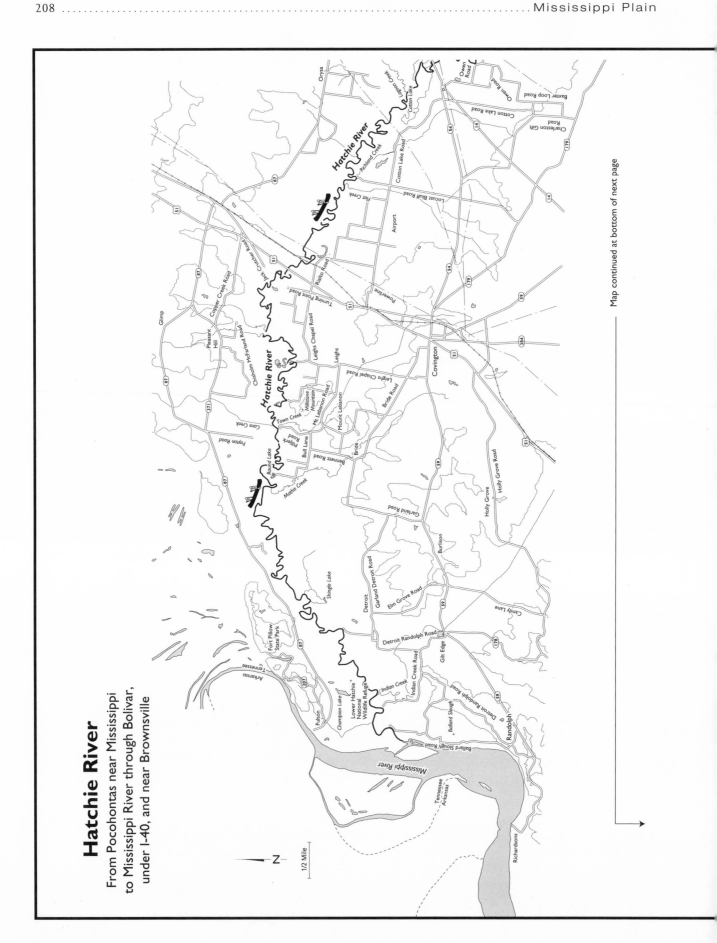

**Hatchie River**

From Pocohontas near Mississippi to Mississippi River through Bolivar, under I-40, and near Brownsville

Map continued at bottom of next page

1/2 Mile

N

Map continued on next page →

N

1/2 Mile

Note: The network of Hatchie Bottoms unnamed roads may be impassable.

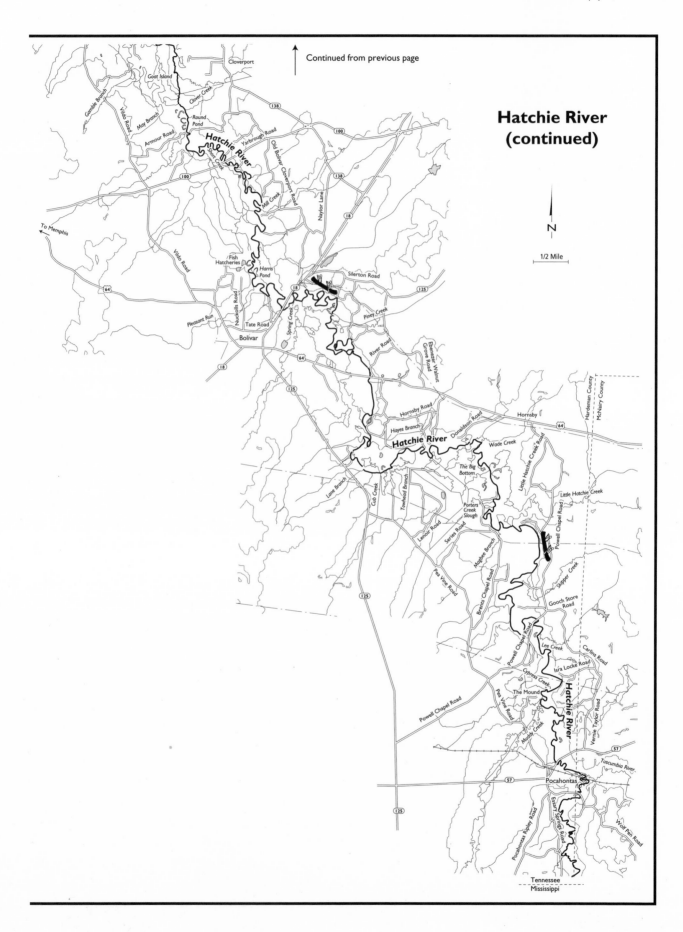

Continued from previous page

**Hatchie River (continued)**

N

1/2 Mile

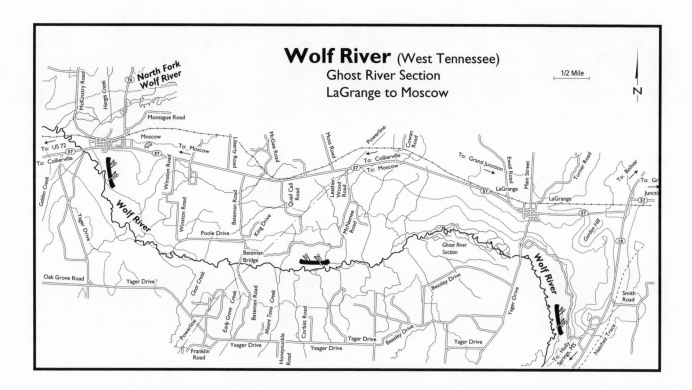

the west side of Memphis, where it resumes its original course for a scant few miles before reaching its mouth. A highway around the circumference of Memphis follows the floodplain of the downstream portions of the Wolf. The scenery includes cultivated land with sparse patches of woodland. Flowing into Memphis, industry and some habitation are visible along the banks. To the west of Memphis the setting is largely industrial. The level of difficulty is Class I, with occasional brush jams and deadfalls being the only hazards to navigation.

Although the Wolf River is more obvious to most people as a floodplain providing an easier corridor for construction of an Interstate highway around Memphis, the Wolf River is actually a rare metropolitan greenway. Enough so that, years ago, a group of forward-thinking river conservationists formed the Wolf River Conservancy (P.O. Box 11031, Memphis, TN 38111-0031), a non-profit organization whose purposes are to protect, enhance, and educate the public about the Wolf River as a wetlands and a greenway (which is visible from space) from its source in northern Mississippi to its mouth upstream of Mud Island in the Mississippi River in Memphis.

There are over 40,000 acres of intact forests and wetlands along the 90 miles of the Wolf. And, to date, the Wolf River Conservancy (WRC) has been involved in placing nearly 12,000 of those acres in some form of protected status.

The WRC actively reaches out to provide hands-on environmental education for area schools, and one of the group's favorite places to host a field trip is along the "Ghost River" section of the river between LaGrange and Moscow. This is true cypress swamp with only the hint of a current providing any clue as to navigation through the watery courses between the trees. Be aware that it is easy to get lost on this section of the river. You could end up paddling more backwater miles than you drove to get to the river. But you will enjoy the scenery. Due to efforts by the WRC and its friends, that section of the river near LaGrange is now the Ghost River State Natural Area.

# Appendix
## Easy River and Canoeing Terms

**Backstroke**: using the paddle to slow the forward motion of the canoe, generally to a slower speed than the current or rapids.

**Beam**: the width of the canoe at its widest.

**Blue hole**: a deep pool, a fishing or swimming spot in the river.

**Bow**: the front of the canoe. Usually only discernable through observation of seat placement.

**Brace**: the paddle as an outrigger-like stabilizer to avoid capsizing of the canoe.

**Broaching**: to "pin" a canoe sideways against a rock within a rapid.

**Capsize**: turn the canoe over, often occurring during a difficult maneuver within a rapid.

**cfs**: measurement of fluid flow in cubic feet per second.

**Chutes**: clear passages of deep, fast-moving flows between obstructions.

**Current**: flow of the river.

**Downstream**: going with the flow.

**Draw**: a stroke to move the canoe in the direction of the side in which the paddler is paddling.

**Drop**: a ledge or fall of up to about five feet within the run of the river.

**Duct tape**: a complete wilderness canoe repair kit on a single roll.

**Eddy turn**: maneuvering the canoe under control through an 180-degree turn from the fast-moving downstream flow direction into an upstream eddy pool.

**Eddy**: a still pool or one with an upstream current behind a rock or obstruction in the middle of fast-moving flow or rapids or along the edge of that flow.

**Ferry**: maneuvering the canoe under control sideways across the flow of the river.

**Flare**: an opposite curvature to the sidewall from that of tumblehome where the gunwale may have the greatest beam measurement.

**Freeboard**: the height of the canoe that is normally above the waterline.

**Grab loops**: tied-off rope or webbing hand holds positioned in place of painters for more positive control during rescue and handling.

**Grab the gunwales**: Don't! A natural (but absolutely wrong) reaction by a beginning canoeist. When the canoe hits turbulence and rocks violently, a novice paddler will grab onto the gunwales of the canoe to avoid being pitched out. Generally this act only results in the paddler pulling the canoe on over into a capsize. The correct reaction is to drop the paddler's center of gravity while reaching out to brace with the paddle against the water.

**Gradient**: the elevation drop along the run of a river.

**Gunwale grabber**: a novice canoeist about to capsize the canoe.

**Gunwale**: the top sidewall edge of the canoe.

**Haystacks**: same as standing waves.

**Hydraulic**: a downstream flow forming a standing wave that falls back upstream on itself.

**Keeper**: a strong souse hole which can "recycle" a floating item keeping it from moving downstream.

**Kneeling**: the proper position for paddlers while maneuvering in whitewater to keep the center of gravity low and centered and to allow flexibility of the body of the paddler.

**Lining**: to lead the empty canoe through the rapids from the bank by control of ropes tied to each end of the craft.

**Paddle** (verb): to propel the canoe; (noun): the implement used to propel the canoe.

**Painters**: ropes tied to the canoe's bow and stern to aid in rescue and handling.

**Peel out**: maneuvering the canoe under control through an 180-degree turn from an upstream eddy pool direction into the fast-moving downstream flow.

**PFD**: a Personal Flotation Device, the life jacket that *all* whitewater paddlers wear.

**Pillow**: water flow over rocks and boulders near enough to the surface to raise the flow above and over those boulders. Pillows are stuffed with rocks.

**Pool**: a still area with slow downstream flow between rapids.

**Portage**: to carry the canoe along the banks to avoid running the rapids.

**Pry**: a stroke to move the canoe in the opposite direction of the side in which the paddler is paddling with the paddle. A difficult stroke.

**Put-in**: the spot along the river where the canoeing trip will begin.

**Rapids**: fast-moving, broken-up water flows.

**Riffle**: small, non-effective flow disturbances to the river surface.

**River**: a flowing stream big enough to navigate a canoe downstream.

**Rocker**: the bow to stern curvature along the "keel line" of the canoe making the craft shaped like a banana.

**Rockgarden**: an area of rapids littered with exposed boulders containing offset chutes between them, causing the necessity for considerable maneuvering for passage.

**Roll**: skilled paddlers in properly outfitted whitewater canoes can turn the capsized canoe upright while still at their paddling stations.

**Rollers**: same as standing waves.

**Run the rapids**: to paddle the canoe through the chutes and standing waves using appropriate maneuvering and control from the paddle strokes.

**Scout**: to walk the bank and inspect the upcoming "blind" part of the river rapids.

**Shoals**: shallow sets of riffles over rock or gravel riverbeds that can stop a canoe's progress downstream.

**Shuttle**: moving cars about so that the canoes are at the put-in and the cars are at the take-out.

**Solo**: a canoe paddled by one person.

**Souse hole**: a wrapped around, multisided hydraulic forming a hole.

**Standing waves**: chutes lined with choppy, splashing, rolling waves.

**Stern**: the back end of the canoe.

**Strainer**: A downed tree in the flow of the stream. Very dangerous. Water flows through branches, but people and craft can get caught in that obstructed flow.

**Take-out**: the spot downstream where the canoeing trip will end (near where the cars ought to be parked).

**Tandem**: a team of two people paddling a canoe. There should be no passengers in whitewater river running.

**Thwarts**: direct cross bracings between the gunwales along the length of the top of the canoe.

**Tumblehome**: the "bilge" curvature in the side of the canoe as seen by tracing from the bottom/waterline area up the side to the gunwale, which may be tucked-in with less beam than midway up the bilge.

**Undercut rock**: a place in the river where there is no pillow of water where the river flow hits the rock because flow is passing underneath the obstruction. Very dangerous. People have been sucked through and under undercut rocks.

**Upstream**: going against the flow.

**Whitewater**: sufficient rapids to intimidate the cautious. Generally, foamy water within the rapids will be white in color.

**Wrapping**: when a broached canoe fills with water and collapses around the rock.

**About the Author:** Bob Lantz is associate professor of technology at Cleveland State Community College in Tennessee. He founded and operated the Blue Hole Canoe Company for many years and served on state- and nationwide river organizations. Lantz published canoeing and river-conservation articles in paddling magazines including *Canoe, American Whitewater, DownRiver,* and the old classic, *Wilderness Camping.* His conservation efforts included testifying before Congress to gain protection for Tennessee's Obed as a National Wild and Scenic River and filing as a local petitioner in the successful effort to protect the Frozen Head State National Area watershed by designating it as one of the "Lands Unsuitable for Mining."

*Tennessee Rivers: A Paddler's Guidebook* was designed and typeset on a Macintosh computer system using QuarkXPress software. The body text is set in 11/15 Joanna with display type set in Helvetica Neue. This book was designed and typeset by Cheryl Carrington and manufactured by Thomson-Shore, Inc.